REAL FOOD PLACES

A Guide to Restaurants that Serve Fresh, Wholesome Food

by Lawrence Block
and Cheryl Morrison

Rodale Press, Emmaus, Pennsylvania

Printed in the United States of America on recycled paper, containing a high percentage of de-inked fiber.

Art Director K. A. Schell
Book Design by Joan Peckolick

Library of Congress Cataloging in Publication Data

Block, Lawrence.
Real food places.

Includes index.
1. Restaurants, lunch rooms, etc.—United States.
2. Restaurants, lunch rooms, etc.—Canada. I. Morrison, Cheryl. II. Title.
TX945.B53 647'.957 81-10599
AACR2
ISBN 0-87857-362-3 paperback
2 4 6 8 10 9 7 5 3 1 paperback

Contents

Introduction

According to a recent news item, one-third of the entire American food budget goes for fast food. Of all the billions of dollars spent on food, in supermarkets or produce stands, health food stores and restaurants, one dollar out of every three goes to buy Big Macs, Whoppers, Kentucky Fried Chicken, pizza, hero sandwiches, and whatever the latest coast-to-coast franchise operation is offering.

That's an astonishing statistic, but it becomes considerably more believable once one has spent a little time on the road. Perhaps the most striking evidence of this country's transformation in, say, the past twenty years, lies in the proliferation of fast-food franchises. Whether the background is mountains or plains or desert, the neon is the same. One can drive from Maine to California and eat every meal at McDonald's.

To do so is, certainly, a legitimate choice. But for those of us who would choose differently, difficulties abound.

Diners and coffee shops can be an inexpensive alternative to the franchise chains. The service is often more personal, the atmosphere can be a little homier, and the food may be a little less boring if only because the menu offers more than formula fare. A hamburger might be topped with baked beans in a New England diner or chili in a Texas eatery, but a McDonald's hamburger in Boston will taste (or lack taste) exactly the same as a McDonald's hamburger in Dallas. The problem with diner food, while it at least allows for a surprise now and then, is that it is likely to be just as calorie-laden, no less processed and every bit as bland as franchise fare; hash-house cooking tends to be less than skillful.

Finding real food is a problem even for those who aren't on a strict budget. Many a time we've gone to expensive restaurants in search of it only to find that there, too, one is likely to encounter canned or frozen vegetables that have been purged of all flavor and texture (let alone nutritional value), salads based on limp iceberg lettuce and hothouse tomatoes, and fluffy, tasteless "air" bread that's served hot and unsliced so you think it's homemade.

It's difficult enough to find food that tastes good and looks interesting, let alone fare that's prepared according to whatever your nutritional or philosophical demands might be. If one avoids fried foods, eschews white flour and abjures refined sugar, eating in transit becomes tricky. If one wishes as well to avoid chemically sprayed and fertilized produce, to stay away from caffeine and alcohol, the problem is compounded. If one is a nonconsumer of meat and fish and perhaps of eggs and dairy products as well, it sometimes seems easier to stay home.

Perhaps the greatest hope for food-conscious travelers—natural-food fans and vegetarians as well as the merely selective—is provided by the health-food and vegetarian restaurants that have been sprouting like mung beans all over North America for the last decade or more. Here, at least, the vegetables one encounters are likely to be fresh and not cooked to death, and the seasoning is apt to have been done by hand, not by a salt-spreader in a fast-food factory. Virtually all of them make an effort to obtain organically grown produce and to prepare it with some concern for retaining its nutritional as well as its aesthetic value. Those that serve meat may buy it from producers who don't raise their animals on drugs and chemicals, and their menus are likely to reflect the management's awareness that some customers don't want to eat flesh. Some of these restaurants are unequivocally successful, providing excellent food in hygienic surroundings at moderate cost. Others are less successful at achieving their aims. But almost all of them constitute a highly preferable alternative to the Pizza Huts and Burger Kings that dot the landscape.

There are other oases, too, from the franchise food and fried nasties that dominate American cuisine, especially outside big cities. Tucked into some of the most unlikely crannies of the landscape are restaurants where the food is attractive, reasonably priced and unusually wholesome, even though the places may not tout themselves as health-food emporiums.

The trick is to find them, especially if your concerns are primarily nutritional or philosophic rather than aesthetic.

The standard guides aren't much help, especially to travelers with definite notions about what constitutes a healthful meal. Books like the Mobil guides, invaluable for locating an acceptable motel, do a variable job of pointing out decent restaurants of any sort, and they have almost nothing to offer a natural-food vegetarian.

The Yellow Pages are rarely useful. It's almost impossible to tell from the listings whether a restaurant's fare is anything you'd consider acceptable, regardless of whether your primary concern is the culinary skill of the chef or the chemical content of the salad dressing. Only occasionally does one find a separate phone book listing for "health food" or "vegetarian" restaurants, and when such listings occur their coverage is spotty at best. The listing probably won't tell you, for example, whether a "vegetarian" restaurant uses dairy products in its cooking, whether a "natural foods" restaurant uses refined flour in its pie crust.

Many of the establishments where one might find a simple and wholesome meal are just the sort that aren't given to eye-catching display ads. Their advertising generally is limited to word-of-mouth, perhaps abetted by small notices in local underground newspapers. As a result, many of the restaurants we're talking about are not widely known even among their neighbors, let alone to the tourist who's just passing through.

And that's why this book was written.

Samuel R. Delaney, the science fiction writer, has said he tries to write the books he looks for but cannot find on library shelves. And that's just what we've done. We decided to compile this volume because we've often wished for just the kind of aid it offers in finding a decent meal in unknown territory.

The original inspiration came to Lawrence Block, who is a vegetarian. He returned from a trip marked by one grilled cheese sandwich too many, only to learn that there had been an excellent vegetarian restaurant within walking distance of his hotel.

"Well, how was I supposed to know that?" he protested. "There ought to be a guidebook. These places ought to be listed somewhere."

And now they are.

Our listings aren't limited to vegetarian restaurants, however, nor those that purport to serve natural foods. They also include a number of restaurants that don't make any pretense of that sort but where the food is wholesome, attractive, satisfying and reasonably priced. Some of them offer the cuisine of a particular ethnic group, and others feature eclectic menus where the emphasis is on real food, not processed oddments. At virtually all the restaurants we've covered, the menus include meatless meals. And the cooks are likely to use fresh, if not organic, ingredients rather than ersatz chemical concoctions.

Cheryl Morrison isn't a vegetarian, nor does she have any consistent nutritional policy other than varying her diet and avoiding food that's badly cooked. On a trip through New England, she found herself wanting desperately to avoid yet another batter-coated, deep-fried seafood platter at an inexpensive restaurant but unwilling to splurge on a meal at a place where she could expect crisp, fresh vegetables and a main course that hadn't been resting in a steam table for a week. Her companion, who had vegetarian tendencies, suggested that they try a health food restaurant. Cheryl reluctantly consented, thinking that even a slab of gluten with a dose of wheat germ, which is the sort of dish she imagined was served in vegetarian restaurants, would be better than another plate of fried greasies.

What she found was a restaurant that offered the hominess and low prices of a diner but where the broccoli offered some resistance to her teeth, where the entree was an aromatic concoction of herbs, grains and vegetables rather than an unrecognizable glob of soggy, French-fried batter, and the blueberry pie contained recognizable berries, not dyed goo bound with cornstarch. What's more, the meal didn't leave her feeling as if her nose was going to slip off her face, as greasy-spoon specials often do.

Ever since then, she has sought out health food or vegetarian restaurants when she has traveled, especially to rural or suburban locales, where even the expense-account places are likely to offer canned spinach and iceberg lettuce.

With the revelation that health food restaurants often serve the most interesting food in town, however, came another discovery: that there are nearly as many definitions of the terms "health food," "natural" and "vegetarian" as there are of the restaurants themselves. People who are more committed than Cheryl is to a diet of unprocessed foods would be appalled by what some natural foods restaurants purport to be natural. At many of them, for example, the cooks routinely use white flour, which is arguably a less-than-natural substance. One of the services we're providing with this book is to help our readers determine just what individual restaurants mean when they say natural, health food or vegetarian.

Rather than just list the restaurants and offer an opinion on whether the food tastes good, we've also tried to provide information of concern to people of varying nutritional persuasions. A great many vegetarians also don't eat eggs or fish or dairy products, for example, so we've tried to find out whether the cooks use those ingredients. We've also made inquiries about whether the dishes include white flour and sugar and whether the produce is organic.

The reviews also will let you know a little about the atmosphere of the places. Cheryl once used the Washington telephone book to locate a health food restaurant near her hotel. She went there expecting to sit down for a leisurely meal; what she found was a lunch counter. If this book had been available then, she might have gone to a more suitable place just a few blocks away.

We're providing other information, too, that will go a long way toward preventing the kinds of problems that arise when a vegetarian is trying to have lunch with a carnivore, or when you want to wash down your health food with three martinis. Most of our listings tell whether the restaurants serve meat as well as vegetarian dishes, if smoking is permitted and whether there's a smoke-free section for those who want clean air, if coffee is served, and if alcohol is allowed on the premises.

HOW TO USE THIS BOOK

The first step in making optimum use of this book is to keep it handy. You might want to stow it in the glove compartment of your car when not actually reading it. Make it an automatic reflex to tuck it into a suitcase when packing for a trip by bus or plane. The book won't do you much good if you're hungry in Seattle and it's on your bookshelf back home in Indianapolis.

On the long road trip, this book might have a role in your advance planning. Perhaps you have some choice in the route you're going to take. By referring to the listings, you may find that one route will allow you to fuel up at several whole-foods oases, while another winds you through an unrelenting desert of Taco Belles and Jack-in-the-Boxes. (Jacks-in-the-Box? Never mind.) Even when your route is predetermined, you may be able to schedule meal stops to your advantage by using this book to investigate your options.

We've arranged the listings by state, then city or municipality, then in alphabetical order. If you don't find a suitable restaurant in the particular hamlet you're visiting, be sure to check the listings for nearby towns. Perhaps a native can tell you which towns are nearby; otherwise, it might help to determine which towns are covered by the local telephone book.

Do call ahead when it's convenient. While we've endeavored to list hours of operation, restaurants are apt to change their policies from time to time. Relatively few of the listed restaurants require reservations, but a phone call can book you a table if the chosen restaurant accepts them, and it can let you know if crowding is to be expected at certain hours.

WHERE THE REVIEWS COME FROM

Scores of reviewers have collaborated to produce the listings that comprise this book. Rather than attempt to cover the country ourselves, we enlisted people throughout the United

States and Canada, who have reported in detail on restaurants on their home ground that might be suitable. What better way to provide a comprehensive listing, we asked ourselves, than to solicit reviews from people across the continent about restaurants in their own backyards? Someone who may have visited the restaurant often (and knows of its local reputation) can give a broader picture than an out-of-town reviewer who's just passing through. And a reviewer who knows the local restaurant scene can tell us how a particular establishment stacks up against whatever else is available, just to keep things in perspective. In addition to more thorough coverage than we could have undertaken alone, the reviewers give the book a welcome diversity of viewpoints and writing styles.

Who are our contributors? Some are professional writers. Others have never previously written for publication. Many have a definite nutritional or culinary consciousness, and some are vegetarian, but some began thinking about wholesome dining only while preparing their reviews. If there is anything to be said about our reviewers as a group, it is that they do not run to type. They come in all ages and many occupations, and their only common denominator has been their enthusiasm for this project.

For the most part, their reviews tend to be informative rather than critical. While they have felt free to express their own opinions on the quality of food and service at the establishments they've reviewed, we trust you'll bear in mind that such evaluations are a highly subjective matter, whether they come from a small-town freelance writer or a sophisticated critic on a big-city newspaper staff. The observation that one man's meat is another man's poison is also true for Zucchini-Oat Flake Loaf.

Furthermore, any restaurant can have an off day. In one trip, Larry stopped at a long-established vegetarian enterprise and was profoundly disappointed with his meal and the manner in which it was served. He returned to New York prepared to write a negative review only to discover that we had already assigned the place and that our reviewer had given it a rave. Cheryl, meanwhile, returned from a jaunt of her own through the same territory. She, too, had visited the restaurant in question, and her judgment echoed our reviewer's. Evidently Larry had hit the place on a bad day. Even the best of restaurants fall short of their usual standards now and then, so it's possible that you'll disagree with a negative review. If your experience disagrees with our reviews in any significant respect, we hope you'll let us know about it for subsequent editions.

Because we perceive our function primarily as informative rather than critical, we also have included a considerable number of short listings. Unlike our signed reviews, these represent restaurants which have not been personally visited by ourselves or our reviewers. Some have been brought to our attention by correspondents who did not undertake to review them. Others came to notice through advertising or listings in alternative media. In many instances, our information on these establishments is incomplete, but we included them to enlarge the scope of this book, to give you as much help as possible in avoiding the golden arches.

Please note that none of our listings or reviews constitutes an endorsement on the part of Rodale Press.

THE NATURE OF THE BUSINESS

While compiling this book, we were distressed and discouraged by two problems inherent in our task—the impossibility of including every worthy restaurant and the tendency of establishments of this sort to close their doors and go out of business moments after they've been reviewed.

The first dilemma, we realized, is one our readers will help us resolve for future editions. Further on, we'll explain how you can help us enlarge the scope of this book by reviewing restaurants you feel should be included.

The second problem is likely to linger. While we have attempted to assure that the restaurants we have listed are in operation as we go to press, it would seem to be inevitable that a percentage will have ceased operation by the time this book is in your hands.

The tendency of vegetarian and natural-food eating places to wink in and out of business could be viewed as a sign of the industry's strength rather than as a weakness. This is such a burgeoning new area of enterprise that a predominant number of restaurants in it have opened within the last few years. With all new businesses, the survival rate is highest once the initial few years are past. It is in the very first year of operation that most new retail businesses fail, and restaurants are no exception to this rule. The mortality for new restaurants, whether they sell alfalfa sprout sandwiches or hog jowls fried in axle grease, is dishearteningly high.

This is especially true for our sort of restaurant, because it is so often started as a labor of love. Typically, one becomes nutritionally aware, begins cooking for oneself and friends, laments the difficulty of obtaining a proper restaurant meal in the area, feels a real calling to bring good food to one's fellows—and suddenly finds oneself signing a lease and pricing kitchen equipment without having acquired any business acumen.

Innumerable fine and enduring restaurants have been born in just such circumstances. But when a new business is started by an inexperienced proprietor, the odds against it are higher than normal.

The odds go up, too, when someone opens a restaurant in an area where an insufficient demand exists. Large cities, resort areas, college towns and art colonies all tend to support health food restaurants more enthusiastically than do regions where it's a rare person who knows tofu from tahini. Not infrequently, entrepreneurs entertain faintly messianic visions of themselves bringing nutritional awareness to the masses, and every once in a while this works, with a fine restaurant thriving in unlikely soil. More often than not, such a place limps through one sad season and shuts its doors.

Even when a restaurant proves to be a commercial success, its lifespan may be a brief one. All the factors that lead people to open new-era restaurants—youth, energy, openness to new experience—may eventually lead them to lock the doors and move on to other frontiers. Many an excellent and commercially viable counterculture restaurant has disappeared overnight because its proprietors have realized that they are no longer into feeding people and feel a profound vocation to go homesteading in Nova Scotia.

Sometimes restaurants change hands. The new owners may change the establishment's name. They may retain the old name but make sweeping changes in cuisine, either to reflect their own nutritional convictions or in an attempt to offer the public something closer to what it wants. They may, finally, stop feeding people altogether and sell sporting goods instead.

For all those reasons, it's not unlikely that you will experience some disappointments while using this book. We trust that you will minimize such disappointments by calling ahead if a visit to a particular restaurant will take you out of your way. We trust, too, that the occasional disappointments will be more than offset by the great satisfaction of sitting down now and then to a superb and health-giving meal prepared and served by loving hands in a warm and inviting atmosphere.

SOME NOTES ON THE LISTINGS

Geographical considerations have been a factor in our deciding whether or not to include a particular restaurant. A restaurant that would automatically be listed if it were in a small Midwestern city might not make the grade if situated in California; there, the abundance of suitable restaurants has made our standards rather more rigorous. A sandwich-and-salad place that would be omitted from the New York City listings might be included if it were in an area where the choices were more limited.

While our reviewers reported the prices of various entrees and complete dinners, we ultimately decided to eliminate prices altogether from our listings. The rate of inflation is such that prices at all restaurants tend to change almost before the ink on the menus is dry. Were we to publish prices, they would be obsolete before the book reached your hands, and they would very likely suggest that the restaurants we've listed were cheaper than is actually the case.

As it happens, vegetarian and natural food restaurants tend to be quite modest in price, and so are most of the other places we've listed. In the few instances where prices are above the moderate range, we have so remarked in our listings.

HOW TO GET ALONG WITHOUT THIS BOOK

Even if you keep this volume always at hand, there will be times when you have to get along without it. Perhaps you'll find yourself in a city for which no restaurants are listed. Does this doom you to a grilled cheese sandwich and a bowl of sugary cole slaw in the local equivalent of Rosalie's Good Eats Cafe? Not necessarily.

There are some tricks for survival. First of all, you can investigate. There may be a suitable restaurant that has escaped our notice, or which sprang up since we went to press. (If so, we hope you'll let us know about it.) How to find out if such a restaurant exists? Well, the Yellow Pages are worth a glance. Check the white pages of the phone book, too, to see if Good Earth or Golden Temple Conscious Cookery has opened a branch in town. See if there are any restaurants listed with names like Nature's Way or Natural this-and-that. To be sure, our kind of restaurant doesn't always tip its hand with its name; Arnold's Turtle and Susan's Cafe don't unmistakably proclaim themselves as the vegetarian natural food establishments that they are, but it's not hard to guess what sort of cuisine Spring Street Natural Foods is likely to serve. If a name seems promising, a phone call can clear up the confusion.

If the phone book fails to provide a vegetarian restaurant, don't abandon it. Instead, check the listings for health food stores, and make a call or two. While there's no iron-clad guarantee that the personnel at such stores will be nutritionally sophisticated, the odds are pretty good. If there's a natural food restaurant in the area, someone in the store will very likely know about it and have an opinion on its merits. If not, you may at least learn of a regular restaurant nearby where the food is relatively wholesome.

Many health food stores have juice and sandwich bars that will do nicely for a light meal. We have made no attempt to list all of them, but we certainly recommend them if a quick bite will suffice. If your gustatory ambitions run higher than that, however, there's often no need to settle for a quick glass of carrot juice and a sprout sandwich.

Ethnic restaurants, especially in larger cities, often afford good possibilities. Any number of cuisines can provide a welcome alternative to steak and potatoes.

Italian restaurants are usually a good bet, and are a bit more ubiquitous in America than other ethnic establishments. Vegetables there are usually fresh, and ingredients tend to be of high quality. Pasta, while almost invariably a white-flour product, can make an acceptable entree for vegetarians who don't insist on whole grains; if the tomato sauce is unavailable without meat, a simple butter sauce or one made of garlic and olive oil may always be requested. A tip: eggplant parmesan, a staple at many health food parlors, is often available at Italian restaurants even when it's not listed on the menu. Ask the waiter.

Chinese restaurants employ fresh vegetables, too, and their stir-fry cooking inflicts minimal nutritional damage. The liberal use of peppers, sesame oil and garlic may provide a welcome change from Middle-American blandness. Most offer a vegetarian dish, either a vegetable chow mein or a chop suey or the melange of stir-fried vegetables known as Buddha's Delight. We're not sure Buddha would be delighted to learn that the dish is more often than not prepared with a chicken stock, so beware if you're a vegetarian. Chinese restaurants tend to add monosodium glutamate to everything, but one can easily say "no MSG." And it's equally easy to pass up the gummy white rice and the deep-fried noodles.

Indian restaurants are a natural for anyone who favors cuisine that's punctuated by intriguing blends of herbs and spices, many of them exotic indeed to the American palate. There is a long tradition of vegetarianism in India, so it is a rare Indian restaurant that does not have several meatless entrees on the menu, although most of them also offer an interesting array of flesh foods, especially chicken, lamb and fish. The rice is almost invariably converted a la Uncle Ben's, which seems to be nutritionally superior to plain polished rice, though a hefty cut below natural brown rice. Indian dishes generally get long and thorough cooking, which destroys some of the vitamins and enzymes even as it enhances the qualities of the aromatic herbs and spices. A couple of caveats: some places do use meat stocks in the preparation of vegetable dishes, especially in soups like mulligatawny, so ask before you order if this is important to you.

Middle Eastern restaurants generally feature food that's not too far removed from its natural state, and some are fertile ground for vegetarians. Greek and Armenian restaurants often have a meatless dish on the menu, while Arab and Israeli places, which have appeared increasingly in the past few years, offer a wide choice of meatless options. For nonvegetarians, too, the heavy emphasis on fresh vegetables (especially eggplant and zucchini) and legumes (like sesame seeds and chickpeas) may offer relief from standard American restaurant fare. Felafel, a deep-fried nonmeatball made of ground chickpeas, and hommus, a chickpea and sesame spread, are widely available, with various restaurants offering other regional specialties. A sandwich of hommus or felafel with salad and sauce served in a pocket of pita bread is the ultimate fast-food item for whole-foods adventurers.

Spanish restaurants are no help for vegetarians, but they're a godsend for fish lovers. Mexican restaurants can prove acceptable to vegetarians and fussy carnivores alike, however. Mexican fare relies heavily on fresh vegetables, and it's generally not too greasy. While the chili is almost always con carne, one can make a good high-protein meal out of cheese enchiladas, refried beans, guacamole and other alternatives. Increasingly, Mexican restaurants have been offering vegetarian combination platters to simplify the selection process.

Japanese restaurants frequently offer the most unprocessed food in town, serving fare that pleases the stomach and the palate as well as the eye. The cuisine employs fresh vegetables as well as dried seaweeds, and the flavorings tend to be subtle. The menus generally include numerous fish dishes as well as a few meat offerings; some Japanese restaurants have taken to offering special vegetarian dinners, and a good choice they are, commonly including vegetable tempura, seaweed, miso soup and tofu. If you don't eat flesh, however, watch out for sushi parlors offering nothing but various forms of raw fish, as well as the western-influenced Japanese steakhouses that cater solely to carnivores. A happy note: it is almost impossible to gain weight at a Japanese restaurant.

German and Middle European restaurants are difficult. The food's likely to be laden with fats and refined carbohydrates, and there's rarely a vegetarian dish on the menu. But you never know. Larry recalls a Rumanian restaurant where he had something called *mamaliga,* a tasty and highly unusual affair of potatoes and onions and sour cream; it was delicious, even if it did lie in the stomach like lead.

Scandinavian restaurants seldom offer much in the way of vegetables, but they generally offer a tantalizing array of fish dishes.

Getting By in the Lion's Den

Best laid plans notwithstanding, sooner or later everyone winds up in a restaurant where every last entree is a meat course and the rest of the menu resembles nothing that is found in nature. Perhaps other members of your party have made the choice. Perhaps you're stuck in your hotel-chain restaurant with no alternative within twenty miles and gale-force winds are blowing. You can still dine without compromising your standards too much, whatever they might be. Indeed, occasionally you can dine remarkably well.

The first step is to make your special requirements known to the person who waits on you. Explain your wishes without apology and ask if she or he can suggest a viable alternative. Many kitchens can prepare innumerable dishes besides those featured on their menus, and the waiters can help you communicate with the kitchen.

Now and then a request of this sort succeeds beyond one's wildest dreams. Larry won't quickly forget a dinner in a pre-Revolutionary restaurant in northwestern Connecticut, where the menu listed eight or ten meat entrees and nothing else. His omnivorous companion ordered a ham steak, while Larry, with lowered expectations, requested "some sort of vegetable plate." They both ate superbly, consuming appetizer and salad, rolls and cornsticks, fresh-baked bread. Larry's vegetable plate sported a baked potato, an ear of corn, and four or five other vegetables, all well prepared. Dessert was included.

When the check came, the meat eater's meal was a bargain at $8.95. Larry's, on the other hand, cost $1.75. Astonishing. He couldn't have bought the ingredients at the supermarket for that price. Evidently the management had assumed that a meal without meat was no meal at all, and had set the price accordingly.

This does not always happen. The other side of the coin is the restaurant that provides a plate containing two kinds of potatoes and a woebegone clump of boiled green stuff and charges as much as if they'd brought you a Maine lobster.

The menus in more and more restaurants, though, are reflecting the public's growing concern with nutrition as well as its rising culinary sophistication. With the sharp increase in vegetarianism in the past few years, even steakhouses have taken to listing vegetarian alternatives on their menus. Indeed, a recent meat industry newsletter cited this fact with alarm, pointing out the number of traditional restaurants in Chicago offering their clientele the option of a meatless entree. (And this in Sandburg's "Hog Butcher of the World"!) Similarly, more and more restaurants have become familiar with vegetarians and can provide a passable vegetable platter upon request. Persnickety carnivores, too, are pleased to note that menus across the land are being influenced by the public's increasing preference for anything that's natural or handmade over counterparts that are mass-produced.

Larry has even found evidence of this new consciousness at banquets, where his expectations for a decent meatless meal are so low that he usually eats before he goes so he won't feel overly deprived if he can do no more than gnaw on a hard roll. Just recently, however, a Holiday Inn in upstate New York supplied a perfectly adequate vegetable plate at a high school reunion. The times, indeed, are a-changing.

Not all restaurants have a sufficient selection of vegetables to make a plate of them particularly appealing, or the vegetables they do offer are canned or otherwise unappealing even to those who will be eating them with meat. When there's only one vegetable available, one's enthusiasm for a whole plate of it is apt to be limited. Worse yet is the prospect of devouring an entire platter of green beans that came from a can. In these places, the appetizer list may offer hope, and the vegetable lover may do well to order several of those dishes in lieu of a main course. Similarly, one can order a dinner-sized portion of a suitable appetizer. Most restaurants will accommodate such a request.

Salad entrees are increasingly available in our diet-conscious civilization. While many of these include meat or fish, it's easy enough to order the popular spinach salad, say, with the bacon omitted if you wish. If there are no dinner salads available, you may ask for a dinner-sized portion of the tossed salad that's normally furnished as a side dish.

In those restaurants with the most severely limited kitchens, establishments offering steak and lobster tail and a baked potato and nothing else, a rescue frequently appears in the form of a salad bar. Customers are encouraged to make as many complimentary visits to this salad bar as they wish in between bites of their surf 'n' turf special. A diner is almost always given the option of skipping the entree altogether and feeding exclusively on the salad bar's offerings, and the cost is usually quite reasonable.

To be sure, the salad you can put together is a healthy cut below what's available at a natural food restaurant, as a rule. The greenery is rarely anything beyond iceberg lettuce, and there will be innumerable offerings one would prefer to avoid, either as a vegetarian or for other nutritional or purely aesthetic considerations. But there usually are enough other selections on hand to provide an acceptable meal, and the all-you-can-eat aspect is not without appeal to those of us with a marked bent toward gluttony.

A few of the franchised fast-food operations have even taken to installing salad bars recently, trying them on an experimental basis in various locations. Whether this trend will continue, and whether alfalfa sprouts will join the pickled tomatoes and Bacobits, will no doubt depend on public response.

For all we know, the quality of food across America will improve so dramatically as part of the trend toward the "natural" that the need for this book will no longer exist. That doesn't seem to be on the agenda for the next few years, however, and we hope in the meantime that this book will assist you in circumnavigating the poison palaces in your quest for real food.

—Lawrence Block and Cheryl Morrison

HOW TO BECOME A REVIEWER

As you use this book, we hope you will help us improve it and make it more comprehensive in its future editions. Perhaps you'll come across restaurants that ought to be in this book. If so, we hope you'll review them for us.

While you needn't be a Pulitzer Prize winner to break into our pages, a few guidelines might be helpful. Try to write your reviews to the approximate length and format of those in the pages that follow. Make sure you cover the following points: Name, address, business hours, telephone number. Is meat served? Fish? Coffee? Alcoholic beverages? May customers bring their own wine? Is smoking permitted? If so, is there a special section for nonsmokers? Are the desserts sweetened with sugar? Do the cooks use white flour? Organic vegetables? What credit cards, if any, are accepted? In addition, try to convey the atmosphere of the establishment and tell what, if anything, makes it special. Mention any dishes you particularly enjoyed—or found lacking.

As they say in the slogan contests, all submissions become the property of the authors of this book and cannot be acknowledged or returned. If your review is included in a future edition, you will receive a complimentary copy of the book, will see your name in print, and will have the satisfaction of being part of a great information-sharing process. You may not help save the world, but perhaps you will be sparing some kindred spirit from the ignominy of cold French fries in Missoula, Montana.

Send your reviews to Lawrence Block and Cheryl Morrison, Rodale Press, 33 E. Minor St., Emmaus, PA 18049.

Alaska

ANCHORAGE

The Bread Factory Restaurant
835 I St.
907-274-2882

The Bread Factory Restaurant in downtown Anchorage boasts of an "incredibly warm and friendly atmosphere." Entering the small, cozy room furnished with second-hand, mismatched tables and chairs, you are greeted by the aroma of delicious home-cooked meals. The all-vegetarian menu is promptly brought to your table by a friendly waitress probably wearing a T-shirt, jeans and a butcher's apron. During the busy lunch hour, seating at common tables encourages old-timers to suggest menu choices to the newcomer who is bewildered by the large selection of omelets, crepes, salads, soups, sandwiches and specialties.

The Meal-of-the-Day, which consists of a hot entree with bread, salad and tea, may vary according to the whim of the cook and the ingredients on hand but is consistently delicious. On our last visit it was a combination of refried beans, yogurt, cheese, sprouts and tomatoes entitled Tostados a la Mexico.

The Factory Worker's Special is a tofu-burger with sauteed mushrooms, tomatoes, sprouts and salad. Great any time of the day is the Factory Omelette, which includes cheese, mushrooms, avocados, tomatoes and sprouts. One of our favorites, the sauteed vegetables, comes in its own cast-iron frying pan. The servings are generous, so customers often share portions.

The delicious 100% whole wheat bread is baked daily, and loaves are available to go as long as the daily supply lasts. Desserts include yogurt with nuts and raisins, cookies made with honey, and apples and cheese. Our choice is the fruit crepe, which is large enough for two. Beverages include beer, wine, coffee, herb tea (a large selection), apple juice and smoothies.

No smoking. No credit cards.

Hours: 6 A.M.-3 P.M. 7 days a week, November to March; 6 A.M.-11 P.M. 7 days a week, rest of year.

—Sheary Suiter

ANCHORAGE
The Cauldron
328 G St.
907-276-0592

It's a big room filled with tall tables and chairs and coffeehouse atmosphere. During the day, service is over a long wooden counter that lines the wall in front of the kitchen. At night, friendly waitresses serve you at your table while you take in live folk or classical music. The music accounts for slightly higher evening prices, but the portions are plentiful and flavorful and the entertainment is good.

Sandwiches such as the avocado, cheese and sprout special are a good choice at lunch, along with one of the 35 varieties of soup the cooks concoct from fresh vegetables. One meat soup and one vegetarian soup are served every day. Try the clam chowder if you're not a vegetarian; if you are, try the cream of cauliflower, cream of broccoli, Italian vegetable or minestrone.

Fondue dinners consist of cheese with apples, vegetables and bread cubes, or two kinds of meat with two kinds of sauce. Sautees of vegetables and cashews or meats and one of 25 quiche recipes (some with meat) are offered on the evening menu in addition to all the dishes served at lunch. Dinners come with fresh salad and whole wheat-honey bread, baked there daily.

Beverages include wine and beer, featuring a dark steamed beer. Try the hot spiced cider, our personal favorite, or the fresh-roasted coffee, herb tea, juice or lemonade.

Also baked daily are all desserts but pie (skip it; it's frozen and sugared). Carrot cake and cheese cake are good, and the cashew-coconut cookies—big ones—are delicious.

Smoking section. No credit cards.

Open 11 A.M.-11 P.M. Monday-Saturday in summer; 11 A.M.-10 P.M. in winter (October-April).

—Ann Kacsur

ANCHORAGE

The Warehouse
1140 E. 74th Ave.
907-344-2032

A church building on the south edge of town has been converted into one of Anchorage's most original natural food restaurants. A down-home atmosphere is encouraged by common seating at large wooden spool tables. Cold beer and wine are served, surprisingly, in pint jars, and the best local folk music groups play Wednesday and Thursday from the large pulpit-stage to the clapping and stomping of full-house crowds. On weekends the music is provided by larger groups from the states.

Warehouse patrons record their own orders on an "inventory sheet," which lists the menu. By far the most popular item on the menu is the generous Bulk Sandwich. To order it, you simply circle your choice of fresh meats, cheeses, vegetables, condiments, and bread, then sign your name on the sheet and hand it to your waitress. The price includes your choice of homemade potato salad, especially yummy, or tossed salad, or soup. All breads are baked daily; our favorite is the sweet Indian Oat, which melts in your mouth like cake. Homemade soups, salads, carrot cake and the meat, cheese and fruit plates are listed as "Excess Freight." The Warehouse provides daily vegetarian specials, among them a vegetarian pizza, which include a salad. All pasta is strictly whole wheat.

Besides a good selection of beer and wine, you'll find freshly roasted coffee, milk, fruit juice and herb teas.

Reservations are recommended on weekends, and there's a cover charge of $2.50 on Thursday evenings and $3.50 on Friday and Saturday evenings that goes to the musicians.

Smoking is allowed in the lobby only, but it's discouraged even there by a grotesque silver papier-mache man who permanently occupies the only chair.

Hours: All year, 11:30 A.M.-2 P.M. Monday-Friday; 6-10 P.M. Wednesday-Saturday. The Warehouse is occasionally open for dinner Monday and Tuesday, when there is special entertainment.

—*Sheary Suiter*

FAIRBANKS

Hungry Dog Cafe
3374 College Rd.
907-479-3787

The Hungry Dog Cafe is housed in a log cabin as properly rustic and organic as you might expect from a natural foods restaurant in Alaska. Its inner walls are covered with mellow rough-cut planks and work by Fairbanks artists. The service is relaxed, efficient and friendly.

Try eggs and assorted vegetables for a breakfast special; the vegetables vary according to what's readily available. Another tasty choice would be a continental breakfast—one of the whole grain, naturally sweetened desserts or cinnamon rolls, the cheapest cup of coffee in Fairbanks or herb tea, and maybe a tall tumbler of unfiltered apple juice. Milk, lemonade (the only item in the place that's sweetened with sugar), grape juice and V-8 are also offered.

The cheese and mushroom sandwich, served on fresh whole grain bread, makes for a delicious lunch, as does the olive and cream cheese sandwich. Nonvegetarian sandwiches such as tuna salad also are served.

You can choose from two main courses in the evening, one for vegetarians and one that's not. These vary according to what's fresh and available. Meat meals have included seafood quiches or salmon steaks (from Alaskan shores, of course). Vegetarian meals, offered in two sizes, are filling. Steamed zucchini with white sauce, a fresh salad with sprouts and seeds, and a delicious apple-carrot-raisin-nut stuffing are particularly good in the summer. The quiches are imaginative and varied.

A word about the fresh-baked desserts: the blueberry-banana cream cheese pie is fantastic, and so is the strawberry cobbler. Fresh, wild berries are used whenever possible. The cheesecake cookie is another original winner.

No smoking, beer, wine or credit cards.

Open 9 A.M.-9 P.M. Monday-Saturday.

—Ann Kacsur

Arizona

YUMA

Nature's Way
250 S. Madison Ave.
602-782-1120

Nature's Way is located next to a restored adobe home housing a museum of early Yuma history. While the restaurant has some indoor seating, the bulk of its tables is arranged in a terraced garden overlooking the museum's aviary. Offerings include vegetarian sandwiches, soups and salads, frozen yogurt and herb teas.

California

ARNOLD

The Natural Patch
1225 Oak Circle
209-795-3262

The Natural Patch is tucked into the heart of the Sierra Nevada "Gold Country." Started as a natural foods store, it has become an excellent place to eat on the mountain. An expansion of the building and the addition of a deck have added an airy feeling to the casual atmosphere.

Any offering on the luncheon menu is a good bet for adults, but for a really generous portion, try the Pigout, a pocket bread topped with fresh vegetables. The kids will love the Gooshy Goober, a peanut butter sandwich with honey or jam; bananas and raisins are extra and may be too filling.

Desserts are limited to fresh fruits, sherbets and ice cream, all sweetened with honey or fructose.

The dinner menu is flexible, offering two or three specials each night. The Turkey Chapatis are delicious. Friday is "Mexican night." Salad comes with the meals, and be sure to order the "Cosmic" dressing, a house blend of oil, vinegar, thyme, marjoram and a few other things that make it outstanding. A child's plate will be made up on request.

Beer and wine are served, along with fruit juices, some specially blended fruit concoctions, coffee and tea.

Entertainment is impromptu in the eclectic atmosphere of the Natural Patch. The outdoor deck is a perfect stage for guitar playing, and patrons are encouraged to share their talents.

Smoking permitted. No credit cards.

Tuesday-Saturday 11:30 A.M.-2:30 P.M.; Thursday through Saturday 6-10 P.M.

—Virginia Ryan

CANOGA PARK

Follow Your Heart
21825 Sherman Way
213-348-3240

"This is a lacto-vegetarian restaurant in a natural foods supermarket, which sells everything from shoes to toothpaste—bulk grains, fresh organic produce, kitchen utensils, fabric dyes, and almost everything connected with the earth-improvement lifestyle. The restaurant is part of the store, well staffed and well stocked," writes our correspondent. "The menu selection is large. There are daily specials, and the hearty soups are particularly noteworthy. Organically grown food is used whenever possible. This is the most popular vegie restaurant in the San Fernando Valley."

No smoking. MasterCard and Visa accepted.

Open 10 A.M.-7:30 P.M. every day.

CARMEL

Cornucopia
3590 The Barnyard
408-625-1454

Cornucopia struggles to combine high ideals of natural/vegetarian food preparation with the commercial realities of a tourist shopping-center location. The result seems more of a success than a compromise—international cuisine with entirely natural foods, and a listing in Livingston's Top Ten Restaurants in the Monterey Bay area.

Some of the appetizers on the menu are sufficient for a small meal. The raw vegetable plate, for example, offers cauliflower, mushrooms, celery, carrots, bell peppers, tomato wedges and daikon (Japanese radish) sprinkled with almonds and cashews and accompanied by a tasty house dressing.

Luncheon choices include Eggplant Burger, pita-and-hommus, and several kinds of large sandwiches. All are served with soup or salad, pickles and chips.

Complete dinners are large—you might want to skip lunch and dine late. There are Mexican meals and other international choices ranging from Monk's Dream (steamed vegetables over brown rice) to Mushroom Stroganoff. All dinners are served with soup and salad and a basket of warm whole grain bread.

Dinner salads are large, too, and they're available with a choice of three dressings, all very special and all made in the Cornucopia kitchen. The house dressing is yogurt and tahini with a little honey; the French is an oil-and-vinegar base with herbs and tomatoes; San Francisco Blue has chunks of blue cheese suspended in a mixture of several oils, vinegar and herbs.

Most desserts are made with honey, but you'd better ask.

Cold beverages include milk, juices straight or mixed, and yogurt and ice concoctions; nonalcoholic sangria and ginseng wine are available, and you may bring your own wine if you drink it in the patio dining area. A full line of herb teas is offered, too, as well as cappuccino, espresso, hot Dutch chocolate, a house blend of coffee, and a black tea-of-the-day.

No smoking. MasterCard and Visa accepted.

Monday 11:30 A.M.-3 P.M.; Tuesday-Thursday 11:30 A.M.-9 P.M., Friday and Saturday until 9:30 P.M.; Saturday and Sunday 9:30 A.M.-1:30 P.M. for brunch.

—Marlene Anne Bumgarner

CHULA VISTA

Lettuce In
618 E St.
714-420-4951

Along the side of a parking lot between Yum Yum Donuts and Wendy's Old-Fashioned Hamburgers, there is Lettuce In, the only natural foods establishment in Chula Vista. The atmosphere is cozy and informal. Lots of live plants enhance the white, orange and brown interior, accented by a row of stylized trees painted on the top portion of the walls. There is natural wood on counters and chairs, and all tables have fresh flowers on them.

Lettuce In is a self-help place where you can prepare your own salad from a bar of freshly cut vegetables. Besides the usual salad dressings, a Lo-Cal house dressing made with yogurt is available. There is a different homemade soup offered daily, or you can order one of the delicious pita-bread sandwiches, which are heaped to capacity with shredded lettuce, alfalfa sprouts, tomatoes and whatever else you choose from the list of skin-and-boneless turkey, tuna, mushrooms, avocados, eggs or grated cheese. All come dunked with a good measure of house dressing that makes eating them a mouth-watering delight.

For dessert there is carrot cake and several flavors of frozen yogurt; desserts contain sugar. Drinks include an assortment of herb teas and canned or bottled natural fruit juices. Milk, black tea and a few diet sodas are available, too. No coffee. No alcohol allowed.

Smoking's permitted but not encouraged. No credit cards.

Open Monday-Friday 11 A.M.-6:30 P.M.; Saturday 11 A.M.-4 P.M.

—Anja Hovland de Sanchez

CUPERTINO
The Garden of Life
10933 N. Wolfe Rd.
408-255-3643

"Located in the Vallco Village Mall, the attractive, greenery-laden Garden features a different soup daily, natural lunches and dinners, and the vegetarian Waldoburger," writes our correspondent.

Nonsmoking section. No credit cards.

Open daily 10 A.M.-4 P.M.

CUPERTINO
The Good Earth
20813 Stevens Creek Blvd.
408-984-0960

See listing for Santa Clara.

DEL MAR

The Gatekeeper
Interstate 5 at Via de la Valle
714-481-8861

Also in San Diego.
The Gatekeeper in Del Mar is a rare experience from first glance. The building itself is half-buried, with its south side a 45-degree dichondra roof from ground level to solar skylight. Cut-glass corner windows and ceiling stained glass provide ample light for dozens of exotic green plants arranged to accent the antiques that decorate this unusual 40-table popular restaurant.

Soft classical music or jazz serves as a background for a menu that ranges from fresh fruits to zucchini souffle au gratin. Whole grain waffles are a favorite of the brunch menu; Fillet Almandine is a top choice of the dinner entrees. A variety of omelets and tostadas, everyone's favorites, is offered on both menus.

Red meat is not served, nor are sugar or preservatives used in food preparation. Only fresh, certified-organic vegetables are served. The Gatekeeper bakes its own breads. It is the only restaurant I have found in California that serves raw milk.

Beer and wine available. Smoking not permitted. There's a $2 minimum at dinner. American Express, MasterCard and Visa accepted. Reservations suggested.

Opens at 7 A.M. every day. Lunch served from 11:30 A.M.-4:30 P.M. Dinner follows until 10 P.M. weeknights, 11 P.M. Fridays and Saturdays.

—Arlene Cook

ENCINO

Lettuce Patch Saladeria
15601 Ventura Blvd.
213-986-9430

See listing under Los Angeles.

ESCONDIDO

Frazier Farms' Country Fare
13th and Centre City Pkwy.
714-745-2141

Old-fashioned wallpaper, stained glass and hanging plants create an atmosphere of country warmth in this fresh addition to the area's finest and most popular restaurants.

Country Fare serves food most readily available in season. The menu always includes a fish dish, a vegetarian casserole, and beef and poultry selections. All beef and poultry, grown by Frazier Farms, are raised naturally without steroids. All produce is grown naturally, too. No refined sugar is used in the kitchen or bakery.

Both the restaurant operation and the continental menu are under the direction of Bill Stewart, who for 11 years was food editor of *Ladies Home Journal*.

Luncheon offerings range from salads to Seafood a la Newburg, but sandwiches and omelets are the favorites of the noon crowd.

Highlight of the week is the Sunday brunch, which features complimentary champagne, a choice of soups, a selection from five entrees, hot rolls and a drink. And it's topped off with fresh strawberry tortoni.

Beer and wine are available. Smoking not permitted. MasterCard and Visa accepted.

Luncheon Tuesday-Saturday 11:30 A.M.-3 P.M.; dinner Friday and Saturday 5-9 P.M.; brunch Sunday 10:30 A.M.-2:30. P.M.

—Arlene Cook

FULLERTON

The Greenery
119 E. Commonwealth Ave.
714-870-0981

The Greenery offers decorative greens for the eye and delectable greens for the palate. It is comfortably informal, its seating consisting of a random assortment of wooden armchairs. The service is usually informal, too; waitresses tend to be young and unprofessional, but genial. Dinner at peak hours could take a bit longer than you'd planned, but the ingenuousness is disarming, and the food is worth a wait.

There seem to be no poor choices on the menu (though occasionally one of the experimental items on the chalkboard doesn't quite pan out). The Un-Burger is delicious and satisfying, as is the Neato Burrito. Both contain a meatlike mixture of ground nuts, brown rice and seasonings. Children enjoy the peanut butter, banana, apple and nut sandwich; so did we.

Fish and eggs are the nearest things to meat that you'll find here. The only fish items are the tuna salad and the tuna sandwich, both baroque with additions, and the shrimp boat—half an avocado filled with shrimp, chopped celery, eggs and a dressing, all on a bed of (what else?) greenery.

For dessert, try the carrot cake unless you object to sucrose. If you do but don't mind fructose, the frozen yogurt is made on the premises and comes in a different flavor every day.

Beverages include coffee, herb teas and a caffeine-free regular tea. Nothing alcoholic is offered or encouraged. As for the burning leaf, an amusing sign threatens organic reprisals on those smoking on the premises. No credit cards.

Monday-Friday 10 A.M.-7 P.M.; Saturday 10 A.M.-5 P.M.

—John J. Brugaletta

GAVIOTA

The Farmer and the Fisherman
Hwy. 101
805-685-2657

The Farmer and the Fisherman is owned and operated by the Brotherhood of the Sun, a local communal group whose three supermarkets, juice factory and bakery dominate the South Coast natural foods scene. Aiming to bring an "earthy vibration" to the McDonald's crowd, the brotherhood offers organically grown foods (from their nearby ranch) and original recipes (from their *Sunburst Family Cookbook*). Seating in the two colonial-style dining rooms is at counter or tables, where views of rolling hills and the blue Pacific provide visual hors d'oeuvres.

Meals come with cornbread; some might prefer it sweeter. Entrees range from beef to vegies. Fish is local and fresh. Abalone chowder is a good example of the creative seasoning we found here (but less gristle, please). The abalone steak dinner is delicious and eye-catching—broccoli rosettes arranged just so by careful hands, with a fluffy mountain of the best brown rice we've ever tasted. The Ploughman's Share, a baked potato covered with herb butter, vegies and cheddar cheese, is too large and too bland.

Breakfasts are a specialty here. Saint John's French Toast is a fine way to start the day—carob-date bread (excellent), fried just right, and homemade applesauce. Served with fried potatoes, whole wheat toast and strawberry jam, the omelets are hearty meals.

The desserts alone are worth your visit. "Almost overwhelming" is the menu's accurate description of the fudgy chocolate cake, and the avocado cream pie deserves rave reviews.

No alcohol. Coffee available. Major credit cards accepted. Smoking section.

Weekdays 7:30 A.M.-7:30 P.M.; Friday-Sunday seating until 8:30 P.M.

—Judy Thomas

GLENDALE
Foods for Life
504 E. Broadway
213-249-2660

Natural wood is the decorating motif of this attractive natural foods restaurant. The tables and chairs (wood with padded seats) are custom-made. Bright lights permit reading, and the surroundings are clean and neat at all times. Mostly women dine here; there are very few children, and few men.

The foods and drinks are top-quality; they seem slightly high-priced but are apparently worth it because sales volume is high. Sandwiches are a big seller, assembled to order and served with a mixed green salad including chopped walnuts. Menus are posted on the walls, and they're so extensive it takes a while to absorb them. Tuna with sprouts is very popular. There are many delightful desserts, made without sugar; carrot cake is the most popular, but others come close.

Coffee and a substitute are available; no beer, wine or liquor. Finding a place to sit at meal time is a problem; it is recommended that you arrive early or late.

—Alan W. Farrant

HERMOSA BEACH

Conversations
934 Hermosa Ave.
213-372-5906

Tucked into a row of shops just a block from the beach, this small, cozy restaurant's white stucco walls are pleasantly accented by warm wood paneling, copper plaques, bright earthenware platters, and plants. It serves an assortment of sandwiches, salads and entrees. No meat or sugar is used in preparation; the only fish served here is tuna. Organic produce is used whenever possible.

Artichoke cheese pie, a delicate quichelike dish made without the crust, is the specialty here. Mushroom-Broccoli Stroganoff is another popular dish; the vegetables are combined in a rich sour cream sauce and served on brown rice under a layer of melted cheese. The salads are interesting combos of fresh vegetables, which include some surprises like jicama. All salads are served with Irish brown bread. Sandwiches are the typical avocado-sprouts-cheese things. Carob mousse ends the meal on a sweet note. Coffee, herb teas, a variety of smoothies and juices and hot cider round out the menu.

No alcohol. No smoking. No credit cards.

Noon-3:30 P.M. and 5-10 P.M. Tuesday-Saturday; noon-5 P.M. Sunday.

—Jamie Shoop

HERMOSA BEACH

The Spot
110 Second St.
213-372-1294

Creating innovative dishes with an international flavor while working within the confines of strict vegetarianism is the goal of The Spot. No meat, eggs, fish or sugar is used in this tiny restaurant. All produce is organic.

The atmosphere here is warm and friendly, the dining room a charming jumble of old tables and chairs and mismatched tablecloths. White-washed walls, plants, a fountain and the smiling staff complete the picture.

The menu is extensive. Entrees run the gamut from a vegetable tempura dinner to Hunza Pie—cooked spinach, cottage cheese and cashews baked in a whole wheat crust and served with grilled cheese on top. Especially tasty is the lasagna—cheese and herbs layered with whole wheat spinach noodles and tomato sauce. All dinners include hot vegetables, salad and bread.

The Spot is especially proud of its desserts, which include baklava and fresh fruit pies. The apple pie is a treat, with raisins and honey in a whole wheat crust topped with fresh whipped cream. Beverages include coffee, herb teas, juice and smoothies.

No alcohol, but customers may bring their own wine. No smoking. No credit cards.

Open noon-2 P.M. and 5:30-9 P.M. weekdays except Tuesday; 5:30-9 P.M. Saturday and Sunday.

—Jamie Shoop

HOLLYWOOD

Old World
8782 Sunset Blvd.
213-652-2520

See review under Los Angeles.

HOLLYWOOD

The Source
8301 Sunset Blvd.
213-656-6388

Smack on Sunset Boulevard with a patio wisely shielded from smog and noise by a window-wall, The Source has a small inside room helped out with plants and mirrors, and an even tinier annex. The modest prices make up for the close quarters.

The all-vegetable entrees, which come with fresh soup or a dinner salad, are many and varied. Mother's Eggplant, with grated mushrooms and olives sauteed in garlic butter, topped with pignolia nuts and cheese in tomato sauce and served with brown rice, is a popular favorite. The Magic Mushrooms are sauteed with Spanish onions, topped with scallions, bean sprouts and Swiss chard, zipped up with grated cheese and tomato sauce, and accompanied by cottage cheese.

The salads, presented in big wooden bowls, contain excellent vegetables, nicely dressed. The Chinese-style salad has at least ten ingredients and an elegant sesame oil and tamari sauce dressing. The Greek-style salad features feta cheese and an olive oil dressing. Fruit salads may be had with yogurt or cottage cheese.

There is a fresh fish of the day with brown rice at lunch and a chicken dish on the dinner menu.

The midday menu includes a hot concoction of ground oats, wheat, sunflower seeds and sesame seeds with raisins, banana, apple, nuts and half-and-half; that ought to sustain you through even the most trying day. Or there's a Peasant Lunch special, sandwiches and omelets.

The desserts contain no refined sugar, and the menu pridefully asserts: "Only whole grains and pure honey . . . all our oils are cold-pressed."

Coffee, bring-your-own-wine. American Express, MasterCard, Visa.

Monday-Friday 11 A.M.-midnight; weekends 9 A.M.-midnight.

—Marty Delman

ISLA VISTA

Sun & Earth
6576 Trigo Rd.
805-968-2031

Located on a side street in a student community, Sun & Earth (established in 1967) predates most of the natural foods eateries in the country. Geometric patterns of inlaid wood add a delightful touch to the interior, but the garden's jungle setting—tree stump seats, bamboo, rubber trees and a lily pond—is exceptionally fine.

We find here the type of high-quality food one might expect of a pioneer. The old standbys—eggplant parmesan, broiled zucchini and sauteed vegetables—are expertly done. Nightly specials are Mexican and Italian fare; the lasagna is a rich mound of vegies, noodles, and jack, ricotta and Parmesan cheeses served with a crisp salad (and an excellent tamari house dressing) and roll. Egg rolls and assorted vegetable casseroles are occasionally available.

Local fresh fish is a house specialty; although we are not fish lovers, we enjoyed the char-broiled Italian Snapper with brown rice, tangy tomato sauce and cheeses. Rice and Nut Salad successfully combines those items with vegetables, jack cheese and lettuce. The burgers—snapper, soy and Veggie-Nut—come with soup and salad.

Portions here are large, prices reasonable, and the staff mellow. Coffee, beer and wine available. Smoking permitted in garden. No credit cards. Occasional guitarist.

Lunch 11:30 A.M.-3 P.M. Sunday-Friday; dinner 4:30-9 P.M. Sunday-Thursday; until 10 P.M. Friday and Saturday.

—Judy Thomas

KENTFIELD

Mountains are Mountains
927 Sir Francis Drake Blvd.
415-459-9781

Hanging plants, fresh flowers on the tables, a giant photo mural and smaller framed nature photographs all give this restaurant a feeling of natural wholesomeness. The balcony has a striking view of Mt. Tamalpais, especially impressive at sunset.

The menu offers hot and cold sandwiches, soup and salads. The green salad has lettuce, parsley, cucumber, tomato, green onions, red cabbage and carrots. For an additional charge you can get avocado, mushroom, tofu, rennetless cheese, onion or sprouts.

The chef's attempt at haute cuisine in two nightly specials is not all that special. The Indian dinner would surely be disowned by any self-respecting Indian cook. It's better to stick to regular fare with something like the hearty large felafel.

Desserts are made with honey. They include fruit pies with whole wheat crusts, soybean ice cream, and fruit yogurt. Beverages include coffee, a hot grain drink, herb teas and juices as well as wine and beer.

Musicians arrive every evening around 7 to play classical, folk, country and western, jazz, pop or '50s rock-and-roll. The quality of the music ranges from amateurish dissonance on up.

Smoking on balcony only. No credit cards. No reservations taken.

Monday-Thursday 11 A.M.-11 P.M.; Friday and Saturday until midnight. Dinner served from 5 P.M.

—Wendy Dreskin

LAGUNA BEACH

Oceans
1750 S. Pacific Coast Hwy.
714-497-3730

In an all-too-harried world, Oceans is a refreshing surprise. Even the California speed-demons tearing up the asphalt on the coastal highway could not disturb the serene atmosphere or the smiling hostess. The word here is mellow. Slowly turning ceiling fans cool the wood-paneled dining room; booths are tucked away in alcoves topped by Moorish arches. Al fresco dining is possible on the secluded lattice-walled patio and the front terrace.

As would be expected, Oceans specializes in seafood. It bakes all of its bread and pies on the premises. The seafood menu includes a catch of the day and a few surprises, such as abalone-style squid and shark. All dishes are made from scratch.

For cheap eats, the soup of the day is a bargain. It's served with crusty fresh bread and butter, and you may have seconds.

On Sundays, a number of omelets are available for brunch. Desserts include a chocolate mousse and fresh fruit pies in a scrumptious crust of dates, nuts and coconut. Except for the mousse and chocolate pie, all dishes are sugarless. Beverages include herb teas, smoothies, juices, milk shakes and coffee as well as beer and wine.

Smoking on the patio only. Children's portions available on request. MasterCard and Visa accepted.

Open 5-10 P.M. Monday-Friday; 11:30 A.M.-10 P.M. Saturday; 10 A.M.-2 P.M. and 5-10 P.M. Sunday.

—Jamie Shoop

LOS ANGELES

Aware Inn
8828 Sunset Blvd.
213-652-2555

If your neighborhood is the swank 16th *arrondissement* in Paris, this is the charming bistro down the block. A beautiful small restaurant, divided into tiny rooms for intimacy, the Aware Inn has a full continental menu that includes "vegetarian delights" and "dieting gourmet" selections. The decor features country-French dark wood paneling, lots of beveled and etched glass doors, exotic fabric wall-coverings over padding for acoustical help, white tablecloths, fresh flowers, and oversized wine glasses.

The menu gives approximate calorie counts, says "butter" is

safflower margarine and "cream" is whipped cottage cheese. The Vegetable Curry L'Indienne is beautiful, served with homemade chutney, and there are low-calorie chicken, veal and fish dishes. Salads are artistic wonders; the seven-vegetable Aware Inn Salad with sunflower seeds and pignolia nuts is too much to go with dinner, so share it with a friend.

Other vegetarian goodies include walnut-cheddar balls, sauteed savories of nuts, vegetables, bread crumbs and cheddar cheese served hot with sauce, and Eggplant Olympus, which has an herb-and-tomato sauce and is topped with melted jack cheese.

There are fresh carrot, apple and orange juices as well as beer and wine. Homemade desserts include a chocolate mousse-type cheesecake and other indulgences. No refined sugar is used here.

Special seating for nonsmokers. Major credit cards accepted.

Lunch Monday-Friday noon-2:30 P.M., dinner every night 6-11:30 P.M.

—Marty Delman

LOS ANGELES

Everyoung Vegetarian Hoedown
11403 Victory Blvd.
North Hollywood
213-980-9011

A correspondent advises: "This wonder is (are you ready?) a Bolivian vegetarian restaurant! It is run by women. The food is magnificent, well seasoned, cooked to perfection. They use soy meats in some of the more exotic dishes, such as Everyoung's Soy Chicken Dinner. One tasty treat is flaxseed tea, a grain beverage that resembles diluted cereal. These women make the best empanadas (individual soy cheese pies) I have ever eaten. Whole wheat pizza with avocado is their best seller. No animal fats are used, only corn oil, and honey is the only sweetener. Prices are moderate. The decor is simple, even neglected, but the restaurant is clean and the people are very friendly. One of my favorites!"

Beer and wine served. No credit cards.

Open 11 A.M.-10 P.M. Monday-Saturday.

LOS ANGELES
Golden Temple Conscious Cookery
7910 W. Third St.
213-655-1891

Bright yellow paint on the outside makes this restaurant especially easy to find. And finding it is well worthwhile. It is a natural foods restaurant—a high-class one. The decor is beautiful: white tablecloths, high-back wooden chairs with straw seats, gold-color carpet. There are hanging plants, and fresh flowers on each table. Music plays as you dine. You can have your meal on the patio nine months a year, and the indoors is air-conditioned. The menu here emphasizes American and Indian foods, and employees are dressed in white Indian costumes, which lends a nice touch.

A popular feature here is the salad bar buffet, all you can eat. Popular items on the vegetarian menu include eggplant parmesan and enchiladas. The soup changes daily. There is a good choice of juice drinks, including fresh lemon and lime, apple, carrot and coconut and pineapple. Herb teas are also available. House specialty drinks include lassi—blended yogurt, honey and lime juice—and Nectaral Rose, which is red zinger tea mixed with apple juice and sparkling mineral water. Sparkling cider is served, too, but there's no coffee or alcohol.

No smoking. Children are not encouraged but are permitted. Major credit cards accepted.

Tuesday-Sunday 11:30 A.M.-10 P.M.

—*Alan W. Farrant*

LOS ANGELES
Hampton's
1342 N. Highland Ave.
213-469-1090

Entrance is via the parking lot, but don't worry. Inside there is an outdoor room with brick floor, hanging plants, bare wood tables. Nice. The inside dining room has wide planked floors, paintings and more plants.

Service is informal but efficient; the salad bar and hamburger embellishments are serve-yourself. The piped music is classical. Clean-shaven tie wearers may be a minority here, but if the ambience is *muy* casual, the concern with quality food is serious.

"No packaged anything" is Hampton's promise. Meat for the famous and gigantic hamburgers is ground fresh daily on the premises, and the fat content is rigidly controlled.

There are no beef or chicken bases for the homemade sauces, out of consideration for vegetarians.

The 20-item salad bar offers crushed pineapple, marinated goodies that may be piled on the hamburgers, cherry tomatoes, green and red onions, huge chunks of blue cheese, and tuna with several fresh dressings. Hot cheese sourdough bread is a go-with for the salad, which is not as crisp as I'd like but good. Soups include homemade vegetable and gazpacho. Eggplant parmesan is also on the menu.

Drink choices seem unlimited—tap beer, French and California wines, diet drinks, homemade lemonade, wonderful cinnamon coffee.

There's a $2.50 minimum. For Sunday brunch, the classical music is live. MasterCard and Visa accepted. Nonsmoking section.

Sunday-Thursday 11:30 A.M.-10 P.M.; Friday and Saturday to 11 P.M.

—*Marty Delman*

LOS ANGELES
Lettuce Patch Saladeria
908 S. Barrington
213-820-2200

Also in Encino.

The bright green and white decor of this small room and patio is carried through to the T-shirts worn by the help, and the salad theme extends to the restrooms, cutely labeled saLADS and saLADIES. Lettuce Patch was among the pioneers of the straight salad places, but the serve-yourself salad theme has now expanded here to a make-your-own-sandwich bar, crepes and quiche that they'll make for you, and a blackboard with daily specials.

The salad bar is first-rate. There are greens, of course; red and green onions; bean and alfalfa sprouts; kidney, garbanzo and French green beans; cherry tomatoes, enoli and hothouse mushrooms, and the best of the market. Dressings include you-make-it oil and vinegar and a couple marked "lower calorie." You can add nuts, sesame seeds and so on.

Sandwiches are all salads—chicken, tuna, shrimp and egg—and they come in two sizes. They're prepared on white or whole wheat pita or whole wheat or granola bread, and you may add sprouts, pickles, red cabbage, radishes—a nice assortment.

There's homemade soup, lots of fresh juices, mineral water, wine, beers, coffee, herb tea, milk and diet sodas.

There is sugar in the banana-nut and chocolate cakes and in the zucchini bread, which is especially good.

No credit cards. Smoking permitted.

Monday-Saturday 11 A.M.-9 P.M.

—Marty Delman

LOS ANGELES

The Melting Pot
8490 Melrose
213-652-8030

You enter the Melting Pot through a delightful red brick patio, all festive with red-and-white checked tablecloths and bright red directors' chairs. It's an especially pleasant place to have breakfast if you can ignore the close-by traffic. The interior is divided into separate spaces with dark wood, plants and high-style nostalgia. Charming. The help is friendly and casual, the menu extensive, the vegetarian choices ample and excellent.

Vegetarian sandwiches include the avocado melt, with slices of avocado on a whole wheat bun, sprouts and tomato piled on top and cheddar cheese melted over all of it.

Specialties include the popular vegetable quiche—steamed vegetables and cheese in a crust, covered with mushroom sauce and served with a small salad. The Vegetable Garden has pick-of-the season vegetables topped with nuts and cheese, and it's accompanied by salad and a roll. There is a raw vegetable plate with dip.

Beverages include fresh juices and herb teas, and there's also a full bar.

American Express, MasterCard, Visa.

Monday-Thursday 8 A.M.-1 P.M.; Friday and Saturday 8 A.M.-2 P.M.; Sunday 8 A.M.-midnight.

—Marty Delman

LOS ANGELES
Natural Fudge Co.
5224 Fountain
213-661-0511

In the poor and frankly crumby part of old Hollywood, Natural Fudge is working hard to serve strictly vegetarian food in a "hang on, gang, we're going to make it" ambience. The room is furnished in Salvation Army rejects, there is expansion going on in one corner, and only the stunning brown paint on the outside of this old store building suggests that there may be taste, if limited capital.

The extensive menu may someday be the restaurant's financial undoing, but it makes for good buys while it lasts. The nutburger items have long been a mainstay for vegetable protein enthusiasts. The club sandwich is a stack of nutburger, avocado, Swiss cheese, tomato, sprouts and soya mayonnaise, served with potato or garbanzo salad; sharing is suggested. There's an avocado taco and a nutburger taco (made from freshly ground walnuts, sunflower seeds, cashews and sesame seeds with garlic, parsley, tamari and onions) with Natural Fudge's own Mexican sauce, and it's good. The salads, made with organic vegetables when possible, offer a choice of homemade dressings. The spinach salad—with avocado, mushrooms, olives and sprouts—is not enormous, but it's got to be the lowest-priced in town. They also make their own soups and chili.

Several items feature tofu, including a sauteed tofu plate, which comes with soup or salad. A side order of tofu is available grilled or raw.

Desserts include honey ice cream, date-nut bread, carrot cake and pecan pie, and there's no refined sugar in them. To drink there are natural herb teas, beer, and a natural house wine.

Nonsmoking section. MasterCard and Visa accepted. Live entertainment nightly.

Monday-Saturday 11 A.M.-11 P.M.

—Marty Delman

LOS ANGELES
Old World
1010 Westwood Blvd.
213-477-2033

Also in Hollywood, Beverly Hills, La Jolla and Palm Springs.
Old World is posh, laid-back California casual to the teeth. What a kick to find a menu saying, "Our food is prepared with your good health in mind," especially in hedonistic establishments that also serve quality booze.

Decor at the various locations runs strongly to plants, dark wood, quarry tile, little rooms, and lots of music. The staffs are young and informal. The menus are enormous, and so are the portions.

A good choice is the Vegeburger, vegetables merged into a patty served on a whole wheat roll with tomato and onion slices and accompanied by German-fried potatoes. The vegetable casserole has fresh vegetables prepared in a rich cream sauce, topped with melted cheese, served with roll and butter, and embellished with fresh fruit—delicious and filling. Vegetable quiche comes with salad and roll.

Old World's Spartan Sandwich consists of avocado, mushrooms, alfalfa sprouts, and a tomato slice, with melted Swiss cheese and a sprinkling of sesame seeds over all; you might do well to order a half-Spartan. Soups are made fresh daily with only natural ingredients. The Belgian Brunch—a Belgian-style whole wheat waffle served with two eggs or cottage cheese and a cocktail—is a best-seller.

The ice cream and all the elegant cakes, tortes and cookies are free of refined sugar and chemical additives. They've proved so popular there is now an "Old World Natural Bakery and Ice Cream" store next to the Sunset Boulevard restaurant.

American Express, MasterCard, Visa.
Sunday-Thursday 8 A.M.-1 A.M.; Friday and Saturday to 2:30 A.M.

—Marty Delman

LOS ANGELES
Organic-Ville
4177 W. Third St.
213-386-1440

Organic-Ville's slogan: "When available, we use organically grown fruits and vegetables." The restaurant is furnished with bright yellow tables and chairs as well as a counter. It opens into a health food store, which in turn leads into a bakery, where all the restaurant's baked goods are made. The building's a bit seedy, though, and so is the shopping area that surrounds it; don't leave your car unlocked in this neighborhood.

The menu includes meat and fish dishes, and the flesh that's used in them is the same as you'd buy in a regular butcher shop or fish store—nothing organic about them. Vegetarian offerings include sandwiches, a huge selection of meal-size salads, juices and sugarless desserts. There's no alcohol sold here. Coffee's available, though. No credit cards, but the prices are low.

Monday-Saturday 11 A.M.-8 P.M.

—Alan W. Farrant

LOS ANGELES
Rosalind's West African Cuisine
1941 S. La Cienega Blvd.
213-559-8816

In Rosalind's small dining room, surrounded by bamboo and palm trees silhouetted against a yellow African sunset, you will be introduced to the cuisine of Nigeria, Sierra Leone, Ghana and Togo. I imagined the food to be similar to Indian fare; it's not, although some of the spices and ingredients are the same.

Dinner begins with a green salad notable only for the dressing, a coconut milk, curry and lemon juice concoction. There are meat as well as vegetarian dishes. The vegetarian entree is a choice of vegetable sauteed and served with rice. My favorite is the spinach, a Nigerian recipe hinting of curry, nutmeg and peppers (also available with shrimp and fish added). Speaking of hot peppers, the dishes here are mild to medium, depending on what you're used to. Included with dinner are akara (ground black-eyed peas), yam balls, plantains, sweet green bananas called kelewele, pilli-pilli (a hot pepper sauce served on the side) and sweet biscuits.

Health-food fanatics might object to the white flour and white rice, but if you'd like a change from the usual vegetarian fare, Rosalind's is the place to go.

Smoking allowed. Reservations advised. Full bar. Coffee served. Major credit cards accepted.

Tuesday-Friday 5-10 P.M.; Saturday to 11 P.M.

—Colleen Davis

LOS ANGELES

Two Worlds
8022 W. Third St.
213-653-4212

Two Worlds is owned by a Jewish family from Burma who moved to Los Angeles in the 1960s. As its name implies, it serves vegetarian foods from both East and West.

You won't find any meat or fish at this strictly kosher restaurant, but you will find some tasty and unusual dishes, all prepared to order. Try the Burmese coconut sauce with mock fish and wheat noodles or the eggplant platter with nuts, mushrooms, tahini, cheese, rice and vegetables. Other good choices are moussaka, mock chicken chow mein with egg roll and rice or noodles, and chili with beans, rice and cheese. Portions are generous, and all dinners include soup, salad and coffee, tea or juice.

For the undecided, the combo plate is a good bet, with five different items including a curry puff, egg roll and stuffed pepper. There's also a variety of sandwiches, salads and omelets. The

Israeli Salad, available in two sizes, makes a filling lunch. Other Middle Eastern specialties are felafel, an Israeli taco in pita bread, and chatselim—fried eggplant in pita.

Desserts are reasonably priced and are made with honey or turbinado sugar. A sweet ending is the baklava or cheesecake. Wash it all down with tea, coffee or juice from a wide selection.

Our only complaint is the slow service. Three waiters for 25 tables is not enough for the Sunday dinner rush. Two Worlds is a family place, so be prepared at times for screaming children. Come early for lunch or dinner, and plan on a leisurely meal.

Beer and wine are available. No smoking, no credit cards.

Sunday-Thursday 11:30 A.M.-2 P.M.and 4:30-9:30 P.M.; Friday 11 A.M.-sundown; Saturday, one hour after sundown to 11:30. Closed Jewish holidays.

—Hope Chaikin Kosh

LOS GATOS

Peasant Chef
368 Village La.
408-345-8006

We stumbled across this restaurant by accident on our way to a poetry reading in Old Town Los Gatos. We were greeted at the door with, "Would you prefer our nonsmoking section?" As we were escorted to the smokeless larger side of the restaurant, screened by dividers topped with plants, our impression of the pleasant room was that it is real, not plastic. Cloth place mats rest on hewn wood tables, flanked by silverware wrapped in matching linen napkins. Fresh flowers stand in earthenware vases below plants hanging from massive wooden beams. Carpeting covers most of the floor, but the terra-cotta tile is bare in the area closest to the kitchen, which is sparkling clean and visible through the swinging doors.

The owners of this restaurant like style: there is a hostess; waiters and waitresses wear cheerful peasant garb; the mood is relaxing. Soft classical music enhances the quiet but efficient movement of the staff, and there is no clanking of dishes (I never figured out how they did that).

The lunch menu is a list of sandwiches including roast beef, turkey, cream cheese and avocado, Syrian salad, and lox and bagel. A peasant lunch (or dinner) consists of a large bowl of homemade soup and a dinner salad with whole grain bread.

Entrees for the evening meal include soup or salad, hot peasant bread, vegetables and brown rice. The choices differ from month to month but have included quiche du jour, chicken sesame, scampi and sauteed oriental vegetables over rice. There is an International Special and a Vegetarian Special, both of which change each day.

Fresh Garden Delight, the most popular dinner salad, is a medium-size heap of fresh, torn greens topped with lots of sliced carrots, mung and azuki sprouts, red cabbage, tomato, mushrooms, cheese, avocado and ham. The fresh fruit salad includes cottage cheese, yogurt or honey ice cream and a sprinkle of coconut. Stuffed Tomato and Oriental Spinach are rich and hearty. The poppy seed dressing was very sweet, almost too much so, but the herb dressing was lovely, piquant with fresh basil.

Two hearty soups are served daily. The tasty gazpacho was the thickest we had ever seen, the cream of zucchini mild and pleasant.

All desserts except the tapioca pudding are made with sugar; they include cheesecake, carob mousse, French custard and apple crisp. Milk shakes and nondairy smoothies are available, along with a hot grain drink, coffee, herbal and regular tea, carob cocoa, mineral water and several types of bottled beer.

MasterCard and Visa accepted. Between 2 and 5 P.M. there's a 10% discount for elderly customers.

Monday-Saturday 11 A.M.-9:30 P.M.

—Marlene Anne Bumgarner

MENLO PARK

Late for the Train
561 Oak Grove Ave.
415-323-0922

"We try to provide a nourishing environment," says Jessie, co-owner with husband Bob of this cozy and homelike place just a dash across the tracks from the Southern Pacific station. The proprietors have realized their intention. On each of the tables a crocheted mat holds fresh flowers; antique salt, pepper and raw sugar containers; and a small canning jar of jam. Garage sales and Jessie's parents provided the embroidered table linens, antique prints and memorabilia, and old-fashioned china. The lace curtains, flowered wallpaper, macrame, and plants give the impression of lunching at the home of friends who have decorated with love and care. "I think people come here for more than the food," says Jessie. "They want intimacy."

The food itself is reason enough for their turnaway business. The menu features breakfast and luncheon dishes like baked scones, blintzes, eight kinds of omelets, Eggs Piperade (light and fluffy scrambled eggs with sauteed peppers, tomatoes and onions). Accompanying many dishes are fresh fruits and potatoes steamed with onions and grilled with soy sauce—very tasty.

The chalkboard lists soups and desserts, which change daily depending on what kind of fresh, organic produce is available. Some of the soups have been mulligatawny, turkey with summer vegetables, and black-eyed pea.

Desserts, some sweetened with fructose or turbinado sugar, have included gingerbread and peaches, pound cake with fresh pineapple sauce, and berries with ice cream. Completing the fare are salads and very hearty hot and cold sandwiches such as sauteed tofu, tabouli, and fish salad. The salad dressings—curried yogurt, buttermilk dill and honey-lemon—present a difficult choice; they're all delicious.

No microwaves or cutting machines are used. Although the food is prepared to order, there's never much of a wait. The warm and attentive staff is efficient as well, and they'll leave you alone with a newspaper if you wish.

No credit cards. No smoking. Wine and beer served.
Tuesday-Friday 7 A.M.-3 P.M.; Saturday and Sunday 8 A.M.-2 P.M.

—*Meredith Phillips*

MONTEREY

The Bruised Reed
375 Alvarado
408-649-3462

On the ground floor of a new and very classy building near the Monterey Convention Center/Doubletree Inn, the Bruised Reed is reached through an art gallery. The gallery features ceramics, photography and paintings similar to those hanging in the restaurant. Soft classical music and healthy plants refresh the dining atmosphere. Tile floors, white walls and a geometrically arranged wood-and-stucco ceiling provide a clean, airy setting. Even the furnishings, fresh cut flowers and table linens carry through a sort of Scandinavian-in-Spain theme. Service is courteous. Preparation is sometimes a little slow, but it's done with great care.

Salads, served a la carte or as dinners (with soup and dessert), run the gamut from an avocado-citrus plate to a Greek salad. There are about two dozen other selections—entrees, sandwiches and omelets. They range from chili (excellent and served with a tangy Greek rice salad and, sadly, a too-dry cornbread) to the tofu-nut roast (thoroughly filling with rice and vegetable). Some selections seem pedestrian but all are well seasoned and attractively served. Most diners leave feeling well fed at prices that are reasonable for the area. Children's portions are available, too.

There is no coffee or alcohol. Hot carob, a hot grain drink, herb teas, juices and bottled waters rule. Shakes are served, too, such as the delicious fruit-and-coconut Tropicana. Desserts (cheesecake, pies, cakes) are a trifle dear but are fine, rich and totally nontoxic.

No smoking. No credit cards.

Sunday-Thursday 11:30 A.M.-9 P.M.; Friday 11:30 A.M.-2 P.M.

—*Kip Eastman*

PACIFIC GROVE

Sunset Korean Restaurant
2006 Sunset Dr.
408-372-2526

Within easy walking distance of the Asilomar Conference Grounds, the Sunset provides a welcome break from the institutional food offered at the center's dining hall. The tasteful oriental decorations do a good job of disguising the 1950s coffee shop decor that was built into the place, and the tall black-lacquered cabinets with inlaid mother-of-pearl scenes hide the soda fountain that is still in place. As the light dims on one side of the restaurant, the owners come out from the kitchen and pull the heavy drapes, giving diners a magnificent view of the sunset over the water.

While Sunset is not strictly a vegetarian restaurant, a vegetarian will have no trouble getting a full meal here. The owners advertise their vegetarian dinner, and they come through handsomely. I received a bowl of miso soup and eight plates of food, one containing a large mound of vegetables, bean curd and alimentary noodles, the smaller ones filled with spinach salad Korean-style, pickled cabbage (kim-ch'i) and other unusual dishes. Turnip kim-ch'i was the special treat of the evening, and the green tea and orange slices washed down the spicy food very nicely. My dining partner ordered fried wonton, which was excellent. It contained meat, but since it was freshly prepared, it probably could be requested with a vegetarian filling. Drawbacks to the food here are inherent to Korean cuisine—too much salt and probably large amounts of monosodium glutamate.

Imported and domestic beers and wines are available, as well as tea and coffee.

With our second pot of green tea we were served dessert, which I will skip next time. It is highly sugared and only on the menu for American tastes. As the sunset completed its demonstration, several people lit cigarettes, and I noticed that there were ashtrays on all the tables. The spacious dining room and open doors contributed to continuing the breathable atmosphere,

although on a cold day it might not be so pleasant.
No credit cards.
Tuesday-Sunday 5-10 P.M.

—Marlene Anne Bumgarner

PALO ALTO

Barbara's Natural Food Bakery & Coffee Shop
2441 Birch St.
415-329-9222

While still a high-school student, Barbara began selling her home-baked bread door-to-door. By graduation she had so many clamoring customers that she opened a bakery, soon extended by a small coffee shop.

PALO ALTO

The Good Earth
185 University Ave.
415-321-9449

See listing for Santa Clara.

PASADENA

Bee Balser's House of Health
235 N. Lake Ave.
213-796-2351

This restaurant has a slogan—"Delicious Health Foods and Organic Juices Served Daily." People who are demanding about their health foods will be happy here. When a health drink calls for an egg, a fertile one is used. All foods are salt- and sugar-free. All items are daintily served in a relaxing well-lighted atmosphere. Counter motif is yellow with pink stools. Tables are brown and pink.

The turkey used here is raised without chemicals. Organic

juices and produce are featured when it's possible to secure them. The fare includes high-protein drinks, homemade soup, salads, a vast array of nonalcoholic drinks and a large selection of desserts.

No smoking. No rest rooms. No salt on tables or counter. No credit cards.

Monday-Saturday 9 A.M.-3 P.M.

—Alan W. Farrant

REDWOOD CITY

The Country Kitchen
2421 Broadway (at the Southern Pacific tracks)
415-364-7777

You enter the restaurant through the Center Bookstore and take a menu, on which you write your name and circle your choices. Don't be put off by the menu's too-cute style and flowery descriptions: "Thirst Aide," "Sandwich Delight" and "Tummy Yummies." Once you've hurdled this obstacle and found a table, you can relax and enjoy the well-prepared food and the pleasant interior.

It's tastefully decorated with antiques, gingham, old wood and a 1926 Magic Chef stove in which cakes, muffins and the daily special (e.g., mushroom-walnut casserole) are baked.

Choices include homemade soup and vegetable, fruit and seafood salads. The sandwiches on nine-grain bread are lavish: an interesting one is cream cheese, mushrooms, avocado, sprouts and olives. Dagwood Bumstead must have invented The Classic: crunchy peanut butter with jelly, honey, celery, banana, raisins and shredded carrots. The tuna and egg sandwiches are tasty in spite of their respective titles (Sorry Charlie and Production of Chicken Little). No red meat is served.

On Thursday evenings, there is a choice of two entrees served with salad and muffin. At breakfast, the possibilities are granola with yogurt or kefir, muffins, coffee cake, nut bread, smoothies and shakes, herb teas, coffees and espresso. Desserts, including sundaes, are sweetened with honey and brown sugar.

In true California style, you are urged to "say hello to the cashier" and to "share your needs with us." The Country Kitchen is run by a religious community counseling service. The adjoining bookstore (where you pay for the meal) sells Christian books. The proprietors' orientation is not forced on the customers in any way, though, and I recommend the Country Kitchen as a pleasant lunch spot.

Self-service. No alcohol. MasterCard and Visa accepted. Nonsmoking section.

Tuesday-Saturday 9:30 A.M.-4 P.M.; open until 8 on Thursdays.

—Meredith Phillips

SACRAMENTO

Pava's
2330 K St.
916-443-2397

Convenient to downtown Sacramento, Pava's serves breakfast, lunch and dinner and offers a varied menu to the vegetarian and nonvegetarian alike. Flickering candles, hanging greenery and antique wooden tables set the stage for relaxed dining and thoughtful conversation. An informal atmosphere and friendly service ensure that your visit will be pleasant.

Among the traditional egg breakfasts, Pava's also features an assortment of vegetable and cheese omelets. Brandy peach crepes served with real whipped cream are a special breakfast delight.

For lunch, you might try a creation called Crunchy Vegetarian, which is a sandwich of shredded carrots, cucumbers, mushrooms, tomatoes and sprouts laced with Pava's tasty creamy garlic dressing. For those seeking a more unusual vegetarian meal, Pava's offers broiled asparagus spears with cheddar cheese.

Pava's consistently manages to serve up distinctive and well seasoned vegetarian dinners of substantial portions. Entrees are served with homemade soup or salad, fresh vegetables and whole wheat rolls. The manicotti, overflowing with ricotta, gruyere and spinach, is a fine choice. Stuffed, baked zucchini served in a rice sauce of cream cheese, walnuts and fresh mushrooms, with brown rice, will satisfy the most selective taste buds. If these do not entice, there is the omelet of the day, perhaps the savory spinach and feta cheese.

Desserts vary daily and range from the slightly exotic sour cream berry pie, with a cheesecake texture but a somewhat chewy crust, to a slice of honey cheesecake. Some desserts are made with sugar, some with honey.

In addition to quality European beers and white, red and rose wines, Pava's offers dessert wines such as plum and pomegranate from California. Coffee, herb teas and juices also are available.

Nonsmoking section. No credit cards.

Monday-Friday 8 A.M.-10:30 P.M.; until 11 Friday and Saturday; Sunday 9 A.M.-2 P.M.

—Lillieanne Chase

SACRAMENTO

Sacramento Natural Foods Drive-In
2968 Freeport Blvd.
916-442-2120

Distinguished by collective management as well as by its vegetarian natural foods menu, the drive-in is a spinoff of the Sacramento Natural Foods Cooperative. It serves take-out food and provides outdoor seating only. The drive-in uses organically grown produce, whole grain breads, rennetless cheese and honey. White sugar, white flour and meat are not used.

The most popular item on the menu is the Burrito Supremo, a filling and tasty combination of refried beans, cheese, tomatoes, sprouts, olives and sour cream on a whole wheat tortilla. Another favorite is hommus, a spicy bean sandwich spread that also can be had as a dip with chips. And if you're trying to have the best of two worlds, the drive-in offers the Macro Burger, a patty of soybeans, millet, oats, celery, onions, carrots and spices, grilled and served on your choice of bun.

The drive-in also serves inexpensive nightly dinner specials. Shepherd's Pie is a mixture of mashed potatoes, vegetables and cheese. Another good possibility is Vegetable Stroganoff, a dinner of steamed vegetables with a sour cream sauce.

Although it doesn't serve coffee or alcohol, the drive-in does offer one item that could transport you to another plane: the smoothie, a blend of fruit, juice, and crushed ice; orange-papaya-banana is just one of the flavors of this exotic concoction. The drive-in also offers juices, herb teas and homemade soups.

No credit cards.

Open 11 A.M.-7:30 P.M. Monday-Saturday.

—Lillieanne Chase

SAN ANSELMO

Seasons
42 Redhill Ave.
415-454-1400

Seasons, true to its name, changes its menu four times a year, at each equinox and solstice. Connected with a natural foods store in Fairfax, it uses organically grown produce whenever possible.

Seasons is a relaxed dining spot. Almost every table has its own alcove, and all of them have tablecloths and cloth napkins, fresh flowers and (at dinner) candles. A natural wood interior, hanging plants and classical music complete the room's atmosphere.

Seasons uses whole grains and unpasteurized dairy products. The cooks avoid sugar and eggs, and they don't use white flour. Fish is available, but it's prepared in separate pots.

It is possible to assemble a dinner from the large a la carte menu, which offers breads, salads, tofu in various styles, grains, sauces, yogurt, and so on. The vegetable curry comes with rice or millet and a delightful array of condiments including strawberries, bananas, almonds, avocados, pomegranate seeds, raisins, cashews, apples, dates and red bell peppers. Full dinners, which come with soup and salad, can be quite expensive. The tempura dinner, toward the lower end of the price range, is very good, although it is impossible to get the batter as fluffy with whole wheat flour as with more refined flour; it comes with soy-lemon-ginger dip, rice with sauce, and a choice of soups and salads.

Beverages include wine, beer, coffee, coffee-substitutes and herb teas. Desserts change nightly, but there is usually an assortment of pies, rice pudding and ice cream.

MasterCard and Visa accepted. No smoking.

Friday-Wednesday 11 A.M.-11 P.M.

—Wendy Dreskin

SAN DIEGO
The Gatekeeper
Interstate 8 at Waring Rd.
714-287-2770

See listing for Del Mar. Similar decor and menu.

SAN DIEGO
Sunseed
705 Felspar St. (at Mission Blvd.)
714-270-3343

Patrons of this small cafe know that fast food doesn't have to be synonymous with greasy burgers and limp French fries. Sunseed, at the Frazier Farms natural foods store near Ocean Beach, is a take-out restaurant with only three picnic tables and more than its share of begging pigeons. But droves of young, health-conscious Californians seem more concerned with the great food than with the side-street atmosphere and the plastic utensils.

Breakfast at Sunseed is hearty enough for this New Englander's appetite. French toast is two thick slices of whole wheat bread fried in egg batter and served with honey or real maple syrup. We couldn't finish an order of whole wheat pancakes, and the fruit salad (served all day) will serve four as a side dish. Our favorite breakfast is the Mexican omelet, filled with pinto beans, cheese, sour cream and hot sauce, and the most adventurous eye-opener is Huevos Rancheros, a corn tortilla with beans, cheese, two eggs and hot sauce.

The same quality and quantity prevail at lunch. Sunseed

salads feature chopped vegetables on a bed of romaine or red leaf lettuce, cheese, sprouts and Italian or herb dressing. Four custardy quiches are made every day: mushroom, zucchini, spinach and our favorite, broccoli. Sandwiches are huge, healthful and imaginative; other lunch items include burritos, quesadillas and vegie pizza on whole wheat pita bread with mushrooms, onion and avocado.

No sugar is used in the preparation of the milk shakes or fruit smoothies. The variety of fresh juices makes it almost impossible to choose one. For caffeine addicts, Sunseed's coffee is one of the best we've tasted.

No credit cards. No alcohol.

Breakfast is served every day from 7:30-11 A.M., until 11:30 on Sunday, and lunch is served until closing at 6:30 P.M.

—Nan Fornal

SAN FRANCISCO

Denebien's
1338 Polk St.
415-673-9036

Denebien's is San Francisco's only kosher vegetarian cafeteria; all dishes are prepared in accordance with Jewish dietary laws. Fertile eggs are the only animal products used.

The restaurant's walls are tastefully decorated with paintings (some of which are for sale), Jewish proverbs and quotations from Golda Meir. Two colorful Japanese bridegrooms' robes are stretched across the center of the ceiling.

It's difficult to recommend a particular dish, since everything we had was delicious. Several entrees are offered each night, and each comes with salad, a slice of bread and a serving of slightly sweet pilaf.

Some suggestions are the vegetarian "sea scallops" or the vegetarian cutlets, both made from gluten. The mushroom, bean and barley soup is almost a meal in itself. And the vegetarian "chopped liver," made from azuki beans,is a tasty side dish.

Desserts change frequently, but they usually include several of the following: walnut, pecan or apple pie, cheesecake and halvah. My favorite is the rich honey-carob mousse.

Wine is served. No smoking. No credit cards.

Open 8 A.M.-10 P.M. Monday-Friday; 10 A.M.-10 P.M. Saturday and Sunday.

—Michael Ketcher

SAN FRANCISCO
Diamond Sutra
737 Diamond St.
415-285-6988

The blond and light brown birch furniture, the large windows across the front, and the clean white walls decorated with a few Japanese kites give Diamond Sutra a bright, airy atmosphere. The menu is a balanced mix of vegetarian, meat and seafood dishes.

I had the spinach-and-walnut lasagna dinner, which included satisfying servings of salad, soup, rice, vegetables and bread. The only weak link in that chain was the somewhat insipid leek-and-potato soup. Fortunately, the restaurant also offers a pungent tomato-onion soup.

Several tasty desserts are available, including a Swiss honey-walnut torte. And for the bibulous, there are four brands of beer and 14 different wines, including sherry and champagne.

The weekend brunch features, among other dishes, a create-your-own omelet, with a choice of nine ingredients.

In the evenings, there's often live music, usually a flamenco or classical guitarist.

Although it's not the custom to talk about rest rooms in restaurant reviews, the ones here are worth mentioning. Rather than being labeled for men and women, they're designated for "graffiti" and "non-graffiti." The division has encouraged a better-than-usual collection of rest room witticisms and artistry.

Smoking permitted, but there is a nonsmoking section. MasterCard and Visa accepted.

Open 5:30-10 P.M. Monday-Thursday; 5:30-10:30 P.M. Friday and Saturday; 10:30 A.M.-3 P.M. and 5-10 P.M. Sunday.

—Michael Ketcher

SAN FRANCISCO

Dipti Nivas
216 Church St.
415-626-6411

Owned by rock star Carlos Santana and run by disciples of Indian spiritual leader Sri Chinmoy, Dipti Nivas (Sanskrit for "abode of light") serves meatless meals cafeteria style.

"Good food in a divine atmosphere" is how manager Ratna King states the restaurant's philosophy. Immaculate cleanliness and courteous, friendly service add to the pleasure of dining here.

The menu rotates among about 25 casseroles, with two offered at any given time. Also available are curries, soups, sandwiches and salads. Customers can call ahead to find out the day's selections.

Recommended is the sampler plate, which includes a portion of each entree, or one entree plus the curry of the day. The walnut croquettes were delicious. Apparently, so is the lasagna; they ran out of it while I was there, and several people waiting in line postponed their dinner until more was brought out.

Although the eggplant curry was so spicy it brought a tear to the eye, the Heavenly Broccoli Soup was rather bland. I'd recommend staying away from the soups. The tomato bisque, also flavorless, was cold enough to be gazpacho.

Desserts, however, are tasty and reasonably priced. Especially recommended are the freshly baked cakes and pies, including gingerbread and sweet potato pie.

No coffee or alcohol. No smoking. No credit cards.

Monday-Friday 11 A.M.-10 P.M.; Saturday 1-10 P.M.

—Michael Ketcher

SAN FRANCISCO
Good Earth
2323 Powell St.
415-433-3174

The Good Earth, with seating for 250, is large enough for smokers and nonsmokers, teetotalers and drinkers, and vegetarians and carnivores to dine in harmony. In short, the restaurant has something that will appeal to almost everyone. It's near San Francisco's famed Fisherman's Wharf.

The extensive menu has several breakfast dishes, including ten-grain sourdough hot cakes, Swiss-style French toast and seven omelets, and they're served at all hours.

For lunch or dinner, several large, full-meal salads are available. Other vegetarian dishes include the Good Earth Burrito, the Good Earth Tostada and the Magic Eggplant Casserole. A number of imaginative sandwiches also are offered, the most interesting being the Small Planet Burger made from a grilled patty of nuts, grains, lentils and azuki beans and covered with melted cheese.

Amenities include free parking at the garage across the street, half-price tickets to a nearby movie theater and occasional cooking classes in the evening.

Beer and wine are available. Special section for smokers. No credit cards, but checks are accepted.

Open 8:30 A.M.-10 P.M. Sunday-Thursday; 8:30 A.M.-11 P.M. Saturday and Sunday.

—Michael Ketcher

SAN FRANCISCO
Greens
Building A, Fort Mason
415-771-6222

An old Army warehouse may not sound like the most appealing spot for dining, but the San Francisco Zen Center has done marvels with Greens. Bright white walls, some redwood burl tables, and practically floor-to-ceiling windows with a view of the colorful marina and the Golden Gate all make this a very attractive restaurant.

The brochette, served with herb rice, is always available and is very good; the bamboo skewers of tofu, tomato, onion and mushroom are charcoal-broiled. There is a pasta special daily. Entrees are served with a salad dressed with oil and vinegar (the lettuce would be happier with some companions) and bread.

There's also a selection of sandwiches, including a tasty pita stuffed with feta cheese, olives, Bermuda onion and lettuce.

Desserts, which come from the Zen Center's own bakery, are a highlight. Most do not ascribe to the ascetic philosophy and use such ingredients as real chocolate, white sugar and cream cheese, although there are one or two made with honey. They are indecently delicious. The Reine de Sabe chocolate cake is especially fine. Beverages include plain and fancy coffees (decaffeinated), regular and herb teas, juice and wine.

Reservations are a must. There are always lines for this popular place; an un-Zenlike bustle prevails. Smoking permitted. MasterCard and Visa accepted.

Hours: 11:30 A.M.-2:30 P.M. Tuesday-Saturday. Open Friday and Saturday nights for dinner—call for new hours.

—*Wendy Dreskin*

SAN FRANCISCO

Harvest Moon Vegetarian Restaurant
339 Judah St.
415-664-3044

Canary-yellow walls decorated with prints of birds and flowers and a tank of tropical fish brighten this small natural foods restaurant two blocks from Golden Gate Park. Harvest Moon serves foods made with organic whole grains, unrefined honey, rennetless cheeses, organic soybeans and, when possible, organic produce. In addition, Quyen Van Nguyen, the new owner, plans on expanding the menu to include oriental vegetarian cuisine.

The dinner special is always a tasty, hearty, well-balanced meal; it includes an entree such as vegetable crepes with cheese sauce or cheesy vegetable souffle with a mushroom sauce, a salad of lettuce, tomato and sprouts, and soup, possibly bean or lentil-vegetable. If two people are dining and splitting their entrees, the sauteed tofu, tomatoes and mushrooms or the sauteed nuts and greens, both served over rice, or the sour cream tacos made with avocado, chili, sprouts, tomatoes and sour cream are good second dinner choices.

Beverages include a large selection of teas, mineral water, a special blend of South American coffee (not too strong) and freshly squeezed juices. No alcohol is served, but you can bring your own wine. Desserts—fruit pies and yogurt—are strictly natural.

Whole wheat pancakes and sometimes whole wheat French toast, a special of two eggs with home fries and toast, and an excellent combination of eggs scrambled with cream cheese and spinach are offered for breakfast.

No smoking. MasterCard and Visa accepted.

Open 11 A.M.-2:30 P.M. and 4:30-9 P.M. weekdays; 9 A.M.-9 P.M. weekends.

—Patricia Smith

SAN FRANCISCO
The Hungry Mouth
11 Clement Ave.
415-386-9792

For years Walt and Magana Baptiste have advocated calm souls and enlightened minds in well-nourished bodies. One of their incidental discoveries is that vegetarians have taste buds, too, and are as threatened by inflation as anyone taking out a meat loan. Labor donated by their devotees helps keep prices laughably low at the Hungry Mouth, and only thought and dedication could produce the uniquely varied menu.

Lunch items include such rarities as a lentil sandwich plate and a mineral broth with mushrooms, kelp, dulse and sprouts. But it's with the dinners that the Hungry Mouth comes into its own. Complete meals—with 11 vegetarian entrees to choose from—include salad, soup, whole grain bread and herb tea. You can't go wrong with any of them, but one good choice is the vegetarian combination plate, with brown rice, spicy red beans, a delicious stuffed pepper in hot Indonesian peanut sauce, and more. Whatever you have will bury the canard that vegetarian food is bland.

The hotter dishes might be enhanced by one of the good foreign or domestic beers, served in a chilled glass. Sherry and honey-flavored fruit wines are served, too.

Desserts, none of them sugar-sweetened, include ice cream, carrot cake and pies, but we've always been too full to sample them. When's the last time you could say that about a low-priced dinner?

Section for smokers. MasterCard and Visa accepted.

Open 10 A.M.-10 P.M. Monday-Friday; 11 A.M.-10 P.M. Saturday; noon-10 P.M. Sunday.

—Joseph Kostolefsky

SAN FRANCISCO
Real Good Karma
501 Dolores St.
415-621-4112

Real Good Karma looks like a vegetarian restaurant should look. Large picture windows let in plenty of sunlight; tables, chairs, benches and counters are unmatched and unfinished; colors are all earth tones. Hanging plants and fresh flowers add to the unpretentious atmosphere. The emphasis here is on food rather than fancy decor.

Everything is prepared without chemical additives or preservatives, using only whole grains, cold-pressed oils and rennetless natural cheese. Except for the tomatoes in an occasional can of paste, all fruit and vegetables are organically grown.

A good bet, especially for those who can't make up their minds among the wide range of salads and entrees, is one of the large combination plates. The one I tried consisted of salad, rice, stir-fried vegetables, tempura and grilled tofu with sesame sauce. Parties of seven to ten people might want to try the Maha Grande Salad.

For dessert, the specialty of the house is fresh fruit pie. Somewhat less successful is the Hot Chai Float, a blend of Darjeeling and Ceylon teas, milk, brown sugar, ginger, cloves and cardamom with a scoop of ice cream. Coffee is served, but no alcohol. Customers may bring their own wine.

No smoking. Live music occasionally. No credit cards.

Open 5-11 P.M. every day, but the kitchen closes at 10 P.M.

—Michael Ketcher

SAN FRANCISCO

Sunshine Juice Bar
1718 Polk St.
415-441-3313

Two tiny tables and four chairs in front qualify this as San Francisco's only vegetarian sidewalk cafe. The small restaurant's interior, tastefully decorated with landscapes, plants and ferns, and red and white checked curtains and tablecloths, is homey.

The food, too, has a home-cooked flavor. Each night a different international dinner special is offered. Dishes range from quiche to spanakopita; a salad and a slice of bread are included. Soups are thick and flavorful, with a different one on the menu each day. Salads range from the low-priced Garden Greens to the Big Sur, which is the most expensive item on the menu.

The low prices here are balanced by small portions, making this an excellent stop for those seeking a quick snack or a light meal. Such a person may find the Inflation Fighter Special ideal; it consists of half a soy pate, egg salad or hommus sandwich and a cup of soup.

Only a limited variety of desserts is offered, with the most interesting being an insipid yogurt pie. For those who don't mind drinking their dessert, however, a wide assortment of juices (bottled and fresh), natural sodas and smoothies are available. Coffee is served, along with beer and wine.

No smoking, no credit cards.

Open every day 11 A.M.-10 P.M.

—Michael Ketcher

SAN FRANCISCO
Today's
216 Stockton St. (at Union Sq.)
415-362-3377

Through a health food store and up a flight you'll find a waiting line and, beyond it, a handsome room where lunch and tea are served and where single diners can feel comfortable. Even with disposable dishes, the total effect is bright and elegant. Everything, including the attentive waiters, is decorated in beige and tan. More to the point, most of the food is inviting.

The menu's main shortcoming is sameness. With no daily specials, the only variables are soups, desserts and fresh fish. Fish, like chicken, is offered only in, or accompanied by, salads, which dominate the brief bill of fare. At Today's prices, that's a lot of lettuce. Still, the Al Dente Salad of barely cooked vegetables in yogurt dressing has nice tang and texture. The one hot dish is outstanding: a salad of matchstick-cut parsnips, zucchini and other impeccable vegetables over puff pastry in a delicious cheese sauce. Vegetable soup and such specialties as puree of lettuce are served with an excellent nine-grain roll, raw sweet butter and the good house vinaigrette salad.

After a sensible light lunch, your resolve may be challenged by the pastries, which are sugar-sweetened, look fantastic, and don't last long. The usually available crushed-almond torte with creme fraiche is lovely. The frozen yogurts, at least, are honey-sweetened.

Good beverages here are the coffee, house wine, steamed beer or porter and the refreshing Cherry Perry (Perrier and cherry juice).

No smoking. Minimum at lunch $4. MasterCard and Visa accepted. Reservations advised, especially before 2 P.M.

Lunch 11 A.M.-3:30 P.M. Monday-Friday, until 4 P.M. Saturday. Tea 3-4 P.M. Monday-Friday.

—Joseph Kostolefsky

SAN FRANCISCO

Le Tournesol
1760 Polk St.
415-441-1760

Le Tournesol (The Sunflower), with its soft, classical music, freshly cut flowers on each table, professionally attentive waiters and carefully prepared French country dishes, raises the health food restaurant to new levels of elegance.

While prices here are higher than at most vegetarian restaurants, so is the quality of the food and service. Everything is prepared with fresh, organic ingredients; all breads and pastries are baked daily on the premises.

A wide and inventive array of entrees is served, and they come with the vegetable of the day and a choice of soup or salad. One excellent dish is the Tarte Aux Champignons Gratinee, a pie baked with mushrooms, heavy cream, herbs and cheese sauce. Other interesting vegetarian entrees include spinach crepes with cheese sauce and a creamy vegetable quiche. For nonvegetarians there's a fantastic assortment: baked clams on a bed of spinach, covered with a sauce of white wine and cheese; baked tomato filled with shellfish and mushrooms (excellent!); seafood crepes with lobster sauce; boneless trout with lemon butter, or crabmeat in a white wine hollandaise. Several large whole-meal salads also are offered.

Ten desserts, ranging from homemade hazelnut ice cream to Moka Java Cake, are on the menu. Quite an assortment of beverages is offered, too: wine, beer, six different coffees, six different teas and several fruit-juice concoctions. A favorite drink here is the Natural Fantasy (by the liter or half-liter): watermelon juice, cherry sherbet, marsala and lemon.

Section for smokers. American Express, MasterCard and Visa accepted.

Monday, Wednesday and Thursday 11:30 A.M.-3:30 P.M. and 5:30-10:30 P.M.; Friday and Saturday 11:30 A.M.-3:30 P.M. and 5-11:30 P.M.; Sunday 11:30 A.M.-3:30 P.M. and 5-11 P.M.

—Michael Ketcher and Karen Kardwell

SAN FRANCISCO

Vegi-Food
1820 Clement St.
415-387-8111

Vegi-Food adheres to Chinese Buddhist vegetarian precepts. Meat, eggs, garlic and onion are not used; they're replaced with various combinations of tofu, vegetables, fungi, nuts and gluten.

This tiny restaurant in the Mission District has only red Chinese lanterns and a golden Buddha burning incense to suggest its orientation. Once you've withstood the line, where you might wait 20 minutes for a table at dinnertime, the service is excellent; a second pot of tea even arrives without being requested. On one recent visit, the cook moved from table to table, graciously offering samples of freshly fried wonton and spring rolls.

The fried wonton appetizers, stuffed with mushrooms, ground vegetables and tofu and served with sweet-and-sour sauce, could easily become addictive. The spring roll—an egg roll sans egg—is a less compelling treat filled with a spicy mixture of shredded vegetables and tofu.

Black Mushrooms and Greens Chow Mein is a reliable entree of large mushroom slices, Chinese greens and carrots served over crisp noodles.The sauce is tasty, and the portions more than adequate. More spartan tastes may enjoy Colorful Shredded Vegetables—a dish of shredded tofu, green peppers, sprouts, carrots and mushrooms in a lightly seasoned sauce. Gluten is served up in various flavorful sauces such as black bean and curry. The most exciting entree is the fried walnuts with sweet-and-sour sauce. Whole walnuts are dipped in batter, deep fried and served with the sauce; the combination is as delicious as it is unusual. I found the most expensive entree—Lon-Hon-Jai Mixed Vegetables Deluxe—mediocre and recommend avoiding it.

There are no desserts or alcohol served here. Guests are not permitted to smoke or bring their own alcohol. No credit cards.

Tuesday-Friday 11 A.M.-3 P.M. and 5-9 P.M.; Saturday and Sunday 11:30 A.M.-9 P.M.

—Lillieanne Chase

SAN FRANCISCO

Wellsprings Communion
1123 Folsom St.

South of Market Street, among factories, warehouses and trucking companies, Wellsprings Communion offers the cheapest vegetarian meal in San Francisco.

The communal group that runs the restaurant views it as a community service and serves large portions of food at below break-even prices. While the menu may vary slightly from day to day, depending on who does the cooking, the basic meal—called the Worker's Special—consists of rice, chapati, vegetable and yogurt or spiced milk; for a few pennies extra, you can get salad and soup, too. Cakes are available for dessert.

While most of the dishes are tasty, the chapati and rice I had were too cool, the spiced milk too warm. Apparently the food is not kept at the right temperature while it is sitting out. And at these prices, one shouldn't expect too many amenities. Although there is often live music, usually classical guitar or jazz, patrons are encouraged to bus their own dishes and clean their own tables. Not everyone does this, and there often are crumbs left over from previous diners. Nevertheless, for nutritious meals at the lowest possible prices, Wellsprings Communion can't be beat.

No smoking. No coffee or alcohol. No credit cards.

Hours: 11:30 A.M.-2 P.M. and 5-7 P.M. Monday-Friday.

—Michael Ketcher

SANTA BARBARA

Good Earth
21 W. Canon Perdido
805-962-4463

Also listed under Santa Clara.

With its country-kitchen decor—brass pots and wooden spoons deck the walls—Good Earth has more wood per square inch than most forests. Perhaps more vegetation, too; plants hang from every conceivable spot, doubling themselves in the many mirrors lining the walls. We felt a sense of *deja vu* here and were not surprised to learn that this is a franchised restaurant, part of a chain.

All foods here are free of most refined sugar and overprocessed flour. Bakery goods are made on the premises and sweetened with honey. While the standard vegetarian ingredients are used, more esoteric fixings such as bok choy, tofu, spinach pasta and azuki beans are available.

Our favorite entree is the Country French Lasagna—spinach pasta and mushrooms smothered in cheese sauce; a larger portion would be nice for the price, however. Malaysian Cashew Shrimp is a heartier serving of delicately spiced crunchy peapods, bok choy and water chestnuts laced with shrimp and served over brown rice pilaf.

Salads are adequate but pedestrian, although their names portend more—New Age Spinach Salad, Mediterranean Sunshine. A broad spectrum of sandwiches featuring tamari-marinated tofu, lentil-azuki bean patties, shrimp and cheese makes this a popular downtown lunch stop. Skip the Famous Recipe Carrot Cake; it is dry. Hot Berry Cobbler with frozen yogurt, when available, will better soothe the sweet tooth.

Herb teas, coffee and alcohol are served. Smoking permitted on the patio. MasterCard and Visa accepted.

Open 9 A.M.-9 P.M. Monday-Friday, until 10 Saturday and Sunday.

—Judy Thomas

SANTA BARBARA

Good Shepherd
726 N. Milpas
805-966-6404

The Good Shepherd offers good food, good prices and mediocre atmosphere. If dining next to a busy street on wooden benches is not desired, we suggest phoning in a take-out order, because the imaginative and original menu is worth the effort.

Our favorite lunch choice is the Vegetarian Reuben, a satisfying blend of melted Swiss cheese, onions, sprouts and Thousand Island dressing (made with tofu instead of mayonnaise).

An ever-changing parade of daily specials underscores the spirit of culinary adventure here. Marinated Rice and Vegie Salad is a new twist on an old theme; the recipe for spinach pie was conceived and is happily consumed on the premises, and Vegetable Goulash introduces a rich onion-mushroom gravy.

Chili and cornbread served with sprout and avocado salad is a house special worth more than its price. A raw food dinner stars on Thursday nights (Beet Loaf, anyone?). All ingredients are rigorously natural—beans are cooked sans lard, pizza crust is whole wheat, sugar is banned. Fresh juices, fruit smoothies, herb teas and coffee are served, but no alcohol.

No smoking indoors. No credit cards.

Open 11 A.M.-9:30 P.M. every day.

—Judy Thomas

SANTA BARBARA

Tea House
301 E. Canon Perdido
805-965-4222

The Tea House owes much of its charm to the delightful old building it inhabits, one of the city's originals. The atmosphere is elegant, with muted rose tones, starchy white tablecloths and gracious waitresses.

Curries are a specialty here, and the vegetable curry—chock full of nuts, raisins, vegies and coconut—is especially rich and satisfying. Lunch features Mexican dishes mildly seasoned for gringo stomachs; charro beans are the house's excellent version of the standard refried beans. Enchiladas Verdes is gourmet south-of-the-border fare: just-right vegies and cheese wrapped in tortillas and blanketed with sour cream and green sauce. Spices and green chilis make the cream cheese and cucumber sandwich interesting but not for everyone. Unfortunately, the Chocolate Mousse is not always at its creamy best. Health fanatics may safely opt for the Yogurt Honey Pond, which describes itself precisely.

Beer, wine and champagne are served here. Teas are brewed

with purified water. There's no ban on smoking. MasterCard and Visa accepted. Unobtrusive harp, guitar or flute serenades often accompany dinner; there might be a harpist during Sunday brunch.

Open 11 A.M.-10 P.M. weekdays; 11 A.M.-10:30 P.M. Saturday; 10 A.M.-3 P.M. and 5:30-10 P.M. Sunday.

—Judy Thomas

SANTA CLARA

The Good Earth
2705 The Alameda
408-984-0960

Also in Cupertino, Palo Alto, Santa Barbara and Westwood. Perhaps the most popular natural food restaurants on the San Francisco peninsula, the Good Earth chain offers a wide variety of vegetable, omelet and seafood specialties and bakes its own whole grain breads daily. Nonsmoking seating always provided.

SANTA CRUZ

India Joze
Santa Cruz Art Center
1001 Center St.
408-427-3554

The regulars and passers-through at India Joze reveal the real Santa Cruz in cross section. The gallery and shops of the art center are reached through the restaurant, providing a nearly steady stream of entertainment while you eat. There are two dining areas—one for those ordering the specialty dinners in the evening, the other for quick meals, lunch and after-hours snacks. The service runs from haughty at worst to priceless at best.

Indonesian, Middle Eastern and East Indian selections rotate on the dinner menu during the week. Lunch offers a specials board as well as the regular menu. At lunch and after hours, diners will find themselves with a wide selection of items, all meatless except for a chowder, chili and a single chicken dish. The special dinners, unfortunately, provide for the vegetarian only by including a mushroom entree within each ethnic specialty. Ask about the extraordinary array of side items that come with the dinner to assure that items like shrimp paste are eliminated. At lunch, the menu includes enormous fruit and Greek salads as well as dishes such as fantastic chickpea-fritter felafel, an Indonesian vegetable platter and Joze's amazing hashbrowns. Ingredients are high quality and fresh, prepared with intense concentration (just observe the kitchen for a couple of minutes), and seasonings are rich, authentic and memorable.

Beverages include a variety of coffees, herb teas, beer and wine. To really get into the spirit of the place, try the hibiscus cooler, the chai (hot spiced tea), or the lassi (a cold, tangy yogurt drink). Usually delicious but horribly rich, the desserts contain sugar.

It's rarely done, but smoking is allowed. MasterCard and Visa accepted.

Open Tuesday-Sunday 9 A.M.-3 A.M.

—Kip Eastman

SANTA CRUZ

Nature's Harvest
2-2145 E. Cliff
408-475-9983

A rustic wooden building nestled between a florist's and a candy shop houses Nature's Harvest. Good use of limited space allows pleasant dining at tables and chairs in one room or on the floor around redwood plank tables in another. Healthy plants and creative mobiles combine with the friendly staff and fine service to create an enjoyable atmosphere in which to enjoy the totally natural menu. In the evening there is occasionally good live music; sometimes it is bad live music.

The menu features ten dinner entrees, tofu-mushroom or Macro-burgers, and salads meant to stand alone. Dinners include soup (such as the hearty lentil), fruit or green salad (both with a wide variety of ingredients and generous portions) and homemade bread (often cornbread made with superb, coarsely ground meal). A Just Soup dinner will satisfy, but the menu continues up the price scale to Eggplant Parmagiana or Mongolian Vegetable Saute. The Cashew-Mushroom Stroganoff is excellent and very filling. There are three pasta dishes, leaving the remainder of the menu based on brown rice. Vegetables are cooked until just barely tender. Use of spices is somewhat heavy-handed but always right for the dish.

Fresh juices, coffee, herb teas, beers and local wines are available. Smoothies here can be made with a base of coconut-pineapple, apple juice or milk augmented with yogurt, yeast or protein powder. The desserts are reasonable and free of sugar; the carrot cake is especially good. Marianne's honey ice cream is served, but it's more fun to travel a few blocks after your meal and get it at its source.

Smoking permitted—outside. MasterCard and Visa accepted.

Open every day, noon-3 P.M. and 5-10 P.M.

—*Kip Eastman*

SANTA CRUZ

Pan's
303 Potrero St., #5
408-427-2123

Nestled in the midst of the Sashmill, a restored collection of redwood buildings that used to house cabinetmakers at their trade, Pan's attracts a steady flow of regular customers as well as tourists.

Watched by a three-story mural of Pan, customers select ingredients from a salad bar containing such treats as marinated pole beans, mixed bean sprouts, mushrooms, garbanzo beans, sweet peppers and raw cauliflower, or they choose one of the three soups of the day. We tried the cream of spinach, which tasted more of lemon than of spinach; the black bean, which was quite flavorful and well textured, and the minestrone—excellent. A request brought a plate of hot whole wheat bread, which was fine-grained and deliciously chewy. A combination meal of salad and soup brings you unlimited servings of both, fresh whole grain muffins and butter, and a wonderful full feeling.

Those who prefer a full meal can choose from four tender omelets, which come with crunchy cheese toast, sour cream and fresh fruit, or from a list of fish and chicken entrees such as baked red snapper, scallops, chicken crepes or Chicken Saute Sec. Vegetarian entrees also are available, and all entrees come with muffins and butter, soup or salad, brown rice and fresh vegetables. Everything is served with pleasant remarks from waiters who take a personal interest in your enjoyment of the meal and who enjoy talking about food preparation.

Beverages include beer, wine, fresh orange juice, apple juice and fruit smoothies in tall fountain glasses, and—disappointingly—soft drinks (for regular businessmen, we were told). Herb and regular teas and a variety of coffees are available, as is hot chocolate. Desserts are tasty but expensive and made with sugar; the cheesecake was among the best I've ever had.

Smoking permitted. We ate on tables outside, where smoke was no problem; the three-story ceilings inside may keep the smoke above the breathing space, but we couldn't tell; no one ate inside on the 98-degree day we visited Pan's. No credit cards.

Open Monday and Wednesday-Saturday 11:30 A.M.-9 P.M.; Sunday 4:30-9 P.M.

—Marlene Anne Bumgarner

SANTA CRUZ
Right Livelihood Natural Pizza
1721 Mission
408-425-5045

Seeming as though it might be transformed any day into an auto parts store, Right Livelihood Natural Pizza occupies the most spartan of quarters in an aging commercial building profitably divided into very narrow leaseholds. After coping with that exterior, you encounter the interior—a sad collection of tables and chairs in front, cushions and low tables in the rear, a few hangings and posters on walls leading to a back counter with a view of the kitchen. Don't look. Turn your attention to the large collection of newspapers and comics or to the menu board near the counter.

Should you choose the latter course, you'll encounter an extensive choice of 16 pizzas with mix-and-match privileges and vegetarian hero sandwiches (from refried bean to the cheese hero). Pizzas start with Humble Pie (a basic cheese pizza) and end with The Works (cashews, vegie sausage, mushrooms, etc.). The pizzas are generously endowed with cheese and/or beans as described, and the sauce is well seasoned, something not all pizza parlors can boast. Condiments such as hot peppers are provided. All ingredients are natural (whole wheat crusts, rennetless cheeses), and the pizzas themselves seem to run a bit larger within each size category than is usual. Smoothies, juices and "natural" soft drinks are available.

This is definitely not the best pizza place in town, and many of the local independents serve trustworthy, delicious vegetarian pizzas. But Right Livelihood fills a definite need, and the pizzas are better than those of most of the chains.

No sugar. No alcohol. No smoking. Cash or local checks only.

Monday and Wednesday-Friday 3-11 P.M.; Saturday and Sunday noon-11 P.M.

—Kip Eastman

SANTA CRUZ

Seychelles
1549 Pacific Ave.
408-425-0450

In the heart of the Santa Cruz Mall action, this vegetarian haven has somehow managed to create an ambience reminiscent of tiny colonial restaurants ringing the Indian Ocean. Seating is limited but includes a counter, tables with chairs in semi-private nooks and in the open, and a single table with cushions on a central raised platform. Service is good, but it helps if, before you come in, you remember to look at the blackboard to decide what you want.

The low-priced lunches, satisfying in quality and quantity,

include soups and grain/bean dishes (spiced lentils, white beans and brown rice). Salads and brown rice dishes form the core of the lunch menu. Dinner selections vary from homemade pasta specialties on Saturdays through a variety of Indian, Mediterranean and Mexican dishes. Braised vegetables and brown rice (spiced) with salad or soup are always available. The moussaka is always great, and the cooks do very well with Indian dishes. The menu is based on the availability of fresh ingredients and the mood of whomever is cooking that night. It's always prepared with attention to detail, however.

Seychelles offers a pleasing selection of California wines, domestic and imported beers, coffee and herb teas. Desserts use no sugar and are filling. No smoking. No credit cards.

Monday-Friday 11:30 A.M.-2:30 P.M. and 6:15 P.M.-midnight; Saturday 6:15 P.M.-midnight.

—Kip Eastman

SANTA CRUZ
Staff of Life Natural Food Bakery
1305 Water St.
408-423-8041

If you need to stock up on staples, want a breakfast or dessert goodie or a quick meal at the lowest possible price and are willing to give up the tiniest pretense of atmosphere, then the Staff of Life Deli, Bakery and Natural Food Store is for you. The majority of the building is occupied by the store, and you have to run the gamut of bakery items to get to the deli in back. There you will find a counter and a bare table with half a dozen chairs set in the midst of the store's bins and shelves.

An immense blackboard on one wall describes the offerings. Vegie pizza (usually disappointing), tofu-burgers, vegie tacos, and fruit or vegetable salads. There also is an ever-changing array of more typical deli fare, always vegetarian and natural. Plenty of food is served for the money.

The deli serves fruit juices but no alcohol. No smoking. Cash only.

Open 10:30 A.M.-8 P.M. every day.

—Kip Eastman

SANTA CRUZ

Whole Earth
University of California
408-426-8255

Perched with treehouse allure on a hillside, Whole Earth's redwood interior blends into the dark groves rising behind it. Whole Earth makes an inviting and appropriate lunch stop on a tour of the University of California's avant-garde Santa Cruz campus. You have a choice of a small table inside or one outdoors on a terrace that wraps halfway around the restaurant. In summer you will rub elbows with the workshoppies, language institute people and a few bemused tourists. During the academic year you will be stimulated by the vociferously liberal crowd. At all seasons, you will be served by a variable mix of student help.

Panels on the wall near the serving counter announce the menu selections. In spite of economically motivated attempts to turn the place over to a franchise chain, the menu remains basically vegetarian and healthy. You'll find much of the menu in your home refrigerator—yogurt, cottage cheese, juices. Sandwiches go from peanut butter and banana to albacore and include egg salad and guacamole. Ingredients may no longer be from the campus no-longer-organic farm, but they are fresh and provided in generally good amounts. Desserts are natural, but they're served in frugal portions and are expensive.

No sugar, alcohol, smoking or credit cards.

Open 8 A.M.-4 P.M. Monday-Saturday.

—*Kip Eastman*

SANTA MONICA

Cafe California
2917 Main St.
213-396-4122 or 399-9466

Two blocks from the Santa Monica Beach is Main Street, a chic L.A. hangout, with its expensive boutiques, antique shops and restaurants. Cafe California, although elegant, manages to retain some of the flavor of the simpler, Bohemian style that used to characterize this Ocean Park area.

You can eat in the small indoor dining area or the pleasant, brick-enclosed patio. Lunches usually include good omelets and large, enticing salads. There are a few dishes available all day, every day. The spinach salad is covered with mushrooms and a dijon mustard dressing. Vegetarian soups are always delicious; my favorites are the spicy gazpacho, cream of tomato and cream of broccoli or watercress. A slice of the very light, nutmeg-spiced quiche goes well with any of the above.

For dinner, the eggplant parmagiana is the best I've tasted. A souffle-like Spinach Fritate is equally good. There's also a fantastic selection of fresh fish. Dinners come with steamed vegetables and wheat, rye or white rolls. For dessert, have brandy over fresh fruit or berries. Excellent coffee, espresso, and an extensive wine list. Meat dishes also served.

Major credit cards accepted. Smoking permitted. Reservations advised. A guitarist plays during dinner.

Monday-Saturday 11:30 A.M.-11 P.M.; Sunday
10:30 A.M.-2:30 P.M. and 6-10:30 P.M.

—Colleen Davis

SANTA MONICA
Nature's Power Station
1551 Ocean Ave.
213-395-6220

There is outdoor dining here—dining while you look at palm trees across the street and the boats in the blue Pacific just beyond. This restaurant and snack bar is especially fun for tourists.

There's a good choice of sandwiches and freshly squeezed juices. All food items are reasonably priced. Unusual sandwich complements include cheese, sliced boiled egg, tomato, avocado, alfalfa sprouts and more. Sandwich prices are lower than in most health food restaurants in southern California.

Now for some "no's." No coffee, beer or wine. No ice in

drinks. No credit cards. No checks. No reservations (but usually no waiting for a place to sit).

Many customers are repeaters.

—Alan W. Farrant

SAUSALITO
Trident
558 Bridgeway
415-332-1334

The multi-level seating of this graciously appointed restaurant allows every diner a spectacular view of San Francisco's high-rise skyline across the bay. Hewn arched beams and carved woods add to the classic charm of this favorite of tourists and locals alike. An outdoor seating area hangs over the water. Seagulls perch on nearby pilings as sailboats breeze by.

The Trident's luncheon menu features sandwiches with salads, egg dishes, waffles and entree salads. Added treats are home-made breads and soups.

A twilight dinner at the Trident is the highlight of anyone's Bay Area visit. The menu is for the most part discerning. The evening offering includes a choice of ten vegetarian casseroles and as many beef and fish dishes, including escargot. Home-made desserts are prepared with honey or raw sugar. Espresso, regular coffee, herb teas, fine wines and tap beer are served.

Everything on the menu deserves a try. We found the seafood dishes, omelets and salads delicious beyond comparison. Service and atmosphere were tops, too.

Nonsmoking section. MasterCard and Visa accepted.

Tuesday-Sunday 11 A.M.-11 P.M.

—Arlene Cook

SHERMAN OAKS

Cafe Alma
13362 Ventura Blvd.
213-986-1592

This is a place for those who want a leisurely meal, a meal they can enjoy looking at as well as tasting. The setting is attractive, too. There's a large sidewalk dining area with a colorful roof. Flower boxes line the front of the building. In the two indoor dining rooms, cloths cover the wooden tables in the evenings. It is the sort of restaurant that quickly turns a first-time guest into a regular.

Fresh produce is delivered daily to the kitchen of Cafe Alma, which offers freshly squeezed juices. A popular house specialty is the protein shake. Among the food specialties is Papaya Natalis (baked papaya stuffed with shrimp and water chestnuts in a lime cream sauce). Also popular is the Javanese saute of shrimp, chicken, beef or a combination of the three. The menu is huge, and nearly all the items on it could be described as health foods. The cooking is excellent, and the food is served by pleasant employees.

Beer, wine and plenty of coffee available. MasterCard and Visa welcome. Children not encouraged. Lunch minimum $2.50.

Monday-Thursday 11:30 A.M.-10 P.M.; Friday and Saturday until 11 P.M.

—Alan W. Farrant

SOQUEL

Tortilla Flats
4724 Soquel Dr.
408-476-1754

Away from the hustle of Santa Cruz and only a block from the best bakery in the county (Maddock's), Tortilla Flats offers fine Mexican food prepared with only natural ingredients. Although primarily vegetarian, the menu includes many selections that come in chicken or shrimp versions. There is seating at a counter or at tables in a warm and friendly atmosphere, with healthy plants, cut flowers, classical music and tasteful artwork. Service by a congenial staff matches the restaurant's appearance.

Food is served promptly and hot, and it's arranged attractively. Traditionalists can choose from the quesadilla snack to the guacamole-taco combination plate, since the menu covers the spectrum of California-style Mexican food. A venture into the tofu enchilada, packed with broccoli and zucchini, will delight. For those with a penchant for nuts and seeds, the Flatland series of burritos, tacos and tostadas is superb and very filling.

Everything is prepared with care; even the lowly quesadilla has diced olive and tomato steaming inside it. The sauces have depth, and often the traditional Latin flavors give way to the more popular vegetarian seasonings.

Servings are ample, and most diners have to be careful not to overdo it. Sharing of dishes can be a delightful experience, and the staff is helpful in that regard.

Desserts, made with sugar for the most part, are merely satisfactory, except for the luscious avocado cream pie. Drinks include beers, local wine, coffee, chocolate, teas and soft drinks as well as an agreeable sangria.

No smoking. No credit cards.

Noon-10 P.M. every day.

—*Kip Eastman*

SOUTH PASADENA

Grassroots Health Food & Yogurt Shop
1119 Fair Oaks Ave.
213-799-0156

The restaurant in the front of this health food store can be seen from the street, and its appearance is inviting—attractive tables with plenty of space between them, nice-looking chairs, fresh flowers on each table, bright colors, beautiful pictures on the walls.

Three meals are served each day. All baked goods come from the restaurant's own kitchen, as does most of the other food, and all ingredients are of the highest quality available. Tasty sandwiches are the main reason for eating here, and they include ham, cheese and watercress on rye; tuna salad and watercress on pumpernickel; avocado, cream cheese and sprouts on pumpernickel; turkey breast on wheatberry, and many more. Soup-of-the-day is popular, too, and many customers order seconds. Want some dessert? There's a good selection.

Self-service is suggested at breakfast and lunch, when the place is filled with workers hurrying to get to their jobs nearby, but this doesn't mean customers are rushed. Far from it; the owners like people to dine in a relaxed atmosphere, especially at dinnertime.

Because of an especially high ceiling, the restaurant is quiet; you can chat with your dining companions without straining to hear each other.

No alcohol, but there are juice drinks and coffee. Smoking discouraged but permitted. Major credit cards accepted.

—Alan W. Farrant

STUDIO CITY

Chez Natural
11838 Ventura Blvd.
213-763-1044

This whole-food gourmet restaurant boasts a beautiful interior decorated in brown tones with red brick walls. There are comfortable booths, and padded chairs at the tables. Flowers grace each table. There is some sidewalk dining, and the outdoor flower boxes are in good condition. Chez Natural is a highly attractive place to dine, and on the expensive side.

Salads, sandwiches and full-course meals are prepared from the finest, most natural ingredients available. The dishes are artfully prepared and professionally presented. Chicken and fish are served along with vegetarian entrees, but there are no red-meat dishes. One of the most popular sandwiches is avocado and white cheese, tomato and alfalfa sprouts on whole wheat bread. Eight desserts are offered, all sweetened with honey, as well as vanilla, carob and maple-nut ice creams.

The menu offers 22 beverages, including beer, wine and

blended fruit drinks, which are popular. Fresh carrot and orange juices are served in liter bottles with wine glasses. Bottled fruit juices are served, too.

The waiters and waitresses here are young and capable, and they never rush guests. Dining here is fun.

No smoking in kitchen or dining room. MasterCard and Visa accepted.

Open every day 11:30 A.M.-10:30 P.M.

—Alan W. Farrant

SUNNYVALE

The Greenhouse
190 S. Frances St.
408-738-8320

A favorite with lunchtime patrons, The Greenhouse has expanded the salad bar concept to its ultimate. Accompanying an extensive array of greens and crunchy fresh vegetables are 15 house-specialty salad dressings plus a Salad of the Day—hence its name.

Nonsmoking section. No credit cards.

Open 11 A.M.-8 P.M. Monday-Friday; 11 A.M.-4 P.M. Saturday.

TOPANGA

Inn of the Seventh Ray
128 Old Topanga Rd.
213-455-1311

Up a delightful canyon, perched beside a creek, the Inn of the Seventh Ray is a charmer.

For lunch or Sunday brunch, the terrace and garden room are just perfect. If the dinner hour turns cool, try the small church room (it really was) with a wood-burning stove. There are candles and tablecloths at dinner, the sounds of birds in the daytime and frogs at night.

The inn is serious about food and its preparation. Steak is free of DES (and it's the only red meat on the menu), chickens are organically raised, and even the beer and wine are carefully selected to be free of preservatives.

The kitchen staff cooks with utensils that won't expose the food to toxic metals. Herbs are grown at the inn. Coffee beans are ground fresh daily, and there is Postum and herb tea. All breads are prepared on the premises.

The menus for brunch, lunch and dinner are extensive, expensive and fancy. Who wouldn't enjoy dishes with exotic names such as Artichoke Queen of Light (filled with tofu) or The Gold Chalice (acorn squash stuffed with millet, raisins, almonds and curry steamed together)?

The food is marvelous. Fresh fruit decorates some servings, tenderly steamed vegetables garnish others, and the fresh bread and rolls that come with dinners are very special. Service is sweet and slow. You don't meander up this canyon for a quick bite; you "soak up Saint Germain's violet ray," as the menu suggests, along with the food. A tiny gazebo behind the garden room is often used for weddings. *Muy romantico!*

Smoking outside only. $3 minimum at dinner. American Express, MasterCard and Visa accepted.

Hours: 11:30 A.M.-3:30 P.M. every day; 6-10 P.M. weekdays, to 10:30 P.M. weekends.

—Marty Delman

WESTWOOD

Forty Carrots
10923 Weyburn Ave.
213-477-8547

This is a cafeteria in the heart of the business district, with a huge choice of food and drink. Its highly attractive facade boasts a carrot-colored awning. There are two dining areas: the front room has comfortable booths and a white tile floor; in the rear are tables on a wood floor. Boxed plants hang from the unique ceiling, and fresh flowers adorn each table. The paper napkins have bright carrots printed on them (and make ideal souvenirs). Children are welcome but get no discount.

Sandwiches and salads (served with a carrot muffin) are the

fare here. A nice selection of desserts is also available; most popular are special yogurt dishes like the Healthy Sundae, which has wheat germ, nuts and raisins. There's also a sugarless fruit compote with apricot sauce. Beverages include teas, coffee, soft drinks and milk. Juices are squeezed daily (you can watch). Shakes are made from the restaurant's own recipes with natural ingredients.

No smoking. No credit cards. No rest rooms.

Monday-Thursday 11 A.M.-9 P.M.; Friday and Saturday to midnight; Sunday noon-8 P.M.

—Alan W. Farrant

WESTWOOD

Good Earth
1002 Westwood Blvd.
213-478-0215

Under a bookstore in the heart of Westwood Village is Good Earth, where no preservatives, artificial or refined ingredients is the rule. The spacious and plant-filled dining area has smoking and nonsmoking sections, lots of UCLA students and an occasional celebrity.

Breakfast (served all day) offers the Santa Cruz Omelet, an unforgettable combination of jack and cheddar cheeses, avocado, artichoke hearts and tomato. Ten Grain Sourdough Hotcakes are served with a honey-molasses syrup.

For lunch, the vegetarian burrito or tostada is excellent. Refried pinto and azuki beans are piled on a whole wheat tortilla and covered with cheese, lettuce, tomato, cucumber, sprouts, avocado and sour cream. There's a large selection of salads and sandwiches as well.

Entrees include the uninteresting Olive Branch Eggplant and the unusual walnut-and-mushroom casserole as well as some meat dishes. Dinners come with soup (usually vegetarian) or salad.

Juices, herb teas, mineral water, so-so coffee, beer and wine are available. The house tea is delicious, but it contains some caffeine.

For dessert, try a Berry of the Week Protein Shake, a good-tasting energy booster, or some of the fresh baked goods.

Major credit cards accepted. No reservations taken.

Monday-Thursday 11A.M.-11 P.M.; Friday 11 A.M.-midnight; Saturday 9 A.M.-midnight; Sunday 9 A.M.-10 P.M.

—Colleen Davis

Colorado

ASPEN

The Little Kitchen
315 E. Hyman St.
303-925-1966

Aspen's only natural foods fishatarian and vegetarian restaurant lies in an old ice cream parlor across from the old Wheeler Opera House, one of Aspen's oldest landmarks. The fare is primarily vegetarian-macrobiotic, with fish served daily.

Breakfast starts off the day right with hot cereal or brown rice; waffles or pancakes with apple-cinnamon sauce, malt syrup, molasses or pure maple syrup; an omelet (using fertile eggs, when possible) served with toast and hashbrowns, with extras like mushrooms, cheese, peppers, onions and sprouts when available, or a Japanese-style okomomi yaki made with vegetables and served with miso-tahini sauce. Or try cooked prunes, eggs cooked to order, or a side dish of hashbrowns. Fresh, hot homemade breads are a specialty here. There are also muffins, pita bread and fresh tortillas daily.

Lunch and dinner menus include sandwiches and salads as well as entree specials and daily dessert variations. The specials are never the same from day to day, but you can expect a grain casserole, bean dish and soup du jour. The Nipponese pizza is nice, with tofu, grated vegetables and miso-tahini sauce broiled on a tortilla. The Salade Orientale has watercress and dulse with chickpeas on romaine lettuce with tofu-umeboshi dressing, and is recommended. No sugar is used in any recipe.

Beverages include beer and wine as well as kukicha (twig tea), herb tea (the restaurant's own as well as a commercial line), coffee and a roasted barley coffee-substitute. In addition to lemonade and cider hot and cold, there are orange, grape, apple and carrot juices, spring water, mineral waters and smoothies.

No smoking. No credit cards.

Open 8 A.M.-9 P.M. Monday-Saturday; 8 A.M.-8 P.M. Sundays, with light meals and live music after 9 P.M. Wednesday-Saturday.

—Fred Pulver

ASPEN
Nature's Storehouse
630 E. Hyman St.
303-925-5132

Nestled in among the protein powders, vitamins and nut butters in this little health food store is a juice bar and sandwich shop serving amply stuffed sandwiches on whole wheat bread. There are two outside tables in summer for those who wish to partake of the high mountain air and watch the people in this charming mountain town.

The variety of sandwiches changes from day to day, but the ones listed when I visited were avocado, cucumber, vegie and the Supreme (the works). There are egg rolls, too, as well as frozen yogurt concoctions and a selection of fruit and vegetable juices.

In winter, which can start in August and last until June in Aspen, a vege-chili is available. There are fresh organic pastries, too, and an assortment of nuts, chips and other snacks.

The only items sweetened with white sugar are the Tiger's Milk bars. Otherwise, honey, maple syrup, molasses, malt and brown sugar are mentioned with all items that contain them.

MasterCard and Visa accepted. No alcohol. Terry, the owner, offers all customers free posters saying in bold letters, "Anyone caught smoking on these premises will be pummelled into unconsciousness with an organic carrot."

Open 10 A.M.-6 P.M. Monday-Saturday.

—Fred Pulver

BASALT

Miguel's Crepe and Sandwich Shop
160 Midland Ave.
303-927-4246

A small cafe and juice bar in the back of Basalt Natural Foods, Miguel's is quaint and clean, cozy and warm. Run by Miguel and a female helper, it offers crepes, omelets, sandwiches, salads, ice cream and other desserts and smoothies.

Catering largely to a local clientele, this restaurant is not often crowded except at lunchtime, and it provides a chance to take in the local color of Roaring Fork Valley, a growing attraction for outsiders visiting Aspen, Vail and other nearby skiing areas.

There are four crepes offered at Miguel's; the most expensive is the creamed spinach version, made with mushrooms, onions and Swiss cheese and topped with hollandaise.

Omelets are made with cheese, tomatoes, chili, sprouts and other fillings, and they're served with salad or toast and rice. Eggs are available in other styles, too.

Sandwiches include guacamole with sprouts, cheese and tomato; cheese with tomato, sprouts or lettuce; tuna; and—a rare sensation—cashew butter, dates, sunflower seeds and honey topped with apples or bananas.

Salads include guacamole with olives and cheese, tuna with tomato wedges, and yogurt with fruit and nuts. Beverages include coffee and tea as well as smoothies with or without ice cream.

The only sugar used here is fructose for the whipped cream. No alcohol. No credit cards.

Open 8 A.M.-3 P.M. every day.

—Fred Pulver

BOULDER

The Good Earth in the Commons
1738 Pearl St.
303-449-6223

Larger and more commercial (part of a franchise chain) than most natural foods restaurants, The Good Earth is still a good bet for those who choose carefully. Its cooks do use sugar (not white, but something called Yellow-D, a less refined brown sugar) in some desserts, although most have none. No refined grains, no additives and no preservatives are used. The staff is extremely pleasant and good about answering questions. The decor is light and airy, with skylights and plants, and there's patio seating in summer.

The breakfast menu includes some unusual omelets and the usual eggs, hotcakes, crepes and French toast plus huevos rancheros, a Mexican-style egg dish that has to be tried at least once on any trip out West.

On the sandwich, salad and entree list (the same for lunch and dinner) are dishes with and without meat and fish. The homemade bread is an excellent ten-grain variety. There are also daily specials, and a different homemade soup and quiche are featured each day. The walnut and fresh mushroom casserole (with sour cream, broccoli, green onions, cheeses and brown rice or spinach noodles) is one of the most popular dishes. The vegetarian lasagna is also good, as are the tostados and burritos, available with meat or vegetarian-style. Portions of fresh vegetables and fruit are very generous. Probably the best choice for lunch is the Magic Eggplant Casserole, with all sorts of vegetables and melted cheeses.

Smoking is allowed, but there is an adequate nonsmoking section. Beers and wines available. No credit cards. There is often a wait during peak dining hours (in summer it can be up to 40 minutes for dinner), but you can browse in some interesting shops on the balcony and still hear your name called for a table.

Open 7 A.M.-10 P.M., until 11 on Fridays and Saturdays.

—Harriet Boonin

BOULDER

Hand to Mouth
1087 14th St.
303-449-5373

You really have to look for this small restaurant among the shops on The Hill across from the University of Colorado campus. It's cozy and colorful, and the atmosphere is simple. Self-service and fast service; the longest wait is about eight minutes for the pizza. You can eat here or take food out.

The most popular dishes are the Mexican-style burritos and tostadas, although the vegetarian pizza is also a big seller. There is also a nice selection of always-fresh salads (greens, fruit, tabouli). Try the Kitchen Sink salad and see if you can figure out what's in it; it comes with a generous portion of guacamole, and somewhere in there we spied celery, cucumber, zucchini, cabbage, carrots, peppers, tomatoes and sprouts.

Homemade soups vary according to the season. In summer the gazpacho is refreshing, and in winter there's always at least one hot vegetarian soup made fresh daily.

No sugar is used. Honey is the sweetener in carrot cakes, cookies and bread pudding. The pizza and quiche crusts do contain some unbleached white flour along with the whole wheat, and there are some preservatives in the cold turkey. Tamari is the primary seasoning, but some salt is used in the tofu pizza topping.

Coffee and herbal teas, plus fresh vegetable and fruit juices are available; no alcohol.

No credit cards. Smoking is not prohibited but, according to the owner, "People just don't smoke in here."

Open 8 A.M.-9 P.M. Monday-Saturday.

—Harriet Boonin

BOULDER

Rudi's
1831 Pearl St.
303-443-5630

Rudi's has convinced its large and faithful following that natural foods can be worthy of the description "gourmet." This is not a budget dining place, but it's worth a visit for a special evening. If you don't want to splurge for dinner, try it for lunch.

Faith Stone, the restaurant's chef since its opening in 1975, has won many cooking awards. When she received requests from *Gourmet* and *Bon Appetit* magazines for some of her recipes, she was flattered, but she declined.

The atmosphere is intimate. Rudi's is tastefully decorated, with brick walls, wood, plants and wall and hangings. The more spacious upstairs room features some beautiful stained-glass windows. Total seating capacity is about 50. Without reservations, you can expect a 20-minute wait at peak lunch and dinner hours.

Rudi's began as a vegetarian restaurant but now serves some dishes with fish and fowl. It still maintains a large, quality vegetarian selection. The menus are revised every six months, and there are daily lunch and dinner specials.

One of the most popular luncheon specialties is soup (homemade cream of butternut squash, harvest mushroom, chilled avocado and cucumber, or any number of others prepared daily on the premises according to the season), salad (choice of tossed or tabouli) and bread (baked in Rudi's own oven). We had a tasty Spanakopeta (crispy phyllo dough filled with feta cheese, spinach, green onions, eggs and spices) with tabouli and bread. A variety of salads, sandwiches, quiches and crepes also is offered for lunch.

Dinner entrees include salad, a freshly prepared vegetable and bread. The Chinese Stir-fried Shrimp (seasoned with tamari and rice wine and served over pilaf) is delicious, but its price is steep. The Moroccan Chicken (marinated in a sauce of apricots, tomatoes and lemon) is very popular and more reasonably priced. The house dressing, made with fresh spinach and herbs, is excellent.

About half of Rudi's desserts contain sugar, so be sure to ask. The chef's Coffee-Toffee pie is a locally famous prize-winner.

No smoking. MasterCard and Visa accepted. Coffee, herb and regular teas, beer and wine available.

Tuesday-Sunday 11 A.M.-3 P.M. and 5-10 P.M.

—Harriet Boonin

BOULDER
The Yarrow Stalk
2517 Broadway
303-449-9445

This small restaurant (which seats 36 inside and 18 on the patio) is in a beautifully decorated Victorian frame house. The scrubbed oak tables, benches with colorful pillows, plants and fresh flowers, and the attractive wallpaper give it a light and tasteful atmosphere. The food is the same, and there are no refined grains, sugar or additives in any of it.

The menu, originally vegetarian, now includes a daily fish special. The most popular dinner items are the Yarrow Stalk Special (grilled tofu, brown rice, beans, steamed greens, and sauteed carrots, onions and sea vegetables) and the Hunky-Dorinori Roll (Japanese-style brown rice with vegetables, rolled and wrapped in thin seaweed, steamed and sliced and served with vegetables). The spinach lasagna is nicely done, with spinach noodles, tomato sauce, tofu and an optional cheddar topping; it's served with a salad.

Sandwiches on homemade bread include soyburger, hommus, and meatless chili on tostada. At least two soups are offered every day—the stand-by vegetable miso and another that's made with what's in season.

Beverages include fruit and carrot juices, coffee, a hot grain drink, mineral water and herb teas. Customers can bring their own wine. No smoking. No credit cards.

Open 11 A.M.-3 P.M. Wednesday-Monday. On Sundays, only brunch is served.

—Harriet Boonin

COLORADO SPRINGS
The Lettuce Head
2917 Galley Rd.
303-597-7476

This clean and attractive restaurant in a small shopping center, seating approximately 60, is a popular spot for breakfast or lunch. Breakfasts here hold no special interest for a vegetarian, but lunch offerings include homemade soups, healthy salads, creative sandwiches and specialty coffees and teas. Carrot cake and cheesecake are made on the premises and are very popular.

No alcohol. Smoking permitted. No credit cards.

Monday-Saturday 6:30 A.M.-3:30 P.M.

—Virginia Brossman

COLORADO SPRINGS
Musical Spoon
530 E. Pikes Peak Ave.
303-634-8630

Close to the downtown area, this popular restaurant serves full-course meals as well as salads and sandwiches. Many of their vegetables are grown in a garden behind the outdoor patio, which seats approximately 75. Two inside rooms accommodate 100 customers, many of them regulars. Whole wheat bread is baked daily, and no sugar at all is used in food preparation. Chicken and ham sandwiches are served, along with fish dinners.

The setting's unpretentious, with a fireplace, some booths, a ceiling fan, old-fashioned lamps, and western and Indian pictures. Local musicians play nightly for tips, and Tuesday is always amateur night, with aspiring performers allowed 12 minutes to prove their stuff.

Full bar service. Smoking permitted. No credit cards.

Open Monday-Thursday 11:30 A.M.-2 P.M. and 5:30-9:30 P.M.; Friday and Saturday 11:30 A.M.-3 P.M. and 5:30-10 P.M.; Sunday 5-9 P.M.

—Virginia Brossman

COLORADO SPRINGS

The Olive Branch
333 N. Tejon
303-475-1199

Here's an excellent natural foods restaurant that draws a significant proportion of vegetarian customers. It is a most attractive place, with European decor, and it seats about a hundred people. Features include homemade soups, homemade salad dressings and superb vegetable quiches. No preservatives are used in the breads. At breakfast, the vegetable omelets are highly recommended.

Smoking permitted. No alcohol. MasterCard and Visa accepted.
Monday-Saturday 7 A.M.-3 P.M.; Sunday 10 A.M.-2 P.M.

— *Virginia Brossman*

COLORADO SPRINGS

Poor Richard's Feed and Read
324½ N. Tejon
303-632-7721

The menu here is 60% natural and vegetarian. Poor Richard's is legally prohibited from having a stove or conventional oven, so they use a microwave oven and three hot plates for their meatless soups. Salads and sandwiches are served as well, along with baked goods, wine and beer.

The walls lined with bookcases allow clients to refuel their minds as well as their bodies. There's much trading and selling of books in this homemade rustic setting, and the management has even been known to barter a meal for a sack of paperbacks! Some customers come armed with chessboards for a lengthy stay, though most are considerate during the lunch-hour rush.

Smoking is permitted, with no special section for nonsmokers, but the habit is gently discouraged with ashtrays supplied only on request. No credit cards. A stable of two dozen folk artists supplies evening entertainment.

Monday-Saturday 11 A.M.-11 P.M.; Sunday 11 A.M.-8 P.M.

— *Virginia Brossman*

DENVER

Genesis Natural Foods
1119 S. Washington St. (right off I-25)
303-722-0549

This small, rustic restaurant and store has a seating capacity of about 30. Its menu is vegetarian, and there are no refined sugars or grains, additives or preservatives in anything they sell. They sometimes serve eggs and milk products. The menu is up on a board and always features a daily special like pizza, lasagna or the very popular stuffed peppers.

Along with sandwiches like avocado and egg salad, they also feature soyburgers, felafel burgers, omelets and a changing variety of salads.

The wok-fried vegetables (lightly sauteed broccoli, cauliflower, cabbage, peppers and zucchini served over brown rice with tofu) are probably the biggest seller. The fruit, yogurt and nut bowl is filling and refreshing.

Desserts are reasonable, with cheesecake the most expensive item, and they're made from fresh fruits and whole grain flour.

No liquor, smoking or credit cards.

Restaurant open 8 A.M.-8 P.M. Monday-Saturday; breakfast served only until 11. The store is open until 8:30 P.M.; both closed Sunday.

—Harriet Boonin

GLENWOOD SPRINGS

Cooking Naturally
1001 Grand Ave.
303-945-7180

Beyond the Naturally food store, a cornucopia of grains, vegetables and fruits and a menu announce Cooking Naturally, one of Colorado's finest natural foods restaurants. The fare is inexpensive and good, the atmosphere cafeterialike and relaxed, with seating at natural wood tables. Live guitar music is featured in the evenings. Folks like Clint Eastwood, Steve Martin and Marlon Brando have gone out of their way to eat at this beautiful little restaurant nestled high on the western slope of the Rocky Mountains.

The food is vegetarian (no meat, fowl, eggs or fish), with cottage cheese, mozzarella, cheddar cheese and yogurt used in salads, hot and cold sandwiches, soups, specials and desserts. The pita pizza (tomato sauce and cheese with a choice of three vegetables) is excellent. I enjoyed the Chinese vegetable soup flavored with tamari and ginger and sprinkled with gomo-sio (toasted and ground sesame seeds and sea salt).

The hot specials might be stuffed green peppers (covered with melted cheese), lasagna (using rennetless cheese), or—if you come on Friday or Saturday, Mexican-food nights—green enchiladas, black beans with sour cream, and Spanish brown rice served with tortilla chips, soup and salad.

There are corn and bran muffins made fresh daily, carrot/walnut cupcakes and poppy-seed cake for dessert; they're sweetened with maple syrup or honey, not sugar. Drinks include mineral water, carrot and apple juices, iced or hot mint tea, lemonade sweetened with honey and "organic honey root beer." No alcohol, no coffee; plenty of herb teas and a coffee-substitute are available.

No smoking. No credit cards.

Open 11 A.M.-6 P.M. Monday and Tuesday; until 8:30 P.M. Wednesday-Saturday.

—Fred Pulver

MANITOU SPRINGS

Jonathan's
110 Canon Ave.
303-685-9080

This restaurant, approximately 50% natural and vegetarian, is in the heart of our large summer tourist area. The atmosphere is warm and inviting, with bamboo dividers and large planters affording privacy to the 120 diners who can be accommodated in three rooms. A pit area affords seating for 16. Theater lights outline the large exterior windows.

All food is made from scratch, using almost no preservatives.

Lusty portions are served. Only one item, peanut butter pie, is made with sugar. Baked goods are made daily on the premises with 95% whole wheat flour. Excellent staff. Although summer is their busiest season, Jonathan's never seems to lack patrons.

Full bar service. Smoking permitted; nonsmoking section during summer only. MasterCard and Visa accepted.

Summer hours (April through September): Monday, Wednesday and Thursday 5-9 P.M.; Friday and Saturday to 11 P.M. Winter hours: Wednesday through Sunday 5-10 P.M.

– Virginia Brossman

Connecticut

BRIDGEPORT

Bloodroot
85 Ferris St.
203-576-9168

Bloodroot is a feminist restaurant and bookstore with a seasonal vegetarian menu; it is operated by a four-woman collective. Located on the banks of Cedar Creek, it has a dining room and patio with pleasant views of nearby Black Rock Harbor. With a seating capacity of 52 inside and 20 outside, there is ample room to handle the crowd on a busy Friday night. It operates on self-service; patrons order from the blackboard menu, then wait at a table, in the foyer or in the bookstore for their names to be called before picking up their dinners on trays. Customers return their own dishes to the bus box after dinner.

The menu varies from month to month as fresh fruits and vegetables (many from an on-site garden) come in and out of season. You won't find "vegie burger" substitutes for meat dishes. Vegetarian ethnic dishes are the specialty. The usual fare consists of at least three choices of soups, salads, breads, casseroles or other main courses as well as desserts. No red meat is served; fish is limited to one dish per meal and served only in summer. Beverages include coffee, tea and juices as well as wine and beer. Some desserts are sweetened with sugar; those without it are indicated on the menu.

Recommended specials combine soup, salad, bread and dessert or the main course with the dessert. Or everything can be ordered a la carte. A large bowl of creamed spinach soup was tasty but was served only warm. Unusual salads are offered in generous portions; The Nicoise is an interesting combination of potato salad, garden beans, tuna and herb mayonnaise dressing on a bed of lettuce. Three half-slices of bread may be ordered in any combination; the potato rye bread, baked on the premises, is particularly good. A wide assortment of cheeses is available and recommended as an alternative dessert. Regular desserts are mostly fruit-based; the blueberry peach sundae has just the right blend so that neither of the fruits overpowers the other.

Smoking permitted only in the foyer and outside.
No credit cards.

Hours: Lunch 11:30 A.M.-2:30 P.M. Tuesday and Thursday-Saturday; dinner 6-11 P.M. Sunday, Tuesday and Thursday-Saturday; brunch 11 A.M.-2:30 P.M. Sunday. Closed Monday.

—Susan Hamburger

BRISTOL
Garden Gourmet
Farmington Ave.
Bristol Plaza
203-589-7185

Fish and chicken dishes share the menu with vegetarian specialties at this popular natural foods restaurant. Recommended entrees include stir-fried vegetables and Gourmet Tofu (with onions and mushrooms), both served over brown rice. Desserts are sugarless, and breakfasts include sauteed apples and honey-broiled grapefruit. No alcohol is served, but you may bring wine.

Nonsmoking section. MasterCard and Visa accepted.

Open every day 7 A.M.-10 P.M.

GREENWICH
Love and Serve
35 Amogerone Way
203-661-8893

Bliss prevails in this vegetarian restaurant run by followers of Sri Chinmoy. Prices are low, food attractively prepared. Breakfast offerings include French toast with yogurt, fruit, nuts and honey. Salads and sandwiches are featured at lunch, along with daily special entrees.

No alcohol. No credit cards. No smoking.
Monday 9 A.M.-4 P.M.; Tuesday and Saturday 9 A.M.-5 P.M.; Wednesday-Friday 9 A.M.-7:30 P.M.

HARTFORD

Garden of Eating
76 Jefferson St.
203-525-8189

A popular sandwich at this lunch spot is Maria's Magnificent, with a filling that combines tahini, tofu, miso and walnuts. The room is well appointed, the soups and salads and daily specials carefully prepared. Prices are low.
No alcohol, smoking or credit cards.
Monday-Friday 11:30 A.M.-3:30 P.M.

MYSTIC

Mischievous Carrot
6 Holmes St.
203-536-7126

Its name notwithstanding, the Mischievous Carrot is a natural foods restaurant where vegetarian dishes are taken seriously (although fish occasionally finds its way onto the menu) and skillfully prepared. It's a tiny restaurant; there are five tables in the main dining room, dominated by a nonfunctional wood stove and the salad/dessert/beverage bar, and five more in a second dining room, where a wood stove crackles during the cold months. The cooks turn out an impressive number and range of meals, however.

The lunch menu consists mainly of sandwiches, such as curried egg salad with sprouts and greens; a tostada with refried beans, cheese, onions, tomatoes and greens, and, for the burger crowd, a felafel sandwich. There are an avocado sandwich and a fried tofu sandwich, too, and various soups and salads. A variety of hot and cold nonalcoholic drinks is available all day long.

Dinners are more ambitious and more interesting. Each night there are at least four specials, which come with soup, salad and grainy but light corn and bran muffins. The entrees are borrowed from many cultures. Recent specials included spanakopita, vegetable crepes, Hungarian stuffed potato pancakes, vegetable-cashew curry, eggplant scallopini and oriental fried rice. There are also dairyless specials. Especially versatile, apparently, are the Carrot's enchiladas, which have emerged from the kitchen as tofu enchiladas, zucchini enchiladas and cheese enchiladas. Vegetable pot pie and quiches are also served.

The salad bar entices almost every diner with its gigantic wooden lettuce bowl and its smaller bowls of five or six chipped raw vegetables, garbanzos, sunflower seeds, bran, wheat germ and an assortment of fresh homemade dressings. The dessert bar is likely to include six or seven choices ranging from oatmeal-raisin cookies to banana-yogurt pie to the inevitable carrot cake with Haagen-Dazs ice cream.

Our favorite meal consisted of a delightfully cool cucumber yogurt fruit soup followed by cheese enchiladas with egg and black olives, which were spicy but far from overwhelmingly so. For dessert, we chose butterscotch pie, the sweetest dessert we've yet sampled at the Carrot, where honey and molasses are always substituted for white sugar.

A no-smoking sign reminds diners that Hippocrates said, "Air is the most important nutrient." Bring your own alcoholic beverages. No credit cards.

Monday-Friday 11 A.M.-9 P.M.; Saturday 11:30 A.M.-9 P.M.; Sunday 10 A.M.-9 P.M.

—Amby Burfoot

POMFRET CENTER

New Leaf
Routes 44 and 169
203-928-3839

The menu leans toward the oriental at this former gas station/ variety store. There are a half-dozen varieties of tempura as well as oriental vegetables, eggplant steak, grilled tofu with seaweed, and a vegetable lasagna made with four different rennetless cheeses. There are some seafood offerings as well. Desserts are made with whole grain flour and sweetened without sugar.

Nonsmoking section. Diners Club, MasterCard and Visa accepted.

Tuesday-Saturday 11 A.M.-10 P.M.; Sunday 9 A.M.-10 P.M.

WESTPORT

The Mushroom
8 Sherwood Sq.
203-226-8012

This small, cozy natural foods restaurant serves fresh fish, poultry and vegetable dishes free of chemicals and preservatives. In addition to the 50-seat dining room, The Mushroom offers a garden dining patio seating 20.

The menu changes weekly depending on availability and freshness of the foods. A la carte includes salad and a vegetable; prices aren't bargain basement, by any means. My favorite, and the most popular entree, is the spinach in phyllo, a blend of fresh spinach, broccoli, feta cheese and almonds baked in a buttery phyllo pastry and topped with a smooth mushroom sauce. The bluefish, piping hot, is moist and tender. The chef's salad offers crisp vegetables (cauliflower, lettuce, tomato); also available are cheese, tuna, avocado and hommus. Our serving was overly generous and had to be carted home for a midnight snack. The two soups du jour—Russian potato and cream of mushroom— were tasty and rich without being too filling.

Drinks include juices, mineral waters, tea and coffee, and there's a full bar. The array of desserts includes fruits, ice cream, cakes and pies, and only the pecan pie is made with sugar.

Reservations suggested. Smoking permitted on the patio and in one section of the dining room. MasterCard and Visa accepted.

Open Monday-Friday 11:30 A.M.-2:30 P.M.; Saturdays 12-3 P.M.; Tuesday-Saturday 6-10 P.M.

—*Susan Hamburger*

WILLIMANTIC

Nature's Place
65 Church St.
203-423-2338

The decor is faintly Tex-Mex, and so is much of the food, with eggplant-almond enchiladas an example of the management's vegetarian ingenuity. Other cuisines are represented as well, and there are some seafood offerings.

Major credit cards accepted.

Tuesday-Saturday 11 A.M.-3 P.M. and 6-10 P.M.; Sunday 4-8 P.M.

District of Columbia

WASHINGTON, D.C.

Cloud Cafe
1634 Wisconsin Ave., NW
202-337-7790

A small cafe at the rear of the Golden Temple Emporium health food store, imaginatively decorated with blue sky and white clouds. "A pleasant place to stop for lunch while shopping in Georgetown," a correspondent notes. "Sandwiches, salads, juices, herbal teas and full meals are offered. The yogurt is made on the premises."

WASHINGTON, D.C.

Golden Temple Conscious Cookery
1521 Connecticut Ave., NW
202-234-6134

This peaceful, all-vegetarian restaurant has two flaws that jar the tranquility: the rather high prices and, in my experience, an inadequate kitchen. Stepping off the noisy street into this serene eastern temple with its stained-glass mandalas, green plants splashed against white walls, and hypnotic waterfall over the door is a distinct pleasure. After receiving the menu, however, you stop trying to figure out where the water disappears and start wondering why the prices are so high.

The menu is impressive, touting a daily special which the restaurant is apt to be out of. That is the second flaw. While your eye roves over endless entrees and salads such as the

Mayan Princess (a tantalizing salad of corn cracklings, black beans, lettuce, tomatoes and chunks of cheddar topped with a dollop of guacamole and sour cream) or the Sat Nam (a bowl of alfalfa sprouts, tomatoes, cukes, scallions, mushrooms, cheddar chunks and bell peppers), be prepared to make a second or third choice. Request an herb dressing and if your waitress, gracious in her white priestess garb, smiles and says it will take 20 minutes to prepare, take the oil and vinegar instead.

It's the same old song all through the meal. A dinner special such as Warsaw Casserole—broccoli, apples, walnuts, breadcrumbs and sauteed mushrooms under a blanket of melted cheese—may take as long as 25 minutes.

The dessert menu (which was being revamped as this book was being published) is enough to set your mouth watering—Apple Munchies, cheesecake, bread pudding—but all they had on hand when we visited were peanut butter cookies and homemade honey-sweetened ice cream (no matter what flavor you order, you always seem to get black walnut). The best fruit drinks (apple cider, grape cider, lemon cooler) are often gone even at lunchtime.

No alcohol. No smoking. American Express, Carte Blanche, MasterCard and Visa accepted.

Noon-9 P.M. Monday-Thursday; until 11 P.M. Friday and Saturday.

—Candice F. Ransom

WASHINGTON, D.C.

Health's A-Poppin'
2020 K St., NW
202-466-6616

Located on Washington's "Wall Street," this cafe-style restaurant and carry-out uses all natural foods and fresh vegetables, which are delivered daily. Specialties include salad plates and sandwiches served in pita. A popular breakfast and lunch spot.

No credit cards.

Open weekdays 7:30 A.M.-5 P.M.

WASHINGTON, D.C.

Radishes and Rainbows
1101 Connecticut Ave., NW
202-223-8880

Our correspondent writes: "This recent addition to the Washington health food scene is in an enclosed mall. An extensive salad bar features fresh vegetables, sprouts and homemade dressings. An impressive array of fruit and vegetable juices is available."

Open 7:30 A.M.-6 P.M. Monday-Friday; 11 A.M.-4 P.M. Saturday.

WASHINGTON, D.C.

Vita Food
1010 F St.
202-737-1231

We wondered at first what Vita Food's menu has in common with natural foods. The restaurant is listed with other health food eateries in the Yellow Pages, and it's situated in the back of a landmark health food store, but it serves ham, canned soups, canned baked beans, sugar-laden desserts and any number of other decidedly unnatural foods. We ordered a cup of "homemade delicious vegetable soup" and were disappointed to find white-flour noodles and canned tomatoes floating around in it.

But then we noticed that fresh fruit salads, chopped vegetable plates, fresh vegetable juices, ginseng tea and other healthful items are served up at this humble lunch counter, too. Cardboard signs on the wall announce that smoking is not permitted. A line in the menu boasts that Vita Food uses "only pure water . . . by filtering out the chlorine." When this restaurant opened in 1928, it must have been a pioneer effort indeed. Even today, it's an oasis in a neighborhood of fast food restaurants and greasy spoons.

No alcohol. No credit cards. Tea and coffee are available.

Open 10 A.M.-6 P.M.; until 7 on Thursdays.

—*Cheryl Morrison*

Florida

GAINESVILLE

Hogtown Granary Juice Bar
1124 W. University Ave.
904-372-2050

The Hogtown Granary, a 3,000-member food cooperative, used to operate this health food restaurant at the Gainesville Regional Airport. As this book was being prepared they were in the process of moving into town.

Breakfast foods include bagels, cream cheese, muffins and juice, but it's the lunches that areally stand out here. An assortment of sandwiches is available – pita stuffed with marinated tofu, for example – along with fresh baked goods and homemade soups and stews.

Drinks include coffee and herbal tea, hot or cold, as well as fresh vegetable juices, banana cream and freshly squeezed organic orange juice. The most popular drinks are the smoothies, 12-ounce shakes made with fruit, cashews, honey and wheat germ.

No alcohol. No smoking. No credit cards.

Open 10 A.M.-6 P.M. Monday-Saturday. Evening hours were being considered at the time of the move, so call and ask if you're interested.

– *Mary N. Rathbun*

KEY WEST

Las Palmas del Mundo
Southard and Frances
305-294-7991

Envision yourself at a table for two amid lush tropical vegetation. A palm or banana leaf sways in the breeze over your head. A most congenial waiter pours your wine and offers a list of delectable natural foods, prepared Key West style. That's how it is at Las Palmas del Mundo, where a meal embodies a philosophy of fine eating.

The menu offers fresh fish-of-the-day prepared expertly in a variety of ways. Shrimp and fish tempuras are coated with a light batter. Organic turkey and chicken are also on the menu. Natural delights include Summer Spaghetti made with buckwheat Japanese noodles, fresh wok-cooked vegetables and homemade tofu dishes.

Las Palmas serves an excellent brunch, which features three-egg omelets, scrambled tofus and myriad other delights.

All sweetening is done with Keys honey or Vermont maple syrup. Desserts are hard to pass by when sitting on the windowsill in plain sight is a fresh-baked pear custard pie, its aroma drifting across the table while you eat. Or dessert might be a scrumptious cheesecake still too hot to cut—the selection changes every day.

Organic raw ingredients are used, with the accent on no-cholesterol, by a staff of dedicated vegetarians who seem to truly enjoy what they do. Cuban coffee, cappuccino and espresso, herbal teas, fresh fruit and vegetable juices, wine and beer are available.

Hours: 9 A.M.-2 P.M. and 7-11 P.M.. Closed Monday.

—Ron Laughlin

KEY WEST

Rich's
1015 Fleming St.
305-296-6868

Located at the rear of Eden House, one of Key West's oldest hotels, is Rich's, THE place to start your day with brunch in a relaxed, quiet, outdoor atmosphere.

Herbal tea, fresh fruit cup, an omelet (the vegie omelet is my favorite) and hot blueberry bread make a delightful morning meal. Eggs Benedict is superb. The traditional breakfast and brunch fare is well prepared and delightfully served by a congenial staff.

No alcohol. No credit cards. Smoking permitted; outdoor dining.

Open 8 A.M.-2 P.M. every day.

—Ron Laughlin

MIAMI
Cafe Mendocino
5950 Sunset Dr.
305-665-5468

This indoor/outdoor eatery is at the intersection of Sunset Drive and South Dixie Highway (U.S. 1) in the same building as one of Miami's newer health spas (Bodyworks). The enclosing wooden fence insulates customers from traffic and creates the effect of a quiet sidewalk cafe.

Salads, which come in two sizes, are always a safe choice here. The treat is in the dressings, all of which are homemade. We particularly liked the tahini. The large salads are moderately sized. The entree portions, in contrast, are very generous.

Entrees include cold sandwiches, grilled sandwiches, hot lunch specials, omelets and a small selection of seafoods. Some of the more interesting dishes are the grilled feta, vegetarian pepper steak, spinach and mushroom strudel and coconut-fried shrimp. Daily specials when last we were there included conch fritters and stuffed lobster.

Water is free, but everything else costs. The appetizer list includes, among other things, French fries, nachos and soup (vegetarian or seafood). The soup is good; the nachos are excellent.

Desserts are sweetened with honey. Some selections, such as the rather gooey mango cake, are not listed on the menu.

The juice bar is a pleasure. Particularly pleasing is the Mendocino Marvel, a blend of juice, banana and yogurt, and the smoothie, a mixture of juice, fruit, crushed ice and honey. Wine, beer, coffee and tea are served, too.

Smoking sections. American Express, MasterCard and Visa accepted.

Open 11:30 A.M.-10 P.M. Monday-Thursday; 11:30 A.M.-11 P.M. Friday and Saturday; 6-10 P.M. Sunday.

—Linda Charlton

MIAMI

Granny Feelgood's Natural Foods and Health Products
121 S.E. Second Ave.
305-358-6233

This luncheonette in the hub of downtown Miami's business world caters mainly to the working crowd and knowledgeable tourists as well as the city's top politicos. It is a combination restaurant and health food store with a large horseshoe-shaped counter and a few booths and tables that fill up rapidly during lunch hours.

Their shrimp salad platter attests to the owners' boast of highly selective buying. Everything is made from scratch. The vegetarian pizza and Jive Turkey Sandwich are certain to appeal to the younger set. The Hi-Protein Salad is a terrific energizer in the midst of a shopping spree. Top that off with the yummy hot spinach pie with melted cheese. For a low-calorie, filling meal, try the raw vegetable salad. The menu also features a vegetable cheeseburger and quiches.

The 100% Colombian coffee has a taste that will please the most exacting connoisseur. Many fortunate customers are aware of Granny's papaya, coconut and freshly squeezed orange juices taken from locally grown trees. Herbal teas are also available.

No meat, alcohol or sugar is served here, and there's no smoking allowed. Carte Blanche, MasterCard and Visa are accepted.

Monday-Friday 7:30 A.M.-6 P.M. (the counter closes at 4); Saturday 11 A.M.-2:30 P.M.

—Cynthia Williams Wright

MIAMI

Oak Feed Restaurant
3008 Grand Ave.
Cocoanut Grove
305-448-0076

Under the sign of a huge carrot in the center of this artist-colony village is Oak Feed, a highly attractive establishment with butcher-block decor and three dining areas—your choice of an air-conditioned room, an outdoor patio with a giant live oak and umbrellas shading the tables, or a canopied room with paddle fans. Evening entertainment is provided by soft jazz drifting from a baby grand in a large alcove. On the patio, you can enjoy a classical or jazz guitarist while wine, beer and sandwiches are served.

The finest fresh fish is chosen with care each day by the manager. Usually the blackboard seafood special is that Florida favorite, pan-fried conch seasoned with natural sea salt. Staying with the local popular choices, you won't be disappointed with the seafood salad sandwich. The house salad is another excellent item.

Sunday brunch features natural wheat pancakes with native fruits such as mango, guava, bananas and avocado. Also whole wheat bagels. With at least a day's notice, the chef will prepare his Something Special—an extravaganza of unusual vegetarian dishes of your choice, guaranteed to make a believer out of anyone. No meat is served.

Desserts are sugar-free, with the soybean cake deserving special attention. Coffee, a wide assortment of fruit juices, herbal teas and a good wine selection are offered, in addition to beer.

Smoking on the patio only. American Express, Diners Club, MasterCard and Visa are accepted.

Monday-Thursday 11:30 A.M.-10 P.M.; Friday and Saturday 11:30 A.M.-11 P.M.; Sunday 9 A.M.-1 P.M.

—Cynthia Williams Wright

TALLAHASSEE
Hopkins' Eatery
1840 N. Monroe St.
904-386-4258

Tucked away among the neon lights of Monroe Street stands a simple green and white sign advertising Hopkins' Eatery. Inside, the plants are abundant and thriving. A garden lines the front window. The mirrored walls reflect additional light for the hanging baskets and potted plants all about.

A favorite menu item here is the Garden Sandwich, which won the National Sandwich Idea Contest of 1979. This champion contains three kinds of cheese, spinach, sprouts, mushrooms, tomatoes, sunflower seeds and more, served on a hot pumpernickel bun. A tasty treat!

Other delights include the vegetarian sub, the tomato and sprout sandwich, and even a peanut butter and banana sandwich with honey and alfalfa sprouts. Meat sandwiches are also available.

Salads include greens, vegies, cheese and sprouts. Homemade soups, ranging from gazpacho to cucumber and served with whole wheat rolls, are a good choice. Desserts are frozen yogurt shakes and sundaes (made with sugar) with a choice of toppings from carob chips to trail mix. Seasonal fresh fruits are available, too. Beverages include fruit juices and herb teas as well as coffee. Bring your own wine.

No smoking. No credit cards.

Monday-Saturday 11 A.M.-5 P.M.

—Denise Condon

TALLAHASSEE
Nature's Way
1932 W. Tennessee St.
904-224-2043

Brightly polished wooden tables, caned chairs and hanging wicker lamps add a sense of warmth to the spacious dining room at Nature's Way. Entertainment is offered most weekends, but the big attraction here is pleasure for the palate.

Such pleasures include vegetable crepes and sauteed tofu with vegies, both served with soup du jour, homemade whole wheat bread and a salad. Daily specials include spinach-mushroom quiche, spinach lasagna and shrimp creole. Flounder and trout entrees are served occasionally.

From the wide variety of fruit and vegetable salads, a good choice is the Harvest Garden Salad, with cheese, cashews, eggs, cauliflower, mushrooms and a choice of seven dressings. My favorite combination is a Golden Garden Salad, with avocado and sprouts, and a vegieburger.

Desserts are made with honey or turbinado sugar. My choice is sour cream and fruit crepes. There's also Haagen-Dazs ice cream.

There's herbal tea, fruit juice, smoothies, hot carob, coffee and a hot grain drink. Or bring your own wine.

Breakfast is served only on weekends, when the fresh-fruit whole wheat pancakes topped with pure maple syrup draw quite a crowd.

No smoking. No credit cards.

Hours: Tuesday-Friday 11 A.M.-9 P.M.; Saturday 9 A.M.-9 P.M.; Sunday 9 A.M.-1:30 P.M.

—Denise Condon

TALLAHASSEE

Taproot Natural Foods
Governors Sq.
1500 Apalachee Pkwy.
904-877-3972
and
631 W. Tennessee St.
904-222-7840

The Taproot at Governors Square offers a refreshing break from the standard fast-food snack shops in the area. Place your order at the counter, but be certain to save yourself a table around the fountains in the cafe-styled dining area. Entertainment is offered periodically; call ahead for information.

For a quieter meal, the downtown Tennessee Street dining room is set up as an informal living room, with sofas, floor cushions and coffee tables. It offers a pleasant, unconventional dining experience.

The menu at both locales is strictly lacto-ovo, using whole grains, avoiding preservatives, caffeine and refined sweeteners.

The Garden Salad and the sandwiches are brimming with fresh greens. WWG (Whatever We Got) varies seasonally but is always topped with a delicious secret sauce. Other sandwich items are garbanzo spread, avocado, cheese and egg salad. Salads also include tabouli and Fruit Folly. Homemade soups are added to the menu in fall and winter.

Taproot is known especially for smoothies, boasting numerous original concoctions of fruit, yogurt and ice cream. A favorite is Shake My Tree, with apple juice, frozen bananas and fresh peaches. A wide variety of fresh juices and herbal teas are also offered.

For dessert, try a Snowball, made with cream cheese, granola, dates, honey and raisins and rolled in flaked coconut. You probably will want more than one.

Bring your own beer and wine. Smoking permitted.

Governors Square: open 10 A.M.-9:30 P.M. Monday-Saturday; 12:30-5:30 P.M. Sunday.

Tennessee Street: open 11 A.M.-4 P.M. Monday-Friday.

—Denise Condon

Georgia

ATHENS

El Dorado
199 W. Washington St.
404-549-3663

Be sure to look up when you enter the El Dorado restaurant. Overhead is a whimsical rainbow sky sponged onto the ceiling. Near the kitchen smiles a giant wooden frog. Together, the bright bursts of color and grinning amphibian set an imaginative tone that also is carried out in the bill of fare.

Breakfast features a thick, creamy and delicious egg custard sweetened with honey and spiced with nutmeg. Fresh buttermilk biscuits, cinnamon rolls and whole wheat bread (baked by elves, the proprietors purport) also are offered, along with generous portions of yellow grits. Buckwheat and blueberry pancakes are tasty and filling. Washing down the bountiful breakfast can be experimental, with a nonalcoholic pina colada—a blend of coconut, pineapple, white grape and pear juices—or one of the seven varieties of tea. A never-ending cup of coffee is sold, too.

Low-priced daily lunch and dinner specials combine soup, vegetables, grains and beans. You can also get huevos rancheros with a flour tortilla, beans, red sauce and cheese; burritos; chili and cheese; stir-fried vegetables with tofu, or a luncheon omelet. No meat or fish is served. Entrees vary daily, and three fresh vegetables are available every day.

Desserts include a generous apple cobbler, homemade cookies, Maya yogurt, and honey ice cream.

No smoking. No credit cards.

Breakfast 7-11 A.M. Monday-Friday; 8 A.M.-3 P.M. Saturday and Sunday. Lunch 11 A.M.-3 P.M. Monday-Friday. Also open for late-night breakfast 11 P.M.-3 A.M. Friday and Saturday.

—Sharyn Kane and Richard Keeton

ATLANTA
Golden Temple
1782 Cheshire Bridge Rd.
404-875-0769

The eclectic international cuisine typical of Golden Temple restaurants throughout the country is featured here, with grain-and-bean dishes well represented. No flesh foods.

Nonsmoking section. MasterCard and Visa accepted.

Open Monday-Saturday 11:30 A.M.-8 P.M.

ATLANTA
Nature's Last Stand
1847 Peachtree St.
404-352-1100

Nestled in the heart of midtown Atlanta is a combination Old World sidewalk cafe and modern fast food restaurant known to entice even the most staunch meat-and-potatoes lovers with their delicious meat-free dishes and casual, friendly atmosphere.

Patrons often choose to begin with Super Nachos, made with melted cheese, guacamole, jalapeno peppers and diced onions, the exotic homemade soup-of-the-day, or spicy chili made from organic pinto beans.

There are cheese, vegie and other sandwiches, too. A special favorite is the Peanut Butter Fantasy, an open-face sandwich with banana, peanut butter and honey, topped with whipped cream. Salads come with a wide variety of vegetables, and they're topped with roasted sesame seeds, grated cheese, your choice of dressing, and homemade croutons. There is a super-delicious fresh fruit salad—a delightful combination of strawberries, pineapple and bananas over yogurt, topped with honey and peanuts.

They offer some combination dinners with soup or chili and various extras—sandwich, salad, dessert and beverage—some of which are priced very modestly, are available every day. Entrees like Italian-style stuffed peppers, Cauliflower Con Questo and

Creamy Vegetable Casserole are served from 11 A.M. to 2 P.M. and after 5 P.M.

Desserts are sweetened with honey, except for the apple crisp, which is made with brown sugar, and choosing between cheesecake topped with fresh fruit and fresh apple crisp with whipped cream is a delicious dilemma. Ice cream is available, too. Tea, coffee, grain drinks, fruit and vegetable juices and beer are also offered.

No smoking. No credit cards.

Open 11 A.M.-10 P.M. Monday-Saturday.

—Lynn Willingham

Hawaii

HONOLULU

Laulimi Fine Vegetarian Food
1824 S. Beretania St.
808-947-3844

Laulimi provides highly seasoned fare.
Section for nonsmokers. No credit cards.
Tuesday-Sunday 11:30 A.M.-9 P.M.

MAUI

Bluemax
Front St.
Lahaini
808-661-8202

For gourmet dining, spectacular sunsets and professional entertainment, visit Bluemax. Open-air tables overlook the Pacific and invite the trade winds in. When we visited, birds ventured fearlessly near our luncheon board for crumbs and were not disappointed. Nor were we. "Bluemax is dedicated to Polynesian languor," the menu proclaims truthfully.

There are no strictly vegetarian restaurants on Maui, but there are many meatless possibilities at the Bluemax, and the French cuisine is superb. For lunch, the French onion soup is a real treat at a reasonable price, and the vegetable-cheese omelets are good. The salads vary; ask your waitress. Fresh fish is the Bluemax specialty, and we've heard it's excellent.

For dinner, we enjoyed the spinach-mushroom crepe and the vegetable casserole (assorted vegetables in a tomato-herb sauce topped with two cheeses). Both are served with salad and bread (unfortunately, it's white). We left pleasantly full, not overstuffed—the sign of a good restaurant.

Bluemax desserts are rich and sweetened with sugar. Coffee and alcohol are served, and smoking is permitted—it's all part of the evening entertainment scene, which has earned Bluemax its reputation for consistently good music. Elton John and Linda Ronstadt are among the well-known performers who visit the Bluemax when on Maui. Live music begins at 10 P.M., and there's a $1.50 minimum. American Express, MasterCard and Visa are accepted.

Open daily, 11:30 A.M.-2:30 P.M. and 5:30-9:30 P.M.; Sunday brunch 10 A.M.-2 P.M.

—Bonnie Caminker Mandoe

MAUI

Carlene's Cafe
2010 Main St.
Wailuku
808-242-9003

Right in the heart of old Wailuku town you'll find Carlene's, an Alice's Restaurant type of place—small, informal and homey. The friendly staff is dedicated, creating an atmosphere as good as the food.

The best breakfast on Maui is served here. Choose a spicy jalapeno-cheese omelet with hashbrowns or a Papaya Special with yogurt, fruit and granola. Banana and blueberry pancakes also are a good bet.

For lunch there are tofuburgers on toast with potato or green salad and an eggplant casserole with salad and rice, as well as hamburgers. The grilled cheese sandwich variations are excellent, and so is Carlene's homemade herb toast.

Suppers on Maui aren't cheap, and Carlene's is no exception. But the fish dinner we had here was the most attractive we've ever seen, and there were roses on the table. Carlene's uses almost exclusively local produce; the morning's catch was accompanied by baked Maui sweet potato, baked onions, baked banana and a delicious slice of zucchini as well as a crisp salad. Also on the menu are a lower-priced lasagna supper and a superb Greek salad—large and fresh with feta cheese, olives and a tasty vinaigrette. The dinner rolls are homemade, but they're white.

There's white wine and beer. The coffee's good, and honeyed juices and herb teas are available. Desserts at Carlene's are always good, but sometimes they're sweetened with sugar.

Smoking permitted. No credit cards.

Breakfast Monday-Friday 7-11 A.M., Saturday 8 A.M.-noon. Lunch Monday-Saturday. Dinner Fridays only, 5:30-9 P.M.

—Bonnie Caminker Mandoe

MAUI

The Vigory
Kashumanu Center
Kahului
808-877-7812

If it's an informal meal you're after, walk through Vim and Vigor Health Foods in Maui's largest shopping mall to the Vigory, where you can get anything from a glass of carrot juice to a full, hot meal.

Hanging plants and a spacious dining area provide a comfortable setting for the cafeteria-style service. The lighting is dim, and wooden walls accentuate the darkness, creating a cool illusion even in mid-summer heat.

The Vigory's food consciousness is reminiscent of the early 1960s, but so are its prices. Raw sugar replaces white in most of the desserts; some are sweetened with honey—coconut macaroons, for example, which are a treat and a real bargain. All baked goods are fresh from the Vigory's own bakery, and they can be purchased to go.

The Vigory serves breakfast, but lunchtime is its busiest hour, with shoppers and shopkeepers alike making selections from a tremendous a la carte menu. Salad plates (choose your own combination from a wide variety including fried eggplant, fried tofu, batter-fried fish and potato salad plus an assortment of vegetables and sprouts) are the most popular items.

Dinner includes either white or five-grain rice, salad, and stir-fried vegetables or a vegie loaf, which includes lentils and almonds. It's a far cry from gourmet fare, but it's tasty and nourishing.

Coffee is served. No alcohol. No smoking. No credit cards.

Monday-Wednesday and Saturday 9 A.M.-5:30 P.M.; Thursday and Friday 9 A.M.-9 P.M.; Sunday 10 A.M.-3 P.M.

—Bonnie Caminker Mandoe

Idaho

KETCHUM
Hobbit Inn
619 Fourth St. East
208-726-4303

Hobbit Inn serves steaks and seafood and is a favorite of year-round residents. Inside and outside seating. Mexican specials every Thursday.

Smoking permitted. MasterCard and Visa accepted.
11:30 A.M.-10 P.M. every day.

KETCHUM
The Kneadery
216 Leadville Ave. North
208-726-9462

A correspondent advises: "The Kneadery is a popular restaurant whose menu has been approved by the Sun Valley Executive Health Institute. Offers a wide menu of sandwiches, omelets and homemade soups." There's outdoor dining on the deck in summer.

Smoking permitted. MasterCard and Visa accepted.
7:30 A.M.-2 P.M. every day.

Illinois

CHICAGO

Bake Shop Cafe
2310 W. Leland
312-334-1347

If you still dream about those luscious pastries drenched in cream from a little cafe in Vienna, all is not lost. At the Bake Shop Cafe, Austrian pastries are made from scratch each day and are free of preservatives, food coloring and refined white sugar. The cheerful, petite restaurant holds a handful of tables along with posters of Austria, and its front window is brimming with plants.

While ham and cheese and corned beef sandwiches are on the menu, we preferred the Crunchy Vegie, which heaped avocado spread, tomato, lettuce and a mound of sprouts on whole wheat toast. The Just Cheese is a delicious combination of cheese, tomato, green pepper, lettuce, herb spread and alfalfa sprouts on toast. Or you might choose the Bake Shop Salad, a generous portion of greens, sesame buds, sunflower seeds and sprouts; try it with sesame herb cream, a yogurt dressing. Soups of the day vary; the smooth carrot soup had a little island of yogurt in it for a tart contrast.

You'll find a nice choice of ten or so different pastries. A less cloying version of the famous Sacher torte from the Sacher hotel in Vienna is made here. Or try the tart raspberry linzer, made from a recipe that comes from the owners' hometown in Austria. On Tuesdays and Thursdays, the specialty is buchtel, a huge yeast puff filled with apricots. Drinks include coffee, a coffee-substitute, fruit and vegetable juices and mineral water. You may bring your own alcohol.

No credit cards. No smoking.

Monday-Friday 11 A.M.-7 P.M.; Saturday 10 A.M.-5 P.M.

—Christine Kuehn Kelly

CHICAGO
Bread Shop Kitchen
3411 N. Halsted
312-871-3831

The Bread Shop Kitchen is not-for-profit, and its food is priced accordingly. Natural foods are taken seriously here, and they're prepared with fertile eggs, raw milk, unprocessed oils and whole grains. This unpretentious restaurant, in a neighborhood of weaving and pottery shops and Latino groceries, is much like a home kitchen, only super-organized. You choose from a chalkboard, write up your own order, pick it up from the counter and clear your own tray. In addition to the front room, there's seating in the garden among the vegetable patches.

Specials have included a tasty chop suey on fluffy brown rice and mung beans (dried out, unfortunately, by 7 P.M.) with a delicious sweet potato-apple side dish. The vegetarian pizza, available Tuesdays and Fridays, is rightly popular.

Soups almost overflow the bowls with chunks of vegetables. The potato soup (with skins intact on the generous slices) is a comforting choice. Add some of the dense raisin bread from the Kitchen's own bakery, and you have a satisfying meal.

The creamy cheesecake tastes like it came from the corner deli. There are granola cookies, too. Drinks include mineral water at bargain prices and herb teas; no coffee or alcohol, but you may bring your own wine.

No credit cards. No smoking.

Open noon-9 P.M. Tuesday-Saturday.

—Christine Kuehn Kelly

CHICAGO
Brother Tim's Natural Foods Restaurant and Sweet Bread Shop
1659 W. 79th St.
312-488-6791

Brother Tim started baking in his home kitchen and selling his tasty delights from the back of his Chevy station wagon. That was back in the '60s. Now Tim has his own vegetarian restaurant and neighboring grocery store on the South Side. It's a new-age version of the old snack shop, only everything is meatless and healthy.

You can't beat Tim's all-vegetable "burgers"—delicious, thick and filling. Other meat-substitute sandwiches made from soybean products, such as the "fish" fillets, the Wham (which Tim says tastes like ham) and the so called Bar-B-Q steaklets are low-priced like everything else on the menu.

Tim's pizza on pita bread, in four sizes, is yummy. You can pick your own vegetarian ingredients. He also offers a variety of soups, including homemade chili bean, which is superb. The fruit and vegetable salads are plentiful.

Desserts, such as carob-coconut brownies and honey-oatmeal squares, are made with honey and/or brown sugar. The applesauce and raisin, banana nut, and carrot-raisin breads are made with honey and without eggs and milk.

Smoking permitted. No alcohol or credit cards.

Open Monday-Saturday 10 A.M.-9 P.M.

—*Sandra Kolichman and Albert Swanson*

CHICAGO

Heartland Cafe
7000 N. Glenwood
312-465-8005

There's room to stretch out in the Heartland Cafe's large dining rooms with exposed brick walls, antique tin ceilings and overhead fans. Or enjoy the outdoor cafe, Chicago weather permitting. The cheerful staff spoils young customers and volunteers information about your order. Some nights, there's entertainment (and a small cover charge that goes to the musicians).

Daily specials include vegetarian lasagna, a spicy enchilada bake and crunchy cashew-rice balls. They come with soup and salad; try the yogurt dressing.

It's hard to believe that the substantial vegetarian chili, served with salad and homemade corn bread, is meatless; keep the cornbread drenched with honey, however, to avoid a cafe coronary. Another good bet is the Heartland Special Salad, a truckload of greens, vegetables, cheese, sprouts and seeds. Or you can have chicken in a delicate tamari-herb tea marinade, served with bulgur, soup, salad and cornbread. Rainbow trout, halibut and red snapper are on the menu, too.

Desserts include Haagen-Dazs ice cream and a variety of baked goods made with honey. The coconut milk and raw apple cider go down easily. There's also strong coffee and ginseng tea. You may bring your own wine.

Brunch is served until 3:30 P.M. every day. People come from all over the city to sample the tofu scrambled eggs and buckwheat pancakes with syrup. Another good choice is Huevos Rancheros—eggs with spicy tomato sauce.

Smoking discouraged. No credit cards.

Monday-Friday 8:30 A.M.-11 P.M.; weekends 10 A.M.-11 P.M.

—*Christine Kuehn Kelly*

CHICAGO
Middle East Gardens
2621 N. Clark St.
312-935-3100

Middle Eastern music plays faintly in this attractive restaurant tucked in among the boutiques and bars of New Town. A special vegetarian menu steers you away from the lamb platters.

Start your meal with a dip; there's hommus, Foule Moudammas (ground fava beans) or baba ghanoush, our favorite. The sturdy pita bread supplied with it is an unusually tasty version made with whole wheat.

The vegetarian felafel plate combines highly spiced patties with a Greek salad and pita bread. Or try the vegetarian grape leaves. For eggplant lovers, there's stuffed eggplant with rice, beans and pita bread. Tabouli comes heaped with sprouts.

A variety of interesting fruit juices includes watermelon and cantaloupe, in season. Coffee is available as well as wine, ouzo and other alcoholic drinks.

On your way out, pick up a rolled baklava drenched in honey

and take it with you as you explore the neighborhood.

No credit cards. Smoking permitted.

Open 11:30 A.M.-midnight Monday-Thursday; 10:30 A.M.-2 P.M. Friday and Saturday; noon-midnight on Sunday.

—Christine Kuehn Kelly

CHICAGO
R. J. Grunt's
2056 Lincoln Park West
312-929-5363

There's a singles atmosphere in this popular restaurant across from Lincoln Park, but coming with your mate and six kids won't be frowned on by the professionally cheery staff. R. J. Grunt's is part of a chain of funky but highly successful Chicago restaurants (others are Lawrence of Oregon and Jonathan Seafood).

The cutesy menu ranges from Roast Beef Aw Juice to the Taco that Ate Chicago. The salad bar, one of Chicago's best, is the draw here, however. For a reasonable fixed price, you can fill your plate time and time again. The waitress brings you a loaf of bread, too. Loading down the groaning board are cole slaw, lettuce with several dressings, applesauce, chopped liver, caviar, chickpeas, raw mushrooms, zucchini, bean salads, sprouts, pickled herring, cheeses and eggs. A side table holds baked potatoes and their toppings, and there's a variety of fresh fruit.

You might also try the delicious Eggs La Grunt— zucchini, spinach, mushrooms and cheese mixed in an omelet. Vegetable soups, nicely spiced, are available, but they're made with meat stock.

Drinks include black teas, fruit juices and alcoholic beverages. Desserts are made with refined sugar.

Smoking permitted. American Express, MasterCard and Visa accepted.

Open Monday-Thursday 11:30 A.M.-11 P.M.; Friday and Saturday 11:30 A.M.-1 A.M.; Sunday 10 A.M.-2:30 P.M. for brunch, then until 11 P.M. for dinner.

—Christine Kuehn Kelly

CHICAGO

Tel Aviv
6349 N. California
312-764-3776

You may be greeted in Hebrew at the Tel Aviv, located in the Jewish neighborhood of Rogers Park. This kosher dairy restaurant offers a Middle Eastern menu suitable for vegetarians of all faiths. In a small room decorated with colorful Israeli posters, you make your meal choices from a steam table.

Our recommendation is the huge pizza drenched in cheese over a thick Chicago-style crust. The felafel sandwich is better than average, heaped in a pita pocket and moistened with tahini. The vegetable plate is less exciting—potatoes, zucchini and carrots. The fried cauliflower has been consistently tender. There's also an attractive swirl of hommus and fresh vegetables in pita. Fish is served, too, baked or fried. The infrequent desserts utilize refined sugar. There are coffee and sodas.

No credit cards. Smoking permitted.

Sunday-Thursday 11:30 A.M.-9 P.M.; Saturday 8 A.M.-midnight. Closed Fridays.

—*Christine Kuehn Kelly*

EVANSTON

Pradhans
514 Main St.
312-491-1145

This cozy vegetarian restaurant near Northwestern University had just changed hands at the time of writing. The new owners were retaining the vegetarian policy, and expected some of the old menu to carry over.

Open 11 A.M.-9:30 P.M. weekdays, later on weekends.

MOLINE

Heritage Natural Foods
517 15th St.
309-764-1912

The best thing this sandwich bar has going for it is its tidy kitchen area and pleasant eating bar: both are spotless. The cooking is purely a one-man show, and if there are more than a few customers, a wait is possible. All foods are preservative-and additive-free, and no sugar is used.

There are only a few sandwiches offered, varying from week to week. All are served on seven-grain bread, and most are hot. The avocado and cheese sandwich, topped by a thick slice of tomato, is delicious and very juicy. Other sandwiches usually available are a tuna-and-sprout and an ordinary peanut butter and jelly.

Someone with a good imagination named the shakes. They include the Purple Peanut (made with grape juice, apple juice and a dollop of peanut butter), the Tropical Treat and the Vigor—a mixture of pineapple, coconut, yogurt and papaya, which is decidedly good but could be thicker.

An excellent variety of juices is available, but only the carrot juice is freshly made. Other beverages include herb tea and coffee-substitute. No alcohol.

No smoking. MasterCard and Visa accepted.

Monday-Saturday 10 A.M.-4 P.M.

—Jo Anne Harvey

WHEATON

New Earth
211 Front St.
312-665-5255

The atmosphere in this quiet, uncrowded restaurant reflects its Seventh Day Adventist origins. It is spotlessly clean, the staff is exceptionally courteous, and the menu is graced with an essay on healthful living. Selections are more limited and the portions smaller than at other local vegetarian eateries, but the prices are reasonable and the food is obviously prepared with care. Refined sugar and chemical additives are strictly avoided.

Budget-conscious diners should try the Grainburger, a mixture of bulgur, soybeans, sesame and herbs, served on a bun with lettuce, tomato, onions and sprouts; add a bowl of hearty vegetable soup, and you've got the Peasant Lunch. Got a sweet tooth? Try the fruit and nut surprise: crunchy peanut butter, honey and bananas, topped with wheat germ and sesame seeds and served with fruit-in-season. Two other sandwiches also are good buys: the Emerald Delight—a blend of avocado, tomato, sunflower seeds and sprouts—and the Garden Bonanza, sauteed mushrooms, scallions, and herbs with avocado and tomato.

New Earth serves four entrees: a fresh fruit plate with honey-yogurt dressing, stir-fried rice with tofu and vegies, bean tostadas with avocado and olives, and whole wheat crepes with spinach or ratatouille. There's a salad bar, too.

Drinks include nonalcoholic wine, fruit shakes, fruit juice and herb teas. No coffee or alcohol.

No smoking, either, and no credit cards.

Sunday-Thursday 11:30 A.M.-7:30 P.M.; Friday 11:30 A.M.-2:30 P.M.

—Barbara Bolsen

Indiana

BLOOMINGTON

Tao
517 E. Tenth St.
812-339-6766

Rough-plastered walls decorated with colorful posters and skylights verdant with cascading ferns and spider plants create a cozy and casual dining atmosphere at the Tao. Each wooden table boasts seasonal flowers plus packets of raw sugar and a shaker of sesame seeds with salt.

The cordial staff is composed primarily of college students who belong to the Kundalini Yoga meditative community that owns and operates the restaurant and adjacent bakery. No meat or fish is served, and no preservatives are used.

Besides daily specials, the Tao highlights seasonal fruit with every meal, beginning with breakfast yogurt (homemade) and fruit. Whole wheat pancakes with Vermont maple syrup are popular, too. Several varieties of fresh-ground coffee are on the beverage list, along with mineral water and juices.

The luncheon menu features a selection of generous sandwiches like the Open Heart, with avocado, alfalfa sprouts, melted Colby cheese, lettuce, tomato and mayonnaise on whole wheat, or the Pita, spicy hommus with vegetables. The salads are crisp and tempting; try one with the house dressing, a delectable yogurt, mayonnaise and herb concoction.

You shouldn't miss the most popular daily special, spinach lasagna. The quiche du jour is tasty, too. A Tao dinner of brown rice, sauteed vegetables, beans, salad and whole wheat bread is inexpensive and filling.

Save room for rich Haagen-Dazs ice cream, poppy-seed cake, a fudge sundae, fruit pie or other special desserts made with honey.

No alcohol, no smoking. MasterCard and Visa accepted.

Open daily 7 A.M.-9 P.M.

—Joyce Lakey Shanks

INDIANAPOLIS

Eat It—It's Good for You
City Market
222 E. Market St.

Eat It—It's Good for You is a fast food oasis amid the hustle and bustle of the City Market. The unpretentious, order-at-the-counter, throwaway-plates, booths-and-picnic-table atmosphere draws a young crowd. Plan to go early or late, not at straight-up noon, to avoid a line.

After you get your lentil burger, walk past the small, crowded dining area, and find an ice cream table on the balcony of the old market building; you can watch the action at the thriving produce stands below. In warm weather, you can catch the passing scene at outdoor tables, too. And if you've picked up a bottle of wine at one of the market stalls, no one's going to stop you from savoring it with your meal.

The menu offers basic vegetarian fare—a variety of sandwiches served on whole wheat or pita bread (including cashew butter and banana), a few soups, and good fruit and vegetable salads with an herbal dressing. Best sellers are three of the daily specials—zucchini, broccoli or lasagna casseroles, generously laden with a potpourri of in-season vegetables and heavy on the cheese.

No meat or fish is served; eggs are used in some of the cooking. Honey is the sweetener. There's no coffee; the selection of herb teas is large. Fruit is juiced on the spot, and some fruit-flavored carbonated drinks are available. Yogurt, an occasional apple pie, carrot cake or apple-spice cake is usually within sight.

No smoking. No credit cards.

Monday-Friday 11 A.M.-2 P.M.; open Saturdays in winter.

—Joyce Lakey Shanks

Iowa

DAVENPORT

Ten Twelve Marquette
1012 Marquette
319-322-9417

Situated on the ground floor of a lovely historic house, this pleasant restaurant is loaded with atmosphere and good food. Although the menu is limited, the service is courteous and fast. Fresh-cut flowers gathered from the wooded area around the house adorn the antique oak tables. Except for ham, all food served is additive- and preservative-free.

The sandwiches, all tasty, are served on homemade whole grain bread. A good choice is the Vegetable Special, which is filled with zucchini, sprouts, tomatoes and a sprinkling of sesame seeds. Salads range from the cottage cheese to the vegetable salad; the tossed salad seems a bit expensive, but its crisp lettuce, chives, mushrooms and other fresh vegetables makes it worth its price.

Each evening features a special entree that comes with a fancy tossed salad covered with creamy house dressing. Meatless Meatloaf is excellent and very filling. The vegetable quiche could have a lighter crust, but it's otherwise a delight.

Of the homemade desserts, all sweetened with honey, the crunchy-topped rhubarb pie is a favorite, and it goes fast. When in season, the mulberry soup is a must; it's a luscious blend of berries (picked from a tree on the grounds), yogurt, peaches, honey-vanilla ice cream and lemon juice. Beverages include coffee, herb teas, fresh-squeezed lemonade, tomato juice and beer.

No smoking. No credit cards.

Tuesday-Saturday 11:30 A.M.-2 P.M. and 5:30-8:30 P.M., with drinks on the lawn from 4:30-5:30 P.M.

—Jo Anne Harvey

DAVENPORT
Vi's Health Foods
113 E. Second
319-323-8619

What this sandwich bar lacks in atmosphere it makes up in good food at a low price. Located in the rear of a health food store, it has no tables; customers can sit on one of the few chairs and balance their plates on their laps, or they can take their sandwiches to a nearby park.

The fare includes sandwiches on seven-grain bread, preservative-free hot dogs on whole wheat buns (with or without sauerkraut), tacos made with organic beef, vegetarian tacos and homemade vegetable soup. The cucumber sandwich is served hot and surprisingly thick. There's no scrimping on cucumbers, onions, peppers, tomatoes, sprouts or organic cheese. The vegetarian taco is made on pita bread, and it's called a taco only because of the shape of the bread; it's crammed with tomatoes, onions, green peppers, sprouts and cheese, and it's served hot.

The great variety of shakes includes carob-banana, coconut-pineapple and papaya. The strawberry is especially good, thick and frosty. One of these big shakes could easily be shared by two people. Sundaes are made with honey-sweetened ice cream and topped with sugar-free preserves. Outside of the shakes, the only beverage is herb tea.

No smoking. No credit cards.

Open 9 A.M.-4:30 P.M. Monday-Saturday.

—Jo Anne Harvey

DES MOINES

The Soup Kitchen
2312 Forest Ave.
515-255-8616
and
810 Walnut St.
515-243-2191

The small building that houses the Forest Avenue Soup Kitchen, near the Drake University campus, is as lovely as its menu, with hand-painted murals on interior and exterior walls. The furniture is primitive and appropriate; for example, the bases of some of the plank tables were formerly treadle sewing machines.

The downtown Soup Kitchen, larger and more sophisticated, is in the elegant Shops Building. It's decorated with contemporary art and giant aquariums. Catering largely to a business crowd, it's open weekdays only. At lunchtime, there's live music by performers from all over the world; a piano's available, too, for anyone who wishes to play it. A visit here is less like dining out than being at a party with friends you've never met before.

Alcohol's banned from the Forest Avenue cafe, but the one on Walnut Street serves imported beer. Neither of them serves meat or fish. The food in both places is free of white flour and refined sugar.

Besides the soups that gave the places their name, each offers a wide variety of sandwiches and salads. Try the whole wheat pocket bread stuffed with provolone cheese, vegies and sprouts. Six homemade dressings enhance salads. There are cold fruit soups, which offer a delightful contrast to the daily hot soups such as broccoli cheese. There's a special every day, too, often a casserole with salad and a slab of home-baked bread.

No smoking; no credit cards at either location.

Forest Avenue open 11 A.M.-9 P.M. every day; Walnut Street location open 9 A.M.-3 P.M. weekdays.

—Mary C. Razor

Kansas

LAWRENCE

Cornucopia
1801 Massachusetts
913-842-9637

Meatless dishes comprise about half the menu here, although steaks and hamburgers are also served. They do their own baking and use organic produce.

No credit cards.

Open 11 A.M.-10 P.M. Monday-Friday; 10 A.M.-10 P.M. Saturday and Sunday.

Kentucky

LEXINGTON

Alfalfa
557 S. Limestone
606-253-0014

Alfalfa, the homey restaurant that sits across from the University of Kentucky, is always an eating adventure, whether you're vegetarian or omnivorous. The fare is so varied it will satisfy any palate.

The fantastic quiche is a meal in itself, with sauteed vegetables, Swiss and ricotta cheeses in a rich egg custard, baked in a handmade pie crust. You can choose from a variety of sprawling dinner salads that run off the plate—Caesar, spinach, sprout and Greek, to name a few—served with a cup of soup and homemade whole wheat bread. There are vegetable concoctions galore, including squash or zucchini crepes, depending on the day. Ratatouille, a French vegetable stew, and eggplant parmesan are some of the other specials. The menu also lists a few meat and fish dishes. There's always a choice of delectable soups, too.

Lunch has its own specials, including all kinds of inexpensive omelets, sandwiches, yogurt and fruit. The Hoppin' John—rice with black-eyed peas, tomato sauce, onions, green peppers and cheddar cheese—is especially good and filling.

Desserts vary daily; the sugar-free ones are designated on overhanging blackboards. There are 13 teas, five juices, two kinds of coffee, espresso, wines and mineral water.

Smoking is not encouraged. No credit cards.

Lunch 11 A.M.-2 P.M. Tuesday-Friday; dinner 5:30-9 P.M. Tuesday-Thursday, until 10 P.M. on Friday and Saturday; brunch 10 A.M.-1:30 P.M. Saturday and until 2 on Sunday.

—Sandra Kolichman

LOUISVILLE

Sunshine Harvest Inn
1769 Bardstown Rd.
502-454-5561

Service is cafeteria style at this largely vegetarian whole foods restaurant. Spinach lasagna is a specialty.

No smoking. MasterCard accepted.

Open Monday-Thursday 11 A.M.-8 P.M.; Friday and Saturday 9:30 A.M.-10 P.M.; Sunday 1-8 P.M.

Louisiana

METARIE
Schan's Natural Foods & Restaurant
1414 Veterans Blvd.
504-837-8444

Our correspondent notes: "Schan's opened several years ago in the junk-food mecca of this suburban wasteland. That it has survived attests to its popularity." It's on the highway that runs from downtown New Orleans to the airport.

No smoking. MasterCard and Visa accepted.

Restaurant open 11 A.M.-3:30 P.M. every day.

NEW ORLEANS
Apple Seed Shoppe
346 Camp St.
504-529-3442

Apple Seed is a lunch place in the central business district serving soups, salads and sandwiches. The specialty here is apple-nut salad.

Weekdays 10:30 A.M.-3:30 P.M.

NEW ORLEANS
Back to the Garden
207 Dauphine St.

A well-established place for lunch in the middle of the French Quarter, Back to the Garden serves soups, salads, sandwiches and hot quiche.

Monday-Saturday 11 A.M.-4 P.M.

NEW ORLEANS
Eat No Evil
405 Baronne St.
504-524-0906

A popular lunch spot in the heart of the central business district, Eat No Evil offers inexpensive salads, sandwiches, smoothies and herbal teas.
No alcohol. No smoking. No credit cards.
Weekdays 10:30 A.M.-3 P.M.

NEW ORLEANS
It's Only Natural
4233 Elysian Fields Ave.
504-283-3037

Sandwiches, salads and complete dinners are served here, with the enchilada dinners a specialty.
Open 11 A.M.-8 P.M. weekdays, shorter hours Saturday.

NEW ORLEANS
Nature's Way Salad Shop
5932 Magazine St.
504-897-0511

Nature's Way is a full-service restaurant popular with students and faculty at nearby Tulane University. The bill of fare includes homemade soups, salads, sandwiches, steamed vegetables and seasonal specials, but it's somewhat less ambitious in summer months.
No credit cards.
Monday-Saturday 11 A.M.-9 P.M.

Maine

BAR HARBOR

Town Farm
Kennebec Place on the Green
207-288-5359

While flesh foods are served at this well-appointed natural foods restaurant, the owners are so solicitous of vegetarians that they cook all meats on a separate grill. Salads, quiches and homemade soups and breads are featured, pancakes are popular at breakfast, and a generous selection of pies heads the dessert list.

We had a salad that was loaded with crisp vegetables as well as tofu made right in Bar Harbor by Island Tofu Works. The coffee we washed it down with was strong and rich. Service at the counter was a little slow, but the help was so pleasant we didn't mind. The dining room is filled with plants, sunlight and wood paneling, and there are tables on a patio that looks onto the town green from a quiet corner.

No alcohol served, but brown-bagging is okay. Section for nonsmokers. MasterCard and Visa accepted.

In the summer, Town Farm is open Sunday-Wednesday 7 A.M.-11:30 P.M. and Thursday-Saturday 7 A.M.-2:30 A.M. In winter it generally opens later and closes earlier and stays closed on Monday; in deepest winter, it's liable to be closed altogether for weeks at a time, so call ahead.

—Cheryl Morrison

BRUNSWICK

Corsican Pizza
76 Union St.
207-729-8117

The specialty here is natural whole wheat pizzas and hero sandwiches. Although meats are on the bill of fare, vegetable

pizza toppings and sandwich fillings are featured. Salads, too.
No alcohol is served, but you may bring beer or wine. No credit cards.
Open every day 11 A.M.-10 P.M.

OAKLAND

Food for Thought
21 Main St.
207-465-7451

The walls are paneled with barn siding in this large and well-established natural foods restaurant. There are some meat and fish dishes on the menu, but vegetarian items predominate. Entrees include stir-fried vegies, green fettucini tossed with butter and cheese, and Spanish vegetables in tomato sauce.
Beer and wine served. Live music on weekends. Section for nonsmokers. American Express, MasterCard and Visa accepted.
Open 8 A.M.-10 P.M. Tuesday-Sunday.

PORTLAND

Cafe Domus
10 Exchange St.
207-775-0127

"A unique cafeteria-style eatery," our correspondent advises, "offering natural home-cooked meals, light lunches and an informal, relaxed atmosphere. Live acoustic music is performed on weekends, and the specialty is the wonderfully prepared desserts—date squares, real cheesecake, etc." Some, be it noted, are made with sugar. Other dishes we've heard about include a highly praised black bean soup and an Indian salad with dates and nuts in honey-sweetened yogurt.
Monday-Wednesday 10 A.M.-9 P.M.; Thursday 10 A.M.-11 P.M.; Friday and Saturday 10 A.M.-midnight.

PORTLAND

The Hollow Reed
334 Fore St.
207-773-2531

The largest and most successful enterprise of its sort in the area, although its vegetarian and natural foods orientation has been modified somewhat in recent years.

Alcohol served. American Express, MasterCard and Visa accepted.

Monday-Saturday 11 A.M.-1:30 A.M.; Sunday from 10 A.M.

Maryland

BALTIMORE
Green Earth Cafe
823 N. Charles St.
301-752-4465

A half-flight below the sidewalk of one of Baltimore's main streets sits the Green Earth Cafe, an informal little restaurant that offers a mostly vegetarian menu with an occasional seafood or poultry dish.

Polished light wood floors, a semi-circular mirror covering most of one wall, hanging plants, fresh flowers, blond wooden tables, and light filtering through the front window give the restaurant an airy atmosphere. The restaurant grows cozier in the evening with the addition of candles and brown and white checked tablecloths.

The menu, handwritten on large white chalkboards, is extensive. The spinach salad with herbal Italian dressing boasts a generous sprinkling of raw cashews along with its onions, mushrooms and croutons. Thick with three different kinds of melted cheese and stewed tomatoes, the eggplant parmesan, served with delicious homemade rolls, rates a gold star. The broccoli served with the meal, however, was overcooked. The Earth Sandwich—Muenster cheese, alfalfa sprouts, romaine lettuce and tomato packed between slices of seven-grain bread—is filling and good, but would profit from the addition of a few more spices. Other entrees include a good selection of omelets, sandwiches like tuna melt and shrimp salad, whole wheat pizza with tossed salad, half a honey-glazed chicken with raisins and bananas, and scallops in wine sauce. Soups, salads and side dishes also are available.

For dessert, try the apple pie with raisins with its rich glazed crust, or the carrot-walnut cake. Desserts contain sugar. Beverages include beer and wine, sparkling cider, fruit juices, herb tea and a coffee-substitute.

MasterCard and Visa accepted. Smoking permitted. There's a $2 minimum.

Monday-Thursday 11 A.M.-midnight; Friday and Saturday 11 A.M.-3 P.M.; Sunday 3-10 P.M.

—Julie Raskin and Carolyn Males

BETHESDA

Premlata
7315 Wisconsin Ave.
301-654-4515

The menu at Premlata is ovo-lacto-vegetarian, and the most popular offering is the Fuzzby, a sort of Dagwood sandwich for vegetarians. Other specialties include cream cheese pie, meatless lasagna, broccoli strudel, quiche, baklava and whole grain muffins.

No smoking. No credit cards.

Open 10 A.M.-5 P.M. Monday-Friday; 10 A.M.-2 P.M. Saturday.

Massachusetts

ALLSTON
L'Odeon
116 Harvard St.
617-254-2634

With its particle-board paneling and wooden booths, L'Odeon looks like a neighborhood luncheonette. The pleasant surprise is its natural cuisine. A large and varied menu—plus a chalkboard of daily specials— includes Paella Valenciana, a Spanish specialty with seafoods; a natural pizza with tofu and vegetables, and tamales with wheat meat (seitan). A Japanese influence surfaces in the seven dishes featuring noodles. Try them pan-fried with shrimps and vegetables or in a broth with fried tofu and watercress. Conservative tastes will appreciate broiled fish with rice and salad.

For lighter meals you'll find American miso soup and the daily special, brown rice by the bowl, and a choice of salads, from the small house greens to the jumbo salad platter. There's a vegetarian platter with grains, beans, greens and seaweed, and a range of appetizers and side dishes.

Sunday brunch features crepes with vegetables, fruit sauces or wheat meat, whole wheat waffles and scrambled tofu.

Beverages include herb teas, grain coffee-substitute, apple cider, spring water and Perrier. No alcohol is served, but you can bring your own. Desserts, baked on the premises, are sweetened with maple syrup and barley malt. Blueberry shortcake is a generous piece of sweet, crusty cake smothered in tart, lightly cooked berries topped with tofu "cream." There are also muffins, cookies, squash pie, apple pie and tofu cheesecake. Fresh fruit in season is lighter in the belly and on the purse.

Smoking permitted. MasterCard and Visa accepted.

Open Tuesday-Saturday 12-3 P.M. for lunch; Tuesday-Sunday 5:30-10 P.M. for dinner. Sunday brunch from 11 A.M.-3 P.M. Closed Monday. They also offer classes in natural and macrobiotic cooking several times a year, so call for information if you're interested.

—Joanne Mattera

AMHERST
Zena's Cuisine
N. Pleasant St.

This is a small, intimate cafe, wholly vegetarian, with a menu running to simple dishes carefully prepared. Offerings include vegetable curry and tofu lasagna.

No credit cards.

Open daily 9 A.M.-10 P.M., later on Friday and Saturday nights.

BOSTON
Sanae
272A Newbury St.
617-247-2475

Sanae, which means "little rice sprout" in Japanese, was Boston's first health food restaurant, vintage 1969. It owes allegiance to the Japanese macrobiotic school. These days it's mellowed enough to serve coffee (and refills are free), but you still won't find meat or sugar on the menu (there are dairy products in the baked goods, though).

This is an informal, white-washed basement restaurant with varnished pine tables and vases of yellow daisies. It's self-serve and bus-your-own-table, and a big blackboard informs you what's special today. "Brown rice is nice," proclaims the menu, and there's always another grain, vegetable, soup and bean-of-the-day along with specials like the Macrodeal or the Square Meal (soup, grain, two vegetables, beans and tea).

The small, mixed salads are individually made at the counter. I recommend the hiziki topping with creamy tofu or walnut dressing. If you're in need of something more substantial, there's always a fresh fish, often scrod, baked in a vegetable sauce, perhaps onion, or the light-battered vegetable tempura, or an omelet. Also good are the noodles, *udon* (whole wheat) or *soba* (buckwheat) pan-fried in vegetable sauce. If you're partial to tofu, you can have tofu stew, or miso soup with tofu.

The folks at Sanae don't object to fried food, and they serve English fries and even Sanae fries— tempuraed yam and carrot sticks, good with the soy dipping sauce.

Desserts are sweetened with maple syrup, and they include apple pie, squash pie and homemade cookies, oatmeal corn muffins, sweet rolls and cakes. The homemade sourdough and whole wheat breads are rather dry and light. Beverages include herb teas, bancha tea, juices and coffee-substitute.

No alcohol. No credit cards. No smoking.

Open Monday-Saturday 11 A.M.-9 P.M. Closed Sunday.

—*Carolyn Hall*

BOSTON

Seventh Inn
288 Boylston St.
617-261-3965

The Seventh Inn is the grown-up, elegant sister of Sanae. Across from the Public Garden, it's simply but classily decorated, with exposed brick, natural colors and yellow mums on the wooden tables. And it's popular; be prepared to wait.

The Seventh Inn specializes in vegetarian and fish dishes. It also serves eggs and tofu, but no meat and little cheese. Everything is wonderfully fresh and visually delightful.

Among the appetizers, the marinated vegetables and seafood are refreshingly tangy. Or try the hommus plate, served with homemade whole wheat bread. Side orders of bread come with a choice of butter—sesame, peanut, fruit or dairy.

There's a wide variety of salads and an inventive selection of dressings, including Japanese plum. I recommend the watercress salad with mayonnaise and tamari. Larger appetites might care to take on a fish dish— scrod, flounder or scallops, broiled, steamed in ginger sauce, or tempuraed, served with two grains or vegetables.

The restaurant also offers whole wheat or buckwheat noodles, tempura, and rice dishes as well as memorable sandwiches like hommus, cheese and sprouts. But the most colorful and festive dishes are the house specialties: skillet-dinners of vegies and tofu or seafood, steamed in sake, ginger and tamari and served sizzling in individual gratin dishes. They're not cheap, but they taste as fresh and beautiful as they look.

Desserts here are made with maple syrup, and they change seasonally. In summer, offerings include blueberry pie, strawberry shortcake and peach kuchen.

In addition to interesting fruit juice combinations, you have a wide choice of domestic and foreign beers, sake and wines. The house wine is French. Coffee is served.

Smoking permitted. MasterCard and Visa accepted.

Open Monday-Thursday noon-9:30 P.M.; Friday and Saturday until 10 P.M.

—Carolyn Hall

CAMBRIDGE
Golden Temple Natural Foods
95 Winthrop St.
617-354-0365

The menu here is a nice ethnic mix of Mexican, Middle Eastern and Indian. No flesh foods or eggs are served, and nondairy dishes are so designated for the vegan's benefit. The Square Meal—soup, salad, beans and grain—is a low-cost meal for a small-planetarian.

No alcohol. No smoking. No credit cards.

Open Monday-Thursday 11 A.M.-10 P.M.; Friday and Saturday 7:30 A.M.-10 P.M.; Sunday 9 A.M.-9 P.M.

CAMBRIDGE
The Last Chance Cafe
25 Central Sq.
617-547-8551

One of life's pleasant ironies is that this snug little natural foods restaurant occupies a former hamburger joint. The clean, self-service facility does a brisk sit-down (capacity 14) and take-out business.

Food is seasoned with a light hand. Ordering is a la carte. Staple fare includes miso soup and fish soup every day, plus a soup of the day, along with brown rice, bean-of-the-day, seasonal vegetables sauteed or steamed, and hommus salad. Beyond these basics, you can usually expect fish salad, smoked salmon, a creamy, nondairy chowder, and pan-fried noodles with crunchy vegetables.Sandwiches are on whole wheat or chewy rice bread, and they're filled with hommus or rennetless cheese and served with sprouts, lettuce and tomato.

Coffee, grain beverage, herbal teas, juices and mineral water are available. Breads and desserts, baked fresh daily, are sweetened with maple syrup or honey. They include corn muffins, pear crunch, brownies and sweet rolls. Kanten, a vegetable gelatin made with cooked fruit, is the perfect light finish to a meal.

Although you will not be rushed, the Last Chance is for a no-frills meal rather than a leisurely dinner. One unpleasant note: the new owner, working with a crew of one, has eliminated dishwashing by serving on plastic. This food is too good to be served the way Ronald McDonald likes it. Bring your own bowl.

No alcohol allowed. Smoking is frowned on. No credit cards. Wheelchair access.

Hours: 11 A.M.-9 P.M. Monday-Saturday. Closed Sunday.

—Joanne Mattera

GOSHEN
Stonybrook
Route 9, Berkshire Trail
413-268-7738

This restaurant is an enterprise of the Wildwood Institute, a Christian organization that also sponsors health and nutrition lectures, cooking classes and nonsmoker clinics. Stonybrook's menu is wholly vegan, with no eggs or dairy products used. For all that, the cuisine is American rather than oriental, and "meatless meat dishes" join the grains and vegetables. Our source raves about cashew-oat waffles served with strawberries, fake cream and fresh maple syrup.

No alcohol. No smoking. No credit cards.

Open noon-7 P.M. Sunday-Thursday.

LEOMINSTER

The Whole Eatery
57 Central St.
617-537-4333

Here's a natural foods restaurant in the guise of an old-fashioned diner. The menu's wholly vegetarian. Salads and sandwiches predominate, along with a few vegie and grain combinations.
Open Monday-Friday 11:30 A.M.-2 P.M. and 5-9 P.M.; Saturday 5-9 P.M.

NORTHAMPTON

Paul & Elizabeth's
150 Main St.
413-584-4832

The menu leans toward the macrobiotic at this large and attractively appointed natural foods restaurant. Tofu, tempura and buckwheat noodles are features in many of the dishes. Fish is served, as are beer and wine.
Open Monday-Saturday noon-10 P.M.

PROVINCETOWN

Rags and Roses
Commercial St.
617-487-2568

Breakfast is a best bet here, with selections including whole wheat pancakes, granola and vegetarian omelets.
Open seven days 6 A.M.-1 P.M.

SOMERVILLE

Take Out for a Small Planet
194 Holland St.
617-623-9250

Frances Moore Lappe's writings are the inspiration here for carry-out dishes high in protein complementarity. Prices are low, and selections include enchiladas with yogurt sauce, egg foo yung with ginger sauce and empanadas filled with mushrooms and beans.

Tuesday-Saturday 11 A.M.-8 P.M.

WESTFIELD

The Red Owl
Route 202
413-562-9712

This long-established natural foods restaurant serves meat and fish dishes, although the extensive menu is predominantly vegetarian. Tempeh steaks are a special. Prices are low.

No smoking. No credit cards.
Wednesday-Monday 10 A.M.-8 P.M.

WORCESTER

Annapurna
483 Cambridge St. (I-290, Exit 11, College Sq.)
617-755-7413

Annapurna is a Sanskrit word meaning wholesome or complete food. Since 1976, under the direction of Dr. Yamuna Lingappa, a microbiologist and nutritionist, Annapurna has been serving vegetarian Udipi Indian cuisine as a healthful, economical alternative to other Worcester eateries. Carefully researched scientific and cultural information is available at the restaurant in support of his goal of preserving this precious, time-tested vegetarian culture, which is fast disappearing in India. Notice the original stone wet-grinders, pasters and rollers in the lobby and the whole oregano, cloves and anise seeds available at the cashier to leave a refreshing taste of India in your mouth as you depart. Here in the relaxed unpretentious atmosphere of Annapurna, you will be served wholesome food of great antiquity adapted for today's sedentary living.

Annapurna's menu is based on the idea that Indian dinners involve experimental eating. Small quantities of rice or pieces of roti, puri or parata (breads) are suitably mixed with different quantities of curries, sauces, chutneys, pickles or yogurts. For this reason, we suggest ordering one of the menu specials, which change every day. One dinner special includes roti (unleavened wheat bread), alu matar (potatoes and peas), samosa (vegetable roll), gojju (tamarind sauce), and pachadi (vegetables in yogurt). Luncheon specials offer a similar variety. Bhojan (dinners) include appetizers, desserts, beverages and more. We suggest Benares Bhojan, including: lassi (liquidized yogurt with raw sugar, cardamom and saffron), samosa, Imli Chutni (spicy tamarind sauce), rice dahl (curried lentils), puri or roti, Rasdar (curried vegetables), pickle, papad (lentil wafer), and choice of desserts such as Kheer (vermicelli, milk, nuts, raisins and saffron) or carrot halvah, and coffee or spice tea.

For limited budgets, nutritional eating and adventurous taste buds, this is truly the place to eat in Worcester. The kitchen, which uses only whole, natural ingredients and raw sugar, is open to any special dietary requirements and will season food to your taste.

Alcohol and smoking are not encouraged. Remember, fingers are used traditionally in Indian eating; napkins are provided. MasterCard and Visa accepted.

Lunch 11:30 A.M.-2 P.M. weekdays; dinner 5-10 P.M. daily. Open Saturday and Sunday 5-10 P.M.

—Shelley Reback

WORCESTER

The Garden of Delights Consumetorium
113C Highland St.
617-752-7048

After the fast food, disco and glitter of the expensive boutiques and hair salons of Highland Street, the charm and intimacy of the Garden's very small, patterned tin and dark-stained wood interior are immediate and compelling. Maxfield Parrish prints, oriental carpets, table candles and soft jazz in the background all add to the low-key, comfortable atmosphere.

Dinner specials, posted on a blackboard over the kitchen counter, include soup; choice of green, sprout or fruit salad; entree, and the Garden's own hearty graham bread. The zucchini lasagna and wok-fried sea-vegetable entrees were good choices when we visited. The sprout salad features a generous mixture of Garden-grown sprouts, cucumber, grated carrot and romaine lettuce served with a choice of honey-vinegar blend, oil and vinegar or house dressing. Innovative sandwiches and lentil burgers are available. Soups, entrees and dressings are homemade and change daily. The management tries to include at least one dairyless entree or soup. Organic vegetables are used whenever they're available.

Desserts are homemade, with carob brownies and honey cheesecake (containing a small amount of sugar) especially recommended. You can also have a hot carob sundae. Depending on the season, we suggest you end your meal with a fruit smoothie, a fresh fruit cooler sweetened with honey, or a cup of hot carob. Assorted herb teas, fruit and vegetable juices and coffee are available, too. Bring your own wine.

Smoking section. No credit cards. Music featuring local talent Sundays 8-11 P.M.

Open Monday-Saturday 11 A.M.-9 P.M.; Sunday 5-11 P.M.

—Shelley Reback

WORCESTER

Struck Cafe
415 Chandler St.
617-798-8985

Like Rome, Worcester is built on seven hills. At the top of one, just when you think you're in the suburbs, you'll find the sunny, plant-filled storefront of the Struck Cafe. Inside, the relaxed thrift-shop furniture, natural wood and gingham tablecloths complement the enormous rainbow super-graphic while nothing detracts from the fine gourmet vegetarian food. The food is a joy, if a bit overpriced for the city.

By far the most interesting items on the menu are the vegetarian crepes, offered a la carte at lunch and dinner. We found the scallop and apple crepe to be an intriguing blend of tender spiced scallops sauteed in white wine with apples, onions and herbs in a delicate crepe. A more subtle choice might be the Florentine crepe, a spiced cheese blend with spinach and sauteed mushrooms. Both are served with sour cream and lemon.

Luncheon sandwiches come with a cup of soup, a garnish of fruit ambrosia and tea or coffee. Our favorite is the Lolo, broiled open-face egg salad, tomato, bacon bits, onion and cheese.

Dessert crepes such as the banana-almond also are recommended. The owners have added weekend meat dishes such as chicken with apricots to the menu, but they offer no beef. The Struck boasts one of the few cappuccino-espresso machines to be found in Worcester. The menu is neither sugar-free nor "natural," but the cooks use fresh vegetables at all times. Assorted herbal teas and coffee are available along with mineral water and homemade lemonade. Bring your own wine.

Smoking tolerated. No credit cards.

Tuesday-Saturday 11:30 A.M.-3 P.M.; Tuesday-Thursday 5-9 P.M.; Friday and Saturday 5-10 P.M. Closed Sunday and Monday.

—Shelley Reback

Michigan

ANN ARBOR

Seva Longevity Cookery
314 E. Liberty
313-662-2019

Giant hanging plants, stained glass windows and artwork on wooden walls provide a comfortable atmosphere in Seva, which adjoins the Soybean Cellars natural foods store.

Daily fixed-price specials are the most exciting and worthwhile choices at Seva, which has been serving moderately priced vegetarian lunches and dinners since 1972. Count yourself among the lucky if you show up on a day when the selections include Russian vegetable pie—a whole wheat and cream cheese crust filled with cauliflower, mushrooms, onions and ratatouille. Otherwise, you'll do well to select one of the Mexican- or oriental-style dishes.

Sandwiches include chapatis, open-faced selections and submarines, as well as egg salad stuffed into a half-loaf of bread. Seva uses organic vegetables and whole grain flour (except in the tortillas).

The superb coffee served at Seva is blended in the restaurant's own kitchen. There's a selection of fruit and vegetable juices, too, but no alcohol. The desserts are sweetened with honey or fructose.

No smoking. MasterCard and Visa accepted.

Open Monday-Thursday, 11 A.M.-8:30 P.M.; Friday and Saturday until 9:30 P.M.; Sunday until 8:30.

—*Douglas Heller*

DETROIT

The Push Cart Cafe
1488 Winder St.
313-393-1985

Although it isn't known as a natural foods or vegetarian restaurant, the Push Cart, situated in the heart of Detroit's historical Eastern Market, is definitely a favorite of native greens fanciers. The cafe prides itself on an eye-catching, sumptuous salad bar brimming with fruits and vegetables brought in fresh daily. The motto at the Push Cart is, "Everything Is Always Fresh." They mean it.

Friendliness and warmth abound in the small, old-style eatery. Lunch and dinner are times of hustle and bustle, so reservations are suggested. One can enjoy the pleasant surroundings of the Eastern Market if seated with a window view. Anything from blue jeans to formals is acceptable attire.

Aside from fine steaks, the cafe offers fish and poultry meals fit for royalty (many regulars cite the pheasant and monk-fish as their favorites) and several vegetable dishes that are bound to please. The vegetable platter is loaded with broccoli, cauliflower, mushrooms and almost everything you can think of; the servers, dressed California style, say it's one of the most popular dishes. But don't overlook the salad bar, either as an addition to your meal or as a meal in itself.

Desserts aren't sugar-free, but their appearance and taste make them irresistable—especially the fresh strawberry pie. Beverages include alcoholic and fruit drinks.

Smoking permitted. MasterCard and Visa accepted.

Hours: Monday 11 A.M.-5 P.M.; Tuesday-Thursday 11 A.M.-10 P.M.; Friday and Saturday 11 A.M.-midnight.

—Lori Pimlott

EAST LANSING

Small Planet Natural Foods Restaurant and Grocery
225 Ann St.

Antique stained glass, creations of local craftspeople and framed prints in a varnished-pine interior give Small Planet a light, cheery atmosphere. If you hit the peak hours at lunch or dinner, you're likely to encounter a wait.

The vegetables aren't organic, but the food is first-rate. The lunch special gives you a choice of six entrees plus soup or tossed salad and house tea, and the price is right. The vegetarian lasagna, made with zucchini and spinach noodles, is a good selection. Other dishes you might enjoy are Quiche Alsacienne, spinach-cheese pie and fried rice with steamed vegetables.

Dinner specials are based on a revolving schedule of ethnic dishes. Monday is Chinese day, Tuesday is Greek, Wednesday is French, Thursday is East Indian, and Friday is Italian. Saturday's Mexican special consists of a chili, bean or guacamole tostada and your choice of bean, cheese or sour cream enchiladas. Sunday's standing feature is all the meatless spaghetti you can eat, garlic toast and your choice of soup or salad. The sauteed tofu with mushrooms and the Small Planet Special Salad are available every day, and they're good. The Bean Nachos is another winner.

Desserts include Haagen-Dazs ice cream and homemade sugar-free baked goods. The cheesecake and the banana-date pie are definitely worth sampling. Beverages include coffee, herb teas and fresh carrot juice.

No credit cards. No smoking. No alcohol.

Open 10 A.M.-9 P.M. daily; until 10 Friday and Saturday.

– Tom Jackson

GROSSE POINTE

Harvest Park
15406 Mack
313-343-0679

Expensive art prints and fine silverware, table linens and furniture add more than a touch of class to Harvest Park, just over the border from Detroit.

The menu promises that you'll be served "food in its most nutritional state, in a fashion that's most appealing to your senses." It includes some fish selections, but no meat. The dishes contain no chemicals, preservatives or additives; only whole grain flour is used.

The prices of the appetizers and salads seem high only until you see the servings, which are generous enough to constitute meals in themselves. The entrees, served with a salad and a coveted loaf of the restaurant's own bread, are priced more moderately, and they include a delicate vegetable quiche; broiled albacore tuna covered with tomatoes, Swiss cheese and white mushroom sauce, and a wonderful streudel of vegetables blended with imported cheese, eggs and spices, rolled into a light, flaky, whole wheat phylio dough, baked, and covered with mushroom sauce.

Sandwiches include a quarter-pound grain and soy "burger." A deep-dish vegetarian pizza consists of broccoli, walnuts, sprouts and other vegetables, and two kinds of cheese piled onto a whole wheat, sesame and sunflower crust.

Desserts, which include carob walnut brownies, carrot-pineapple cake and zucchini-banana cake, are sweetened with turbinado sugar, and the large selection of unusual coffee blends, mixed fruit juices, ciders and smoothies go with them perfectly.

No alcohol. No smoking. MasterCard and Visa accepted.

Open Tuesday-Thursday 11 A.M.-9:30 P.M.; Friday and Saturday until 10.

—Douglas Heller

PETOSKY

Mercado Cafe
421 Howard St.
616-347-2630

In keeping with its Mexican heritage, the Mercado forms a pleasant retreat within the marketplace. The market is the Grain Train Natural Foods Co-op, where you can work up an appetite eyeing the wooden bins filled with dried fruits, nuts and grains.

The Mexican dishes here—a few of which contain meat—are *muy bueno.* You can indulge in the deluxe burrito—an over-stuffed tortilla (not made on the premises) filled with beans, cheese and crisp vegetables and topped with spicy tomato sauce and a dollop of sour cream. The enchiladas also are superb, and if you want to save room for dessert (you will), you can order a half-portion.

Other taste treats include the Supreme Salad—a gardenful of fresh vegetables topped with boiled eggs and avocado slices; the Avocado Club sandwich—a triple-decker combination of avocado, cheese, tomato and special dressing; and the broiled trout dinner, a local rainbow trout cooked in a delicate wine sauce and served with soup, salad and beverage.

The desserts are the Mercado's crowning achievement. Honey cheesecake, chocolate pie, fresh fruit and cream crepes and all manner of whole wheat pastries are made fresh daily at the cafe. Some desserts contain fructose. Only whole wheat flour is used.

To drink, there's rich Colombian coffee, a vast array of herb teas, fresh juices and a yogurt-fruit concoction.

No alcohol. Ashtrays available on request. No credit cards. On Friday evenings, there's jazz, folk or classical music provided by local entertainers.

Hours: 10:30 A.M.-4 P.M. Monday-Saturday; until 9 on Friday.

—Helen Prescott

SOUTHFIELD

Healthy Jones
29221 Northwestern Hwy.
313-353-7766

This combination store-restaurant in a trendy open shopping mall is bright and airy, with hanging ferns, butcher-block tables and young waitresses in T-shirts emblazoned with a giant butterfly, the symbol of Healthy Jones.

The menu proudly proclaims that no chemical additives or preservatives are used in any of their foods. In order to keep the air as fresh as the food, there is no smoking permitted.

The H.J. Dinner Salad, with mixed greens, broccoli, red cabbage, cauliflower, carrots, parsley and a touch of sprouts, comes with a choice of tahini, blue cheese or herb dressing, and it's a bargain. No red meat is served here, but they do have organic chicken and there is fresh fish daily, plus full vegetarian meals like baked spaghetti, made with whole wheat noodles, special sauce and cheese and served hot and bubbly. An especially delicious dish is the Garden and Chinese Vegetables, with mung sprouts, tofu and almonds, quickly sauteed in a wok and served over brown rice. Top off your meal with an herb tea or H.J.'s own fresh-ground coffee and a choice of desserts including carrot cake, pecan pie, cheesecake, ice cream and frozen yogurt with fruit toppings.

On Sunday you can take advantage of an all-you-can-eat brunch.

The management has applied for a wine-and-beer license, so call first if you're interested in alcoholic beverages. All major credit cards are honored.

Open 11 A.M.-11 P.M. Monday-Saturday; until 10 P.M. on Sunday.

—Ruth Ryan Langan

Minnesota

MINNEAPOLIS
Blue Heron
1123 W. Lake
612-823-4743

A pleasant environment adds to the delight of eating at this small restaurant, where the all-natural philosophy extends to the decor as well as the food. The pastel tablecloths and the matching fabric in the handmade light fixtures are colored with dye made from sumac berries, hibiscus and other vegetation. Soft guitar music and singing is provided by local musicians.

For a good, hot dinner entree, the daily special is always safe. The enchiladas are tasty and not too spicy; they come with a side of chips and guacamole dip, and the price is right. The sandwiches are served on thick slices of whole wheat bread. Fruit in season is offered for dessert, and the pies are fantastic. The coffee is good, and there's a variety of teas. Beer is served, too.

Smoking permitted. No credit cards.

Open 5-10 P.M. Monday; 11 A.M.-10 P.M. Tuesday-Saturday; 10 A.M.-9 P.M. Sunday.

—Stella Madden

MINNEAPOLIS
Mud Pie Vegetarian Restaurant
2549 Lyndale Ave. South
612-872-9435

Eclectic is the operative word at Mud Pie. The decor includes antiques, Egyptian motifs, beautiful natural woods, a variety of art, a modern outdoor patio and a Mexican room.

The clientele comes from all areas and age groups in the Twin Cities. When it opened nearly a decade ago, Mud Pie drew primarily the young and health-food-oriented. Since favorable reviews began appearing in local papers, however, it's everyone's place.

The menu is the most eclectic of all. Italian, oriental, Mexican, Arabian and standard health food fare such as vegieburgers have two things in common—healthy eating and low prices. The spaghetti dinner features whole wheat noodles and garbanzo balls. The tacos sport sunflower seeds. Tempura is made with selected deep-fried vegetables. Mud Pie has something for everyone, and it's all prepared from whole foods and fresh produce.

Best known for thick, thick soups (you can almost eat them with a knife and fork), Mud Pie is also touted for its selection of herbal teas and fruit juices (no coffee served). If you can't spend enough on food to impress your friends, try the more-than-adequate beer and wine list.

The menu advises diners that preparing food properly takes time; however, the longest wait (for lasagna) is only 17 minutes, which seems reasonable enough.

No smoking. No credit cards.

Monday-Saturday 11 A.M.-10 P.M.; Sunday 9 A.M.-1 P.M. for brunch, with regular menu available from 1-10 P.M.

—*Rosalie Koskenmaki*

MINNEAPOLIS

Seward Community Cafe
2129 Franklin Ave. East
612-332-1011

The decor is early greasy spoon, and you must master a number of house rules in order to eat, but if you like generous portions of healthy food at low prices, this is your place. A small, nonprofit community corporation runs the cafe as an integral part of the neighborhood's determination to rebuild and retain its own character. It's the nonprofit part of that description that has customers taking their own orders, tabulating them (tax tables are provided), taking them to the counter, picking up the food, busing their own dishes, washing the table afterward, and fetching their own Glenwood Spring water.

Breakfasts are a popular item here. The most expensive one is the omelet with tomatoes, sprouts, cheese, green pepper, onions, mushrooms and three eggs, and even it is a bargain. At certain hours everyone in the place seems to be eating the Red Earth Breakfast: potatoes scrambled into eggs with onions and melted cheese and smothered in ranchero sauce; if you ask, they'll give you fresh garlic to go with it.

For lunch, have a sandwich (soyburger, nutburger, peanut butter and banana or Middle Eastern garbanzo) with juice, beer, coffee or a bottomless cup of tea. Follow up with their great fresh-fruit yogurt or a fruit shake. Dinners include Mexican dishes, huge salads and fried rice (with sprouts, onions, tamari, honey and scrambled egg).

Smoking allowed in certain booths until 11:30 A.M. and 2-5 P.M. No credit cards. No alcohol.

Open weekdays 7 A.M.-8 P.M. except Tuesday, when the restaurant closes at 11:30 A.M. for a corporation meeting and clean-up; Saturday and Sunday 8 A.M.-8 P.M.

–Rosalie Koskenmaki

ST. PAUL

Cafe Kardamena
364 Selby Ave.
612-224-2209

Named after a Greek village where the owner spent some time, this vegetarian cafe offers a great Greek spinach pie and large Greek salads. Totally dedicated to the whole-food way of life, the owner does her buying direct from the farms each day so the attractive and well-prepared dishes are often only hours away from the soil.

The menu varies from day to day and reflects the seasons, the availability of fresh produce, the weather and even the cook's fancies. Different grains and vegetables are featured each day, as are two soups—"one from the garden and one from the field."

You might want to wear a bib to eat the sandwiches. Definitely on the generous side, the guacamole sandwich oozes avocado pate, tomatoes, lettuce, sprouts and cheese from between thick slices of homemade whole grain bread. Other menu finds: the Garden Salad with the cafe's secret homemade creamy curry and garlic dressing; Coquilles St. Jacques; walleye pike with herbs; miso pate, a good coffeelike grain drink.

The desserts deserve a most honorable mention. The pastry chef bakes fresh each day, using only honey and natural ingredients. Something of a legend in the area, he is reputed to stop at nothing, turning out nectarine pie that has no equal anywhere, almond cream cake, sunburst cake, orange cake, cherry-custard pie, tofu cheesecake and strawberry cream cakes and pies.

The cafe has a spare, pure look that dramatizes the art on the walls, the classical music and the excellent, inexpensive food.

Smoking and nonsmoking sections. No alcohol except for private parties. No reservations, and there's usually a line at peak hours. No credit cards, either.

Tuesday-Saturday 11:30 A.M.-9 P.M.

—Rosalie Koskenmaki

ST. PAUL

Great Expectations
1671 Selby Ave.
612-644-1836

Warm, dark woods, Victorian wallpaper, ceiling fans, old-time sepia photos and hanging plants are the major attractions here—until a tray goes by. Curiosity about what the folks at the next table are eating makes a lot of people forget where they are.

Enormous open-face sandwiches get the most attention. The Puritan piles zucchini, green peppers, tomatoes, onions, alfalfa sprouts, cucumbers, mushrooms and Monterey Jack cheese on half a long, home-baked roll. The Cattleperson combines roast beef, cheese and coleslaw, and the Pilgrim blends turkey, asparagus tips, gravy and pepper cheese.

Great Expectations offers healthy, attractive soups, salads, sandwiches, malts and a comprehensive breakfast menu at modest prices. Originally vegetarian, the restaurant now includes a few meat and non-whole foods for its neighborhood regulars.

Almost nothing here is ordinary. For your basic grilled cheese, you choose from five cheeses and six breads. They bring you two great slabs of bread topped with melted cheese and tomato slices accompanied by orange sections, grapes and a great garlic-dill pickle spear. Local reviewers and loyal customers rate the French onion soup (made fresh twice daily) right up there with the kind served at the old Les Halles restaurants in Paris. Thick gobs of gooey cheese, hunks of bread and lots of toothsome onions float in a rich beef broth.

Other popular items are the skin-on fries and the multi-ingredient meatless salads. Soda fountain items are homemade with fresh ingredients; the desserts are brought in and aren't too healthy for you. Beverages include coffee, tea, fresh lemonade and the best water in town (they float lemons in it to remove the taste of the Mississippi).

Smoking and nonsmoking sections. No credit cards. No alcohol.

Sunday-Thursday 7 A.M.-10 P.M.; Friday and Saturday to 11 P.M.; closed 10:30-11 A.M. Monday-Saturday.

—Rosalie Koskenmaki

Missouri

KANSAS CITY

Golden Temple Conscious Cookery
4059 Broadway
816-561-6440

See listings of other Golden Temple restaurants in Reno, Los Angeles, St. Louis and Washington, D.C.

No smoking. No credit cards.

Monday-Friday 11 A.M.-3 P.M. and 5-9 P.M.; Saturday 11 A.M.-9 P.M.

ST. LOUIS

Golden Temple Cafe
17 S. Euclid
314-367-0405

In a small, modest room filled with grain bins and colorfully stocked shelves, Golden Temple serves substantial vegetarian food. Meals are simple yet nourishing, and the quiet staff clad in turbans and white robes adds to the slightly solemn atmosphere.

Daily soup and entree specials offer variety to the menu of familiar sandwiches and salads. The Wha Burger (a high-protein vegetable burger) and the felafel (pita stuffed with vegetable patties, greens and tomato) are tasty selections. A reliable salad is the Golden Garden, but the Guacamole Relleno or Mayan Princess provides a pleasant change.

Honey-bean pies, frozen yogurt and honey ice cream, with an assortment of healthful toppings, are served for dessert. Beverages include juices, shakes and smoothies and an unusual hot Yogi Tea, which is a blend of spices with milk and honey.

No alcohol. No smoking. No credit cards.

Monday-Saturday 11 A.M.-5 P.M.; until 6 on Thursdays.

—Christy Abelov

ST. LOUIS
Sunshine Inn
8½ S. Euclid
314-367-1413

Nestled among a crowded row of shops and restaurants in the Central West End, Sunshine Inn offers a variety of delicious and wholesome foods. The cozy, informal setting provides a comfortable place to relax and enjoy a satisfying meal.

Crisp salads and meat-filled or sprouty sandwiches are always available, but the daily specials are usually more popular. A bowl of homemade soup and fresh rolls or a slice of quiche with a Garden of Eden Salad are reliable dishes. Another tasty choice is the Ratatouille Provencale, an array of vegetables over brown rice topped with melted cheese. The dinner menu includes a healthy selection of chicken, seafood and vegetarian entrees.

There is an excellent assortment of tempting desserts, and most are made with honey. A rich dessert called Chocolate Mountain is one of the best in town.

A broad range of beverages is served: coffee, black and herbal teas, juices, soft drinks and special concoctions. There's also a full bar with imported beer and wine.

Smoking allowed. No credit cards.

Open Tuesday-Sunday 11:30 A.M.-10 P.M.

—Christy Abelov

Nevada

LAS VEGAS
Alfalfa's Ltd.
1107 E. Tropicana
702-736-6441

Alfalfa's is a full-service wholly vegetarian restaurant with an international menu. The house special is a vegie Dagwood sandwich served on unleavened bread and called, God help us, a Bible sandwich.

Nonsmoking section. No credit cards.

Open 11 A.M.-11 P.M. every day.

LAS VEGAS
Food for Living
4015 W. Sahara Ave.
702-876-5191

Our correspondent writes: "A fine vegetarian establishment in the middle of Las Vegas. The vegetable couscous was straight out of the Casbah!"

No smoking. American Express, Diners Club, MasterCard and Visa accepted.

Open 10 A.M.-7 P.M. every day.

RENO
Golden Temple Conscious Cookery
902 S. Virginia
702-786-4110

Just eight blocks south of the center of Reno's casino gambling, a few followers of the Kundalini Yoga path serve what they call conscious cookery. The meals exclude all meat, fish, poultry and eggs. Honey is the only sweetener used here, with some dishes garnished with cheese. Coffee, alcohol and smoking are prohibited.

Some of the delights from the menu are Adi Shakti Enchiladas, stuffed with spiced mushrooms, and Mushroom Meadow, which consists of mushrooms sauteed in butter on a sea of sour cream and scallions over a baked potato, surrounded by tender home-grown alfalfa sprouts, avocado and tomato dressed with lemon tahini.

Two of the popular sandwiches are the avocado-and-cheese and the cream cheese with dates, walnuts and sliced apple. All sandwiches are served on the restaurant's own bread, baked daily.

Service is a little slow, but no one seems to mind waiting in such a pleasant and friendly atmosphere. You have only to eat here two or three times before you're treated like friends of the family.

Fresh juices—orange, strawberry-orange and carrot—are the specialties. Other beverages include a date shake and a banana shake, made with the restaurant's own honey ice cream. Everyone has to sample the Yogi Tea at one time or another.

No credit cards.

Open 10:30 A.M.-8:30 P.M. Monday-Saturday.

—Sherman Reinius

New Hampshire

ASHLAND

Suzanne's Kitchen
Main St.
603-968-7614

A correspondent advises: "This restaurant is a second home to me. The vegetarian menu is an international one, with Middle Eastern and Far Eastern specialties. Great desserts, all sugar-free. And where else can you get scrambled tofu for breakfast? There's usually a poetry reading on Thursday night and live music on Sunday."

Open 7:30 A.M.-9:30 P.M.; closed Monday.

CONCORD

The Natural Selection
S. State and Concord Sts.
603-224-4757

Prices are low at this self-service natural foods restaurant. While meat entrees are offered, there's an ample selection of vegetarian items, including quiche, assorted homemade soups and sandwiches on pita bread. Extensive selection of desserts.

Open 11 A.M.-8 P.M. Monday-Saturday.

FRANCONIA

Tatwamasi Natural Foods Restaurant
Main St.
603-823-7722

A part of Tatwamasi Natural Foods store, this restaurant serves sandwiches and salads. Strictly vegetarian at time of writing, they plan to add eggs, fish and dairy products to the menu. Desserts are sweetened with honey and maple syrup.

Open 11 A.M.-3:30 P.M. Monday-Saturday; 10 A.M.-3 P.M. Sunday. Call for information about their evening cooking classes.

PETERBOROUGH

The Folkway
85 Grove St.
603-924-7484

A wood stove provides warmth in this semi-vegetarian restaurant. Vegetable quiche and lasagna are usually available, along with soups and sandwiches and tempting, if sugar-sweetened, desserts. Alcohol is served. There's often music at night.

Open Tuesday-Saturday 11:30 A.M.-2 P.M. and 5:30-8 P.M.

CLINTON

Lazy Daisy Natural Foods Restaurant
21 W. Main St.
201-735-4817

A rustic cafe serving only whole grain and vegetarian dishes with local organic vegetables when available. Entrees, soups and desserts change daily. Baking is done on the premises. No refined foods, additives or preservatives are used here.

No smoking. No credit cards. Alcohol's not served, but bring your own if you wish.

Monday 11 A.M.-3:30 P.M.; Tuesday-Friday 11 A.M.-8 P.M.; Saturday until 5 P.M.

EAST RUTHERFORD

Park & Orchard
227 Park Ave.
201-939-9292

A source notes: "One of the best whole foods restaurants in the metropolitan area. Well worth a visit." Chicken and fish as well as vegetarian dishes. No refined sugar or white flour is used. Baking is done on the premises, and some of the produce is organic.

Liquor served. Smoking permitted. All major credit cards accepted.

Open for lunch Tuesday-Friday 11:30 A.M.-2 P.M.; dinner Tuesday-Saturday 5-10 P.M. and Sunday 2-9 P.M.

HOBOKEN

The Beat'n Path
125 Washington St.
201-653-9457

One cook is macrobiotic, the other was trained at a natural foods cooking school in the Netherlands. So you will find a mixture of the two styles here, especially in the daily specials. Our favorite is the ample dish of scallops cooked in sherry over brown rice. And there is a variety of tofu specials that arouse consistent interest.

Among the dishes on the regular menu, the house salad is quite good. Ingredients vary, and on the day we were there it contained fresh greens, avocado, sliced egg, chickpeas, chunks of cheese and bean sprouts. The Japanese noodle dinner, with whole wheat noodles and seasonal vegetables in ginger sauce, also is worth trying.

On Saturday and Sunday, brunch typically includes waffles and crepes with syrup, yogurt, fresh fruit and nuts, sandwiches, chili, salads and assorted omelets, all served with a bread and butter basket.

The desserts here vary unpredictably from extremely good to somewhat disappointing.

To drink there are juices, teas, coffees and hot cider with rum.

The Beat'n Path has a front room where patrons can eat an evening meal or drink coffee while being entertained by folk, rock or chamber music or poetry readings after 9:00. Sometimes there are plays and other special events.

Smoking frowned upon but not prohibited. No credit cards.

Open 5:30-11:30 P.M. every night except Monday (only drinks and desserts served after 10:30); 11 A.M.-3:30 P.M. for Saturday and Sunday brunch.

—Stuart Suss

POINT PLEASANT BEACH

Wild Oats
1300 Richmond Ave.
201-877-2272

Tucked away in the rear of a health food store of the same name, Wild Oats serves hot dishes, salads and sandwiches for an inexpensive lunch. The decor of the five-table eatery is simple, and paper plates and plastic utensils belie the quality of the meatless cuisine.

A rich Jarlsberg quiche highlights the hot portion of the menu, which also includes chili and stuffed mushrooms. The soup of the day is posted on a blackboard along with other specials; broccoli bisque was the selection on a recent visit.

The only fish on the menu is tuna, and it's served in a sandwich with tomatoes, lettuce and alfalfa sprouts on an excellent seven-grain bread. My personal sandwich favorites, however, are the Wyoming, with Jarlsberg, lettuce, tomatoes, sprouts and dressing, and the Rainbow, which features grated vegetables with the same special dressing in pita bread.

For a light lunch, either the California or Shepherd salad should suffice. The former is basically leaf lettuce, and the latter is spinach with cheese, other vegetables, sunflower or pumpkin seeds and alfalfa seeds. A selection of dressings is available.

The drink choices include organic-carrot, apple or coconut juice, herb teas, and hot spiced cider. Coffee is not available, nor is alcohol, and customers are not encouraged to bring their own wine. The sugar-free dessert menu lists carrot cake, custard, carob or vanilla honey ice cream, and something called Maple Syrup Delight.

Because of limited seating, get there early, especially on summer Saturdays, as this is a tourist town. Credit cards are not accepted, and smoking is not permitted.

Open 11:30 A.M.-3:30 P.M. Monday-Saturday.

—Joe Bilby

New Mexico

ALBUQUERQUE

The Bakery Cafe
118 Yale SE
505-255-0749

The Bakery Cafe (strictly vegetarian) was put together by a collective years ago and has maintained its homemade appearance. In late summer and fall, a semi-wild garden with towering sunflowers greets the patron who enters the high-fenced front yard of the little restaurant. Two long tables sit outdoors under bamboo-covered arbors, as though waiting for a party of sylvan carousers to bang mugs and shout songs.

Inside, there are only four tables, but much sunlight from the large windows which open to the garden. The food is special. The cafe collective (still operating) makes its own bread, yogurt, catsup, mayonnaise, syrup, hommus, tabouli, chili, mustard, sprouts—we haven't exhausted the list, but you get the idea.

Our favorite breakfast is the Huevos Rancheros—two eggs, chili sauce, herbed French fries, cheese and whole wheat toast. Pancakes are good, especially with fruit and yogurt, which can also be ordered separately. There's a variety of teas and fresh organic juices.

For lunch, the soup du jour, salad and bread is a bargain. For those desiring more solid food, there is the tofuburger, the peanut butter and fruit sandwich or the Small Planet Salad with hommus, sunflower seeds, sprouts and dressing.

Smoking is permitted on the patio, but inside it goes the way of sugar, meat, fish (none on premises) and credit cards (not accepted). Alcohol is not served, though perhaps it's occasionally smuggled. Coffee is plentiful.

Open 8 A.M.-3 P.M. every day and 5-9 P.M. Thursday-Sunday.

—*Neal Singer*

ALBUQUERQUE

Homestead Natural Foods
119 San Pasquale SW
505-243-0370

You're driving down Albuquerque's Central Avenue to see historic Old Town and you feel as though you're turning into a Kentucky Fried Chicken. There are franchises everywhere. But wait—what's that? A rainbow painted on the corner of a large cinder-block and glass building. It's Homestead Natural Foods, with a cafe, juice bar and store, all in one place.

Inside, you notice the order and cleanliness. You're buoyed by the flowered wallpaper and that cheerful feeling that only comes from walking on new linoleum. There's some pretty nice woodwork, too. Somebody's done some *work* around here.

There's no meat or fish. If you're hungry, try the California Tostada (whole wheat or corn tortilla, beans, cheese, green chili, a lot of tasty guacamole, all sitting on a bed of green salad). Or if vegieburgers are your style, try the Buddha Delux (soybeans, millet, chopped bell peppers, celery, onions, wheat germ and sunflower seeds form the burger, which is accompanied by beans and the ubiquitous New Mexican green chili).

There is a variety of salads, from a small one of mixed vegetables and sprouts to Global Village Greens (guacamole, tabouli, tofu, hommus and cashews on a European-style green salad with American sprouts). We recommend the tabouli, though the hommus and the Middle Eastern salad (hommus and tabouli on a bed of greens, served with sprouts and pita) have their good points, too.

Prices here are modest; some of the dishes come at reduced prices for a half-order, and it's best to inquire about that if you're only moderately hungry.

Desserts are sugarless. No smoking. MasterCard and Visa accepted.

Monday-Friday 11 A.M.-9 P.M.; Saturday 11 A.M.-6 P.M.; Sunday noon-6 P.M.

—*Neal Singer*

ALBUQUERQUE

Morning Glory Cafe
2933 Monte Vista Blvd. NE
505-268-7040

It looks like a 1950s luncheonette, with its long counter and stools, red vinyl booths and shaded fluorescent lights. It's not the decor, obviously, that brings sleepy Albuquerqueans to stand in the street on weekends waiting for an open breakfast table. Perhaps it's the paintings (a changing collection of work by the more accomplished local artists), or the guitar-playing (classical, folk and original), or perhaps it's the food.

The Morning Glory comfortably accommodates every lifestyle. Although meat is served, it is bought only from a ranch which prides itself on not "shooting up" its animals with water, antibiotics or chemicals before slaughter. There is white sugar out on the table; it sits next to the honey jar. And behind the counter are sugar-free whole wheat desserts as well as truck-stop sweet rolls.

Our favorite breakfast (when we can get in) is the Three Egg Super Omelette (the eggs are fresh from the farm), with whole wheat toast and home fries. We add whole green chilis and cheddar cheese and wash it down with coffee (the cafe's own blend) imported directly from Mexico. Other possible omelet additions are mushrooms, spinach, herbs, tomatoes, onions and sprouts, or chemical-free turkey, bacon or sausage.

The luncheon menu features items like the Pat Garrett—a quarter-pound burger covered with green chili strips on a whole wheat bun (served with fresh French fries, pinto beans or salad) and the Mable Dodge Lujan—Swiss cheese, raw fresh spinach, whole wheat bread and mayonnaise.

At 5 P.M., the lighting gets cut back and candles appear on the tables. No liquor is served (though some patrons are rumored to have smuggled in their own in discreet brown bags). The dinner menu ranges from fresh fish from Louisiana to cooked steak, and from fresh salads to vegetarian dinner plates. One salad, the Decadent, is composed of turkey or tofu, Gouda cheese, hard-boiled egg, avocado, mushroom, lettuce, tomatoes, carrots, sprouts and green chili strips and topped with sour cream dressing. The tofu dinner plate comes with a homemade brown sauce and an individual whole wheat honey bread loaf. In addition there are vegetarian and meat burritos, blue corn enchiladas and other New Mexican staples. From 4 to 6 there's a French Crepes special that changes every night.

Smoking permitted. MasterCard and Visa accepted.

Monday-Saturday 7 A.M.-10 P.M., with breakfast available until 5; Sunday 9 A.M.-4 P.M.

—*Neal Singer*

ALBUQUERQUE

Mother Nature & Son
3118 Central Ave. SE
505-255-7640

Mother Nature's more pleasant aspects are featured nicely in this completely vegetarian restaurant. Plants and vines hang from trellises, which themselves hang horizontally over the room. A charming back patio is built entirely of wood, with upper walls and roof made of wooden slats to let in light and air.

Mother Nature's son, owner Bill Rather, takes his responsibilities seriously. "We don't *own* sugar, just New Mexico honey," he says, and his flour is stone-ground daily on the premises.

The restaurant's most popular dish is a vegetarian casserole called Our Specialty (available in half-orders), the ingredients of which change daily. Our favorite set of ingredients is the Cosmic Casserole, made with organic brown rice, cottage cheese, sour cream, cheddar cheese, green chili peppers and sauteed mushrooms. For those liking less rich food, sandwich plates like the Magic Mushroom, made of homemade whole wheat bread, homemade mayonnaise (safflower oil, eggs, vinegar and spices), melted rennetless cheese, tomatoes and sauteed mushrooms, might fill the bill. Also available are Beanwich and Cheese, 'Nana Nut and Melted Cheese sandwiches, which come with alfalfa sprouts and a choice of tossed or potato salad.

There usually are homemade soups and a variety of salads. Our favorite is the Super (romaine, grated carrots, red cabbage, raisins, sunflower and sesame seeds, sliced rennetless cheese and tomatoes topped with alfalfa sprouts).

For dessert there is a variety of homemade choices like almond cheesecake, bread or rice pudding, zucchini bread, eggless banana bread and others, all cheap. There's natural ice cream, too, as well as vegetable and fruit juices and coffee.

No smoking, no alcohol, no credit cards.

Open every day, 11:30 A.M.-7 P.M.

—Neal Singer

New York

ALBANY

Ribbon Grass
33 Central Ave.
518-465-0248

Subdued lighting playing on old brick walls, a bookstore in the rear of the restaurant (with spiritual and cookbooks), tie-dyed stools along an antique oak bar, an international menu and a casual atmosphere make Ribbon Grass Natural Foods Restaurant a delightful retreat. The corner where the cooks are creating generous portions of imaginative natural foods is separated from the dining area by neck-high partitions.

No meat is served at this vegetarian restaurant, but eggs and dairy products are on the menu. All soups, salads and dressings are homemade. The daily specials (lunch and dinner) posted on the blackboard are reasonably priced and of gourmet quality. There's a choice of ten different entrees at dinner; one of them, the Protein Salad, is a mountain of fresh raw vegetables, nuts, seeds, cheeses, eggs and fruits.

You may order desserts from the blackboard's several options. The carob-nut brownie with maple ice cream was moist and rich. The apple-nut crunch was fresh and delicious. No cane sugar is used at Ribbon Grass; there's a honey pot on each table. Only whole grain flours are used.

Ribbon Grass does not serve alcoholic beverages, but it invites patrons to bring their own wine. No smoking; no credit cards.

Monday-Friday 11 A.M.-2:30 P.M.; Wednesday-Sunday 5:30-9 P.M. The restaurant is closed for a week or so during the summer and sometimes on holidays, so call if you're in doubt.

—*Judith Wooster*

AMITYVILLE
Santosha
40 Merrick Rd.
516-598-2039

Translate Santosha and you come up with contentment—the perfect word for this cozy, comfortable restaurant. The interior is small and warmly decorated with hanging plants, soft lighting and sturdy pine tables. Lovely nature scenes set off the paneled walls. There is entertainment on Friday and Saturday nights—gentle music that lends a pleasant background to your meal.

Dinners come with soup, salad and bread. The soup alone, an excellent vegetable mixture, is worth a visit to Santosha. Try the house French dressing on your salad; it's nicely flavored with lots of herbs. We found the fruit, nut and cheese plate appetizer to be fresh, plentiful and delicious. Seventh Dynasty—stir-fried vegetables over brown rice, topped with melted cheddar cheese—is usually good, with nicely crisp vegetables, but an overdose of onions can sometimes spoil it. Fettucine Santosha is a nice change—pasta in a cream sauce with a crunchy sprinkling of carrots, zucchini and onions. The best bet among the main-course salads is the mushroom-spinach combination. Santosha features a children's menu, too, with basics like a peanut butter and jelly sandwich with a glass of milk.

Sugar-laden desserts such as some rather humdrum ice cream are available, but the daily dessert special is usually sugar-free and worth a try, ranging from acceptable to delicious.

No smoking, no alcohol. No credit cards.

Tuesday-Thursday 11 A.M.-2:30 P.M. and 5-9 P.M.; Fridays and Saturdays until 9:30 P.M.

—Ann Jamieson

BROOKLYN
Francine's
196 Hall St.
212-783-9445

A well-recommended vegetarian restaurant across from Pratt Institute, Francine's has a primarily vegetarian menu that includes some carefully labeled fish and chicken dishes.

Wine and beer served. No smoking. No credit cards.

Weekdays 11:30 A.M.-11 P.M.; open at 6 P.M. Saturday, noon Sunday.

BROOKLYN
Our Daily Bread
316 Seventh Ave.
212-499-3279

Our Daily Bread is a vegetarian restaurant and bulk-style natural food store.

Nonsmoking section. Beer and wine served. No credit cards.

Monday-Friday 11:30 A.M.-10 P.M.; Saturday noon-6 P.M.

BUFFALO
Greenfield Street Restaurant
Greenfield St.
716-836-9035

Located a few doors off Main Street about halfway between the downtown business district and the State University of New York campus, Greenfield Street is more than a good place for a vegetarian meal. It's a strong center for the local counterculture.

And it's a strictly no-frills operation. Customers make their selections from a battery of chalkboards, pick up their trays at the serving counter, and are strongly encouraged to bus their own tables when they've finished eating. Greenfield Street is operated by a 12-person collective, and they take their roles seriously; on a recent visit, a notice had been posted apologizing profusely for the need to increase prices.

The higher prices were still plenty low. Stir-fried vegetables with or without grain, a Soy Macroburger with or without cheese, other sandwiches, a bountiful vegetable salad—all these offerings represented good value. Greenfield Street's food is always well prepared, if a bit pedestrian and underseasoned. You'll eat hearty and get away cheap, but you may not find yourself begging the chef for the recipe.

Beverages include coffee, tea, herb tea and Postum—no alcohol. The desserts are sugar-free. No smoking. No credit cards.

Hours: Breakfast from 9 A.M. Saturday and Sunday; lunch 11:30 A.M.-3:30 P.M. and dinner 5-9 P.M. Tuesday-Sunday. Occasionally open late as a coffeehouse.

—Lawrence Block

BUFFALO

Koinonia Cafe
718 Elmwood Ave.
716-882-3327

Koinonia—the unpronounceable name is a Greek word having to do with Christian sharing and fellowship— occupies the first floor of a substantial Victorian house a couple of blocks north of Ferry. The dining room is comfortable and well appointed, with the works of local artists displayed on the walls.

The food here is imaginative and consistently appealing, with a good selection of salads, sandwiches and hot dishes.

Recent dinners there began with a hearty carrot soup that was a little too rich for our companion's taste and a cold tahini soup made with raw vegetable juices that was light, savory and impossible to fault. For our main course, we passed up the quiche and the sauteed vegetables, both good choices in the past, in favor of the vegetable pie, a melange of vegies, nuts and cream cheese in a chewy whole wheat crust. A companion had a fish entree served with rice pilaf and found the portion exceedingly generous but the fish itself rather bland.

Our dessert was carob cream pie—rich, mellow and delicious, and like all Koinonia desserts, sweetened lightly with honey. Another popular dessert choice is a half-portion of Sunny Orchard Salad, fresh seasonal fruit with raisins, coconut and granolas, topped with a yogurt and honey dressing. Beverages include coffee and a hot grain drink, tea and herb teas. We're partial to a blended smoothie of coconut, pineapple and banana.

Serving persons are bright, young and personable, and the prevailing attitude is one of, well, koinonia, for want of a better word. And the little basket of homemade muffins they bring you when you sit down is very nearly worth the price of the whole meal.

No smoking is permitted in the dining room, but there's an attractive lounge adjoining it where one may sip coffee while having a nicotine transfusion. No credit cards. No alcohol.

Monday-Friday 11:30 A.M.-2 P.M. and 5-9 P.M.; Sunday 11 A.M.-3 P.M. and 5-9 P.M. Open as a coffeehouse with an abbreviated menu Wednesday-Friday 9 P.M.-1 A.M.

—Lawrence Block

BUFFALO

One World Cookery
530 Rhode Island St.
716-886-8466

Ginny and Seth Geller opened One World Cookery in July 1975 and have been doing a steady business ever since. The decor is a tad dull, but the restaurant is immaculate and there's always a fresh flower on each table. It holds about 44 people, though 20-25 are usually eating there, and that seems comfortable for good service.

The mainstays of the menu are a delicious shrimp tempura with brown rice (which is served with everything); steamed vegetables with cheddar sauce, perfectly prepared and generously served; and Greek salad dinner, with avocado, feta cheese, wonderful olives and loads of salad goodies. In addition, Ginny, who does all the cooking, prepares a veal dish such as Roumanian Veal Ragout or Veal Tacino and a chicken dish like Chicken

Saltimbocca or Chicken Crepes each day. There is also a vegetarian quiche almost daily; my favorite is made with fresh asparagus. Each meal comes with a hot, homemade whole wheat roll.

One World has a delicious gazpacho plus a different hot soup each day. The soup, usually vegetarian, might be cream of eggplant or vegetable barley; however, when I ordered corn chowder, the waiter told me it was made with chicken stock. I'd been hoping for a vegetarian soup, but I was impressed that he told me about the chicken.

Dessert is either amaretto cheesecake or a daily special, usually made with fresh fruit, such as cherry custard or strawberry mousse. They are heavenly. Honey and raw sugar are used for sweetening. Everything is homemade, and no additives or preservatives are used.

There is a small but nice wine list and beer, but no hard liquor. Smoking permitted. No credit cards.

Tuesday-Saturday 6-10 P.M.

—Susan Lichtblau

CATO
Greenleaf
Route 34 at Route 370
513-626-2751

Your first glimpse of the Greenleaf is a restored wooden staircase leading to the upstairs dining room, and the restored wood look doesn't end with the stairway. Floors, doors, tables and cabinets scattered throughout the large, simple dining room all have that sheened appearance. In keeping with the restaurant's name, the room is decorated with a ceiling border of green leaves.

This strictly vegetarian restaurant operates weekends only, with dinners on Friday and Saturday and breakfast on Sunday. Complete dinners (with discounts for children) include a choice of soup (corn chowder, mushroom barley or onion, for example); salad (fruit or green), entree (eggplant parmesan, Middle Eastern vegetables with rice, or crepes stuffed with fresh vegetables); and dessert (apple crisp, apple cake or fresh fruit—no sugar in any). Two choices for each part of the meal are always offered, and they change weekly. A la carte dishes are available, too, in large, small or children's portions.

When we visited, a generous serving of fruit salad was full of melon balls, bananas, pears, grapes, raisins, apples and coconut and was topped with a light, tasty mixture of yogurt, cinnamon and orange juice; it is a perfect breakfast dish. Other suggestions are the whole wheat pancakes and the oat muffins. Granola, eggs and bread (not as fresh as it could have been on our visit) also are available. Don't be shy about mentioning a dish you find enjoyable, because the recipes are on the counter for customers' perusal.

Beverages include coffee, a hot grain drink, herb teas and fruit juices. No liquor or carry-in is permitted.

No smoking. No credit cards.

—Molly K. Gramet

CLARENCE

Asa Ransom House
10529 Main St.
716-759-2315

While by no means a vegetarian restaurant, Asa Ransom House deserves inclusion here by virtue of its emphasis on healthfully prepared natural foods and its charm and high quality. This establishment, several miles east of Buffalo on Route 5, still operates as a country inn, with four guest bedrooms available. It is as a restaurant, however, that Asa Ransom most distinguishes itself. Its local popularity is such that reservations are always essential and often must be made days, even weeks, in advance. Such popular success is all the more remarkable in a restaurant that is closed Fridays and Saturdays, in keeping with the religious beliefs of the owners, who are members of the Worldwide Church of God.

We enjoyed both of the vegetarian entrees—a stuffed cucumber filled with wheat germ, walnuts and vegetables and topped with melted cheese, and an excellent vegetable platter. For the omnivore, the roast beef is highly praised, and the menu boasts smoked corned beef slices with apple-raisin sauce and a boneless fricasseed chicken with granola biscuits.

Salads lean toward dark-leaf lettuce, vegetables are always fresh, cheese is a local raw milk product, additives are assiduously avoided, MSG is shunned, honey and herb teas are available, and the quality of everything is impeccable. It's not cheap.

Nonsmokers' dining room. Alcohol served. No credit cards.

Open 4:30-9 P.M. Monday-Thursday; 12:30-8 P.M. Sunday, and for lunch on Wednesday.

—Lawrence Block

FULTON

Keryn's Kitchen
200 Hannibal St.
315-598-7401

This bright and sprightly restaurant is introduced by a colorful sidewalk garden. On the inside, checked yellow tablecloths are accented by yellow rough-spun napkins. Everything is spanking clean and crisp. There is a wall decoratively covered with wicker baskets and a potted foliage plant or succulent on each table. A natural foods store adjoins the dining room.

Diners may wish to try the excellent potato soup when it is offered as a special; garnished with carrot slices and chopped parsley, it is eye-appealing and delicious.

A standard dinner includes entree, appetizer, salad, vegetable and homemade bread. The entrees, which rely heavily on meat substitutes, include "beef" stroganoff, cabbage rolls, cheesy cauliflower and "chicken" crepes, and spaghetti and "meatballs."

Sunday brunches are special. Morning Start is a favorite pancake item, with strawberries or blueberries and a choice of yogurt or whipped cream—Stripples (soy bacon) included.

Whole wheat flour is used for the crusts of the delicious pies. There is sugar in the desserts. A wide range of herbal teas, juices and coffee-substitutes is available. No alcohol or smoking. No credit cards.

Hours: Sunday brunch 10 A.M.-4 P.M., luncheon and dinner noon-4 P.M.; Monday-Friday lunch 11:30 A.M.-2 P.M.; Wednesday and Thursday dinner 5-8 P.M. Closed Saturday.

—Bob Rock

GREAT NECK

Nature's Greenery
8 Bond St.
516-466-4313

Nature's Greenery, with two entrances, is in a building registered as a national historic place on a refurbished brick-paved street. The main room, for nonsmokers, exudes light and warmth from the shining floors and blond tables to the broad windows and reflector lamps used only at night.

Beware the good bread and little tubs of butter, the salad and inviting dressings that fill you up while you wait for the baked or broiled fish of the day, crunchy fresh vegetables with teriyaki sauce, or buckwheat spaghetti al dente with tomato sauce and Parmesan cheese in a glass bowl, all prepared to order.

Try the delicious and imaginative vegetarian pizza: cheese and tomatoes baked in a phyllo crust. Or spend a long, happy midday over a combo platter of tuna salad, egg salad, guacamole, Eggplant Caponata, tabouli, meatless pate, chips and crackers. We find the spinach herb dressing, made from reduced cooked spinach, oil, vinegar and spices, a treat. Some customers come for snacks like fresh melon, hot stuffed mushrooms, protein shakes and side orders of grain-of-the-day and brown rice.

There are some fruity sugarless desserts, sometimes good, sometimes doughy. If you're still hungry after one of the best natural foods meals in the New York suburbs, order a frozen yogurt sundae or some Haagen-Dazs ice cream.

Minimum: $2.50. Major credit cards accepted. No sugar, little salt in cooking and baking. No meat. Customers may bring wine or beer. Live music on Saturdays.

Noon-4 P.M. and 5-10 P.M. every day, later on Friday and Saturday. Closed some holidays.

—Lillian Schiff

GREAT NECK

Salad Encounter
123 Middle Neck Rd.
516-487-1069

Sit on the awning-covered patio or choose the wide-windowed dining room with tasteful carpeting and leafy plants. Then walk along the buffet, putting exactly what you want and how much you want to eat on a strong paper plate. The cashier will weigh your choice and charge you by the ounce, often reminding you to take a complimentary slice of pumpernickel or raisin-walnut whole wheat bread. The price is right, and the coffee price includes a refill.

Dozens of salads, some with dressing and some without, and pieces of cold fruits are attractively displayed on a reassuring cushion of ice. Sincere weight watchers are given every chance to select a hard-boiled egg, a slice of Swiss or Muenster, lots of plain lettuce and tomatoes and chunks of cantaloupe. Nonvegetarians say they would like a real tuna salad but must make do with bits of tuna in pasta shells, slices of salami or sometimes ham.

We recommend the broccoli spears in a secret house dressing, the curry of noodles with raisins, and string beans or peas with mushrooms. Cold vegetables are the stars, and on any given day you're sure to find cauliflower, carrots, kidney beans and onions, spicily dressed, alone or in combos. A crock of soup is always available. There is quiche every day from the famous caterer next door. The few pies and cakes, made with sugar, are good. Apple juice and tea are available.

No alcohol is served, but you may bring your own. There are ashtrays on the tables. No credit cards.

Open 11:30 A.M.-9 P.M. every day except some holidays, later on Friday and Saturday.

–Lillian Schiff

HUNTINGTON

Chez Vegie
14 Elm St.
516-271-1269

In a little brown frame house a few doors from New York Avenue, Chez Vegie greeted the world in September 1979 as an almost completely vegetarian restaurant; some delicious Monterey Jack cheese hides in one sandwich. The clientele is already attached to the high-quality vegetables and grains, the three tiny, inviting rooms, the few tables set with cloth napkins and chopsticks, and the Bach to Rollins playing on the stereo.

Our favorite salad is tabouli, made with satisfying red and white cabbage, cucumber, tomato and bulgur marinated in olive oil, wine vinegar, mint and parsley. A first-rate tempeh sandwich is a savory square of chopped, baked soybeans, special sauce, tomatoes, onions and lettuce on hot whole wheat pita. Add a little tofu dressing, redolent of sesame oil, to salad or sandwich for a pleasing midday meal.

For dinner, two recent visitors planned their own Indian menu: samosa appetizer (mildly spiced potatoes in deep-fried whole wheat pastry with tamarind sauce on the side); dahi vaddi (cold yogurt sauce floating a deep-fried Indian legume, ginger, coconut and coriander); an authentic korma with vegetables, cashew-coconut cream, and spices; dahl (spiced Indian lentils); raita (cucumbers, tomatoes, herbs and spices in yogurt) and chutney.

There is no sugar on the premises, so the pies in their thin, wheaty crusts might contain honey or maple syrup. We enjoyed the smooth, creamy tofu-banana pie.

The servers need more experience and the menu needs more variety. That will happen in time, we are told. Otherwise, this establishment rates high marks for very agreeable ambience and honest food.

No smoking. No credit cards. No alcoholic beverages served (but a few of the dishes contain some spirits); bring your own if you wish.

Tuesday-Saturday 11:30 A.M.-2:30 P.M.; Tuesday-Sunday 5:30-10 P.M.

—*Lillian Schiff*

ITHACA
Cabbagetown Cafe
404 Eddy St.
607-273-2847

Just outside the gate to the Cornell University campus, Cabbagetown Cafe serves vegetarian delights to students and local folk alike. The tasteful stucco and wood trim decor is accented by a long table with benches that extend down the middle of the room. Children are especially fond of the communal atmosphere. Diners who prefer more intimate tables along the walls often have to wait in line.

They line up for the creations of Julie Jordan, the owner, whose vegetarian cookbook, *Wings of Life,* is in its fourth printing. Her Enchilada del Dia, with choice of refried beans or guacamole, tortilla chips and salad, and the Quiche du Jour, with salad and bread, are available every evening. Cashew chili, served over brown rice with melted cheese and cornbread, complements the soup and salad or sandwich specials served at lunch and dinner. Scrambled tofu or Huevos Rancheros (fried eggs over tortillas with cheese and tomato sauce) spices up Sunday Brunch. No meal is complete without a salad topped with Jordan's rugged garlic dressing, created from a creamy mayonnaise base.

A wine list heads the beverage selection. No meat or fish appears on the menu. Coffee is available. Fresh pastries are sweetened with turbinado sugar. No smoking. No credit cards.

Monday-Saturday 11:30 A.M.-5:30 P.M.;
Sunday 10:30 A.M.-2:30 P.M.

– Tom Terrizzi

ITHACA
Golden Temple
150 Ithaca Commons
607-273-7710

Ithaca boasts an outdoor pedestrian mall for its central shopping area, and the Golden Temple occupies a prime location there. Food can be natural and healthy as well as enjoyable and fulfilling, and this restaurant proves it. The decor is not outstanding, but the proprietors make the atmosphere unique. They inspire your trust as they make sure your meal is prepared carefully and served competently. They often stop and chat with patrons about the food—and almost anything else.

The dinner and luncheon buffets include soups, chili, salads, fruit, breads, cheeses and beverages. There is always a daily special such as a mild curried yogurt vegetable platter accompanied by a tossed salad. In addition, an interesting assortment of hot and cold sandwiches is available at reasonable prices. The food is good in its simplicity and doesn't hide behind extra-rich sauces and heavy spices. The diner appreciates the variety of textures in the food as the meal progresses.

Desserts, prepared without sugar, are made on the premises. The cheesecake and baklava are noteworthy. The freshly made honey-sweetened ice cream may beckon one back to the "good weather window," where this and other snacks are sold.

Eating at the Golden Temple is truly relaxing, and the diner will leave satisfied, without a large dent in the wallet, and without heartburn.

No meat, fish or coffee. No alcohol. No smoking. No credit cards.

Monday-Thursday 11 A.M.-8 P.M.; Friday and Saturday 11 A.M.-4 P.M. and 5-9 P.M.

—Linda E. Byard

ITHACA

Moosewood
DeWitt Mall
607-273-9610

Years ago, the large brick building known as the DeWitt Mall served as the local high school. Now it houses a variety of small businesses including the Moosewood restaurant, which is nestled in a basement corner. Operating as a collective since its inception several years ago, Moosewood advertises itself as offering gourmet vegetarian cooking. The diner will not be disappointed. The decor is a little dark, but warmth and informality is the rule.

Menus are posted on two blackboards. There is not a huge variety on any given day, but one can definitely count on food prepared with care, served attractively and in abundant quantity. Lunch choices on one day included Indonesian rice salad with marinated tofu and fruit, ratatouille over rice with salad, cheese and tarragon souffle, and a chili, cheese and lettuce combination on pita bread. Thick soups, hearty breads and dewy-fresh salads are always available. Each Sunday night, food from one ethnic group is featured as well as a precisely cooked fish entree. Curries and Middle Eastern foods are popular on other nights.

Desserts, some of which are sweetened with sugar, are tempting, but you may not have enough room. Coffee and alcohol are available. No smoking. No credit cards.

Lunch Monday-Saturday 11:30 A.M.-2:30 P.M.; dinner Monday-Thursday 5:30-8:30 P.M. and Friday-Sunday 6-9 P.M.

—Linda E. Byard

NEW YORK CITY (MANHATTAN)

Amy's
471 Ave. of the Americas, 212-691-6877
108 University Pl., 741-2170
210 E. 23rd St., 889-2720
1877 Broadway, 265-5191
2067 Broadway, 595-3708
2888 Broadway, 666-1100

A fast-food chain that serves primarily Middle Eastern fare, Amy's is several cuts above the greasy felafel stands that have invaded New York in recent years. The chain has built its reputation on testimonials extolling its nutritious, tasty and wholesome food at budget prices. For the most part, Amy's deserves its reputation.

The several branches share a common decor of fast-cleanable Formica and brusque plastic. The business success of Amy's undoubtedly stems from the similarity of ingredients shared by the various menu items. The main menu offers sandwiches and specialty platters. All platters are served with a meatless Amyburger (felafel), hommus bi-tahini, baba ghanoush, stuffed vine leaves, feta cheese with oregano, black and green olives, tahini and toasted pita. In our considerable experience, the meatless platter, which contains only those ingredients, is the best bet. Other platters add kufta (chopped meat, nuts, spices and wine), fish fillet, hamburger or steak; we have never enjoyed them, as the meats are all frozen and cooked/thawed to order, a method that consistently renders the meat tough and tasteless.

The sandwich menu follows suit. We recommend the Amyburger, baba ghanoush, stuffed vine leaves, hommus bi-tahini, tuna (no mayonnaise) and the salad sandwich; all are served in toasted pita with fresh vegetable salad and tahini dressing. Other sandwiches available are steak, hamburger, kufta and codfish fillet.

At some branches, there's a breakfast menu that offers eggs with melted cheese in toasted pita buttered with tahini at an all-time bargain price. It also features date-nut cake with eggs, juice and coffee.

For dessert there are the typically Middle Eastern bird's nest (phyllo dough, pistachios and honey), baklava (phyllo with nuts and honey) and halvah (sesame and nuts), or the frozen yogurt plain or sundae-style, fruits and nuts and carrot cake. Drinks include coffee, tea, fruit juices, milk, hot chocolate and soft drinks.

No alcohol is permitted, but customers may bring beer and wine. No credit cards, no tipping. Smoking permitted; some branches have nonsmoking sections.

Hours vary from branch to branch, but all are open for lunch and dinner.

—Nancy Chew

NEW YORK CITY (MANHATTAN)

Arnold's Turtle
51 Bank St.
212-242-5623

Arnold's Turtle is a first-rate vegetarian cafe in a quiet section of Greenwich Village. Dinnertime lines attest to the quality of the food here and to its pleasant, if sometimes noisy, atmosphere. The background music at Arnold's is liable to be anything from Bach to the Beach Boys. The waiters and waitresses are friendly (although some are so spacy one suspects they've been smoking the salad greens). The decor is enhanced by brick, wood and hanging plants with two window-walls that give the feeling of a sidewalk cafe without the street noises and smells.

There's one warning that no reviewer could omit in good conscience: the restaurant's name provides a clue to the speed of the service. The food's worth the wait if you're in no great hurry, but stay away if you're up against a deadline.

We've never eaten anything at the Turtle that wasn't good, and we go there frequently. Meals are accompanied by generous heaps of alfalfa sprouts and shredded carrots with a choice of dressing (tachaina's our choice) and a basket of whole grain bread (which is baked on the premises daily, like the pies).

All sandwiches are stuffed into stone-ground whole wheat pita; our favorites are the Total Cheese (Jarlsberg and cheddar melted with tomatoes and sprouts) and California Avocado (avocado slices with tomato, alfalfa sprouts and cheddar).

In addition to a few entrees that are available every day—like a wonderful Russian Vegetable Pie that includes cabbage, carrots, mushrooms, onions, herbs and a thin layer of cream cheese in a light and chewy whole wheat crust—there are daily specials listed on a chalkboard. We usually order the stuffed eggplant with rice, raisins, nuts and tomato sauce if it's available. We're also fond of the Shepherd's Special, always available, which consists of brown rice and the bean-of-the-day topped with melted Jarlsberg; it's especially good with black beans. And we're hopelessly in love with the brown rice pudding, which is made with nuts and raisins and topped with heavy cream. We could go on and on.

Arnold's uses only whole grains. The few desserts that contain sugar are labeled that way on the menu. The coffee's delicious, and there's a vast array of other hot and cold drinks, including beer and wine.

No credit cards. Smoking permitted, but not encouraged.

Open from noon-1 A.M. every day except on Sundays, when it closes for an hour after brunch and reopens at 5 P.M.

—Cheryl Morrison

NEW YORK CITY (MANHATTAN)

At Our Place
2527 Broadway (bet. 94th and 95th Sts.)
212-864-1410

Middle Eastern restaurants, increasingly ubiquitous in New York in recent years, are always fertile ground for the vegetarian and natural foodist. Felafel and hommus and baba ghanoush are a safe bet for either a full meal or an out-of-hand snack.

At Our Place is a step beyond the general run of such establishments, with an extensive selection of elaborate dishes for the vegetarian epicure. In a cheerful split-level room with booths arranged in a mirrored geometric maze, one meets with a choice of seven vegetarian entrees. Moroccan Moussaka consists of rich layers of eggplant, green pepper, tomato and mushroom baked with bechamel sauce. Imam Bayaldi, the popular Turkish eggplant dish, finds that vegetable stuffed with tomato, raisins, onions and nuts. Khodar Curry is a particularly tangy melange of curried vegetables with raisins, apple, coconut and chutney, an unusual blend of sweet and hot tastes. Nonvegetarians have in addition a choice of eight meat entrees, including versions of the moussaka and curry.

Most entrees are served with chickpeas and cracked wheat, and all include a cup of soup and a small salad. The soup on a recent visit was a velvety spinach soup, very tasty and smooth as custard. The salad's nothing special.

Among the appetizers, hommus and felafel are a better choice than the stuffed grape leaves, served warm and drowned in a murky tomato sauce. Desserts include apricot pudding and baklava, both (alas!) made with sugar. Mint tea and Turkish coffee are offered, along with the usual beverages, and the wine list is modestly priced if not overambitious.

Smoking permitted. Major credit cards accepted. Reservations advised on weekends. There's a $2 minimum.

Sundays and Mondays 5-11 P.M., Tuesday-Saturday until midnight.

—Lawrence Block

NEW YORK CITY (MANHATTAN)

Au Natural
55th St. and Second Ave.
212-832-2922
and
37th St. and Third Ave.
212-490-0481

And how natural it is: natural oak floors, natural blond wood and cane bentwood chairs, natural-wood-finished columns and tables. No artificial plants here—green jumbled masses adorn panel and floor, mostly philodendron with an occasional accent of Swedish ivy, dracaena or potted palm.

In this clean, well-lighted, open space are served soups, quiches, salads and hot entrees. Many patrons select from the long salad list. We found the Olivier a tasty and surprisingly light chicken salad. The chicken (seasoned with rosemary and dill) accompanied by potato and egg rested on a bed of lettuce, shredded carrots, shredded cabbage and was garnished heavily with black olives, dill pickles, cherry tomatoes and sunflower seeds. Yogurt salad (with cottage cheese, fresh fruit, dates, nuts and shredded coconut) was intriguing. Hot entrees range from omelets to lemon-sherry sole, flounder stuffed with sauteed vegetables (at dinner only), or scallops sauteed with fresh vegetables. There are hamburgers and cheeseburgers, too, as well as quiche.

Frozen yogurt comprises a large portion of the dessert menu; it can be had in a variety of shakes and sundaes. The dessert list also includes such wonders as Au Natural Honey Cheesecake and mocha walnut torte; fresh fruit is available.

Beverages include natural, caffeine-laden coffees and teas as well as a rather long list of natural, alcoholic wines and a rather short list of herb teas. Juices, milk and "natural" sodas are also available.

This pair of restaurants do a brisk business, so it is probably wise to avoid rush hours. Usually there's a five- to ten-minute wait.

Smoking section. American Express accepted (with a $10 minimum).

Open every day 11:30 A.M.-12:30 A.M., later in summer.

—*Nancy Chew*

NEW YORK CITY (MANHATTAN)

Barry's Place
246 E. 51st St.
212-832-7188

Vegetarian and fish dishes are featured here.

MasterCard and Visa accepted.

Monday-Friday noon-3 and 5-10 P.M.; Saturday dinner only.

NEW YORK CITY (MANHATTAN)

Boostan
85 MacDougal St.
212-533-9561

The vegetarian Middle Eastern food at Boostan is so good (and so reasonably priced) that we'll gladly put up with the looks and location of the place. Boostan is decorated in eclectic ugly—a glaring white fluorescent sign next to the kitchen door, a 1950s diner-style dessert showcase in front of it, light-starved philodendrons strung across the ceiling, hideous wall decorations here and there. It's in a section of Greenwich Village that's swarming with tourists on weekend nights, on a block full of felafel stands, head shops, Indian shirt stores and the like.

Boostan's dishes are prepared without meat stock or eggs. The bread served here is whole wheat pita. The rice is brown, the cooking oil olive. Refined sugar is used only in the Turkish coffee.

The menu includes sandwiches, salads, entrees, soups, and Middle Eastern specialties such as stuffed vine leaves, hommus and tabouli. We tried a soup and two selections from the list of entrees. The vegetable soup was a spicy, aromatic concoction with big chunks of zucchini, onions and other fresh vegetables. Stuffed eggplant was prepared with a mixture of rice, mushrooms, nuts, raisins and tomato sauce packed into half an eggplant and cooked to perfection. Even tastier was the ouzzi, a combination of rice, peas, mushrooms, nuts and raisins encased in a light pastry and served with yogurt sauce on the side. Both entrees were subtly and fragrantly spiced. The overzealous use of garlic that we've come to expect from Middle Eastern restaurants was nowhere in evidence here.

The dessert list includes halvah, baklava and other pastries made with honey (and white flour, sadly, as is the pastry for entrees). You could float a nail in the Turkish coffee, and that's as it should be. Mint tea, a Middle Eastern tea, mineral water and fruit juice are served here, too, but not American coffee or alcohol (although customers can bring their own beer and wine).

Smoking permitted. No credit cards.

Tuesday-Sunday 5 P.M.-midnight.

—*Cheryl Morrison*

NEW YORK CITY (MANHATTAN)

Brownies
21 E. 16th St.
212-255-2838

Brownies, in business in the same spot near Union Square since 1936, is one of the oldest health food restaurants in town, and its menu is among the most varied. Brownies is basically a dairy restaurant, but it also serves a wide variety of fish dishes and any number of ersatz concoctions such as Vegetarian Chicken Liver as well as several interesting vegetable dishes that are offered without apology. The service at Brownies is friendly and efficient, and the restaurant's atmosphere is pleasantly corny—

lots of knick-knacks, captain's chairs, pink fluorescent lighting. There's a lunch counter in the front room for those in a hurry, and there are two spacious and much quieter dining rooms, including one for nonsmokers.

Lunch is a bargain at Brownies. Entree prices include soup or salad, and a plate of whole grain bread, crackers, butter and cottage cheese is on the house no matter what you order. On one recent visit, we chose Eggplant Steak, broiled fish of the day (which turned out to be halibut), a side order of brown rice, a salad and a cup of mushroom barley soup. The "steak" was nothing more or less than tender slices of breaded and sauteed eggplant, lightly seasoned and served with a tomato sauce that, despite Brownies' boasts about it, was bland and uninteresting. The fish (a 4-ounce portion) was fresh and cooked to perfection, which is to say not too much. The soup was steamy, fragrant, and full of fresh mushrooms, the salad was crisp and colorful enough to overcome the so-so creamy French dressing, and the baked rice was a lightly oiled, mildly seasoned treat. At dinnertime, the portions are bigger (8 ounces of fish, for example), and so are the prices.

We washed all that down with a Pitcher of Punch, a refreshing mixture of unsweetened pomegranate, apple, grape, orange and lemon juices that was more than enough for two. Other imaginative fruit and vegetable drinks are offered, too. The menu even touts a "nonalcoholic wine list," but we didn't bother. Desserts include some sugary stuff like brownies (of course) and deep-dish apple pie, but there's also fresh fruit, unsweetened baked apple and whole wheat donuts and muffins.

No alcohol is permitted, but you can bring your own wine. No credit cards.

Monday-Friday 11 A.M.-8 P.M., Saturdays noon-4 P.M.

—Cheryl Morrison

NEW YORK CITY (MANHATTAN)

The Caldron
306 E. Sixth St.
212-473-9543

When the original owners were debating what sort of business to open in 1969, they consulted the oracle of the I Ching. The answering hexagram was "the cauldron," so they opened this macrobiotic restaurant. A few years later, the owners returned to traditional Judaism and took the restaurant with them. The kitchens were completely koshered; the biggest change in the fare was the removal of shrimp from the menu. The regular macrobiotic clientele and the kosher customers have increased, and anyone else looking for a simple, healthy and tasteful meal will also be glad to discover The Caldron. It's very highly recommended for both food and price.

Step into its charming cavelike storefront and sit down to try one of the daily specials. The Caldron offers eight different types of tempura, all delicate and tasty, and numerous fish and vegetable dinners. The Trout Karaage Dinner includes a whole trout, deep-fried with a special ginger sauce, brown rice with tahini and a choice of salad or sea vegetables.

The owner's Russian mother-in-law has developed all the homemade desserts, which satisfy the requirements of both macrobiotic and kosher diners. Apple crunch, fruit kanteon, custard sundaes and assorted pies, cakes and pastries are all a delight, and they're all sweetened with only maple syrup or apple extract. No sugar is used, and all ingredients are natural. A very pleasant and knowledgeable staff is happy to discuss macrobiotic and kosher dining if you're interested, but they do not push. They don't have to; the excellent food speaks for itself.

The Caldron's kitchens have graduated all of this city's macrobiotic chefs who have subsequently opened their own restaurants.

There is a smoking section. No alcohol is served, but you can bring your own with restrictions; all beers are okay because they're kosher, but only certain wines are kosher, so they must be checked at the door.

Sunday-Thursday 12:30-11:30 P.M.

—Shelley Reback

NEW YORK CITY (MANHATTAN)

Dojo
24 St. Marks Pl.
212-674-9821

The noisy and bustling kitchen at Dojo is right at your elbow from almost any point in the dining room, which means that the hearty and pungent aromas of ginger, garlic and vegetables can be a real tease when you are waiting for your dinner to show up. Dojo seems to be crowded at all times, so just relax and enjoy the smells and sounds as you sip from a bottle of Japanese beer or a half-liter of California wine.

The daily fish specials, served with salad and brown rice, are excellent choices; they're steamed with either a tart black bean sauce or a delicate white herb sauce or broiled with a ginger sauce. So is the Yakitori, a Japanese-style barbecue of chicken, beef, shrimp, scallops or vegetables on three skewers with brown rice and salad. The food is prepared without MSG.

Dojo also offers a fine selection of soyburgers served in pita bread with tahini dressing, brown rice and salad. It has extensive salad and breakfast menus as well as omelets and sandwiches, with or without meat. All are reasonably priced and filling.

The real treat here comes at dessert time. The restaurant started out years ago as an ice cream parlor serving homemade fresh fruit and nut ice creams and, lucky for us, they have kept the ice cream menu and quality throughout the years. The ice cream menu changes frequently. Other desserts come from a local bakery and are made without sugar.

No credit cards. Smoking permitted.

Sunday-Thursday 11 A.M.-1 A.M.; Friday-Saturday until 2 A.M.

—Shelley Reback

NEW YORK CITY (MANHATTAN)

East West
105 E. Ninth St.
212-260-1994

This quiet, roomy restaurant serves up vegetarian and fish dishes made only from whole foods—no refined grains or sugars, no additives, no preservatives. The service is efficient and friendly, and the staff is remarkably pleasant to children. Wood paneling gives the place a well scrubbed look without sacrificing a feeling of warmth.

One good bet is the vegetarian special, which includes a cup of soup (perhaps the rice, flavorful miso) and a plate heaped with sauteed vegetables (a bit overcooked), chickpeas with vegetable gravy, and brown rice with bechamel sauce. Another is tempura (with or without shrimp), which features crunchy carrot slices, broccoli spears and green beans in a light, crispy batter. A delicious dinner entree is the Shrimp Scala—large steamed shrimp on brown rice with melted Jarlsberg. If the portions are a little too large, East West accommodates customers who want to share meals or take their leftovers home.

Dessert prices are high, but so is the quality; the carob cream pie was silken. Bancha tea is on the house, and other herb teas are available.

No coffee or alcohol is served, but customers may bring their own beer and wine. Smoking permitted. American Express accepted.

Monday-Thursday 5:30-10 P.M., Friday until 11; Saturday 4:30-11 P.M.; Sunday 4:30-10 P.M.

—Cheryl Morrison

NEW YORK CITY (MANHATTAN)

Farmfood Dairy Vegetarian Restaurant
142 W. 49th St.
212-757-4971

In 1973, the annual convention of Matzoh Brei Lovers met here to indulge in what to their tastes was the world's greatest Matzoh

Brei, a dish so heavy and filling that it cannot be termed a delicacy, although it only makes its appearance once a year at Passover time. At Farmfood, it's available all year round, a meal in itself with a glass of clabbered or sour milk.

For those of us with lighter appetites, Farmfood offers one of the largest selections of cold salad plates in Midtown. These platters have been pleasing customers for more than 50 years, and their delights are too numerous to list. For starters, try the fruit salad special of fruits, figs, nuts, raisins, dates and sour cream or cottage cheese. The Health Dinner includes appetizer, soup, a salad platter, dessert and a beverage. The lunches are the best value, and they're served weekdays until 4 P.M.

Farmfood is also known for its roasts and meat-substitute dishes, made with a soy-protein and nut-meat product. For lunch or dinner, Farmfood serves up such innovations as mock lamb chops, schnitzel and Salisbury steak.

Nothing is fried here, and no animal fats are used in cooking. While the ingredients are not sugar-free or natural, vegetables and fish are fresh. Sandwiches are made with your choice of bread. We suggest Nova Scotia salmon and cream cheese on a bagel, which is a bargain.

With its cheery red and white decor, Farmfood looks as though it has played host to countless Bar Mitzvahs and weddings. Mature and friendly service and a family-style atmosphere make this a most comfortable place to meet for a meal.

No alcohol. No credit cards. Minimum $1.50, and splitting one meal between two people will add $1.50 to your bill. Smoking is okay.

Weekdays 11 A.M.-8:30 P.M.; Saturday and Sunday until 10:30 P.M.

—Shelley Reback

NEW YORK CITY (MANHATTAN)

Fertile Crescent
91 Chambers St.
212-233-5680

This establishment is an inexpensive natural foods restaurant near City Hall.

NEW YORK CITY (MANHATTAN)

Govinda
340 W. 55th St.
212-765-5942

An attractive mural and other art adorn the walls of this buffet-style restaurant downstairs in the Hare Krishna building not far from the Broadway theater district. Soft music provides a pleasant background for diners, who may choose to eat at tables with chairs or in the carpeted pavilion, where lower tables and puffy cushions provide an eastern setting.

Govinda has a fine reputation for its Indian cuisine, which is delicately spiced for American taste. The daily special features all you can eat for a low fixed price. Selections include dahl (mung bean or split pea soup), chapatis (bread), pakora (crisp, batter-dipped fried eggplant or cauliflower with tomato chutney) and two casseroles of vegetables cooked in ghee (clarified butter).

Pastries and cakes, made with sugar, are baked daily on the premises. Diners visiting for the first time receive a large peanut chip, ginger or almond cookie as a special treat. Seven herb teas are available, and there's lassi, a yogurt drink with fruit juice.

No credit cards. No smoking. No meat, fish, coffee or alcohol.
Monday-Friday 12:30 P.M.-9 P.M.; Saturday 5-9 P.M.

—Elizabeth Roberts

NEW YORK CITY (MANHATTAN)

Greener Pastures
117 E. 60th St.
212-832-3212

Go through the health food store, the busy juice bar, the older room and the newer one to the very new, glass-roofed patio with plants in tubs and hanging pots. The young, attentive staff is filling water glasses and serving whole grain bread and flatbread while artists, business people and scholars explain the place's history and cuisine. They beat the waitresses in recommending the special of the day, perhaps broiled sole teriyaki, which comes with hearty soup and dessert. Where else can you get a plump, sugarless baked apple today?

At noon we often make a meal of two appetizers: guacamole (with corn chips) and egg salad, and maybe some of the outstanding homemade frozen, fruity yogurt for dessert. We also recommend the bursting sandwiches: salmon steak; avocado, cheese and tomato; or cream cheese, apple spread and walnuts. A good buy and good eating is the crunchy eggplant steak in light batter over brown rice on its hot plate in an oval wooden plank. If fish are on your diet, don't miss the piquantly dressed cold poached salmon with cucumber salad. Or create your own meal from such diverse side dishes as snow peas in sesame sauce and crudites with house dip.

Greener Pastures' chicken and meat substitutes are better than most because of tasty spicings and sauces. The fresh salads leave us dissatisfied, perhaps because of their unvaried greens, but many of the customers obviously disagree.

The list of sugarless desserts grows ever more enticing. There's pecan pie baked with maple syrup and blackstrap molasses hidden under whipped cream, and there are at least ten other agreeable choices.

No smoking. No credit cards. Minimum: $2.50. Wine, beer, mineral water and coffee are served. Dietary laws observed.

Monday-Saturday noon-8:30 P.M.; until 9:30 on Friday and Saturday. Closed some holidays.

—Lillian Schiff

NEW YORK CITY (MANHATTAN)

Hiro
330 E. Sixth St.
212-475-9274

If ever a restaurant was to be recommended on quantity of food alone, this is the place. Slapping some greasy batter around a chunk of vegetable does not a tempura make, however. Nor does easy access to a bottle of soy sauce qualify one's cuisine as Japanese. But for those on a very small budget with very large appetites, we suggest a meal at Hiro.

We suggest it with considerable reservation. There may be few people hungry enough to truly take advantage of the volume of food served, so bring a friend. Also, we'd prefer our fried vegetables drained prior to leaving the kitchen, not served up in a paper towel package that looks as though someone had forgotten to drop it off in the trash on his way out of the house. Somehow, it lacks the aura of fish and chips swathed in newspaper and, if the British have already abandoned that tradition, perhaps we can nip this one in the bud.

The vegetable tempura dinner includes a bowl of bland miso soup, with almost enough wakame seaweed to be noticeable, a fine homemade Indian paratha bread, and a mountainous vegetable plate appetizer of azuki beans with tahini sauce and brown rice, sauteed vegetables, fresh bean sprouts and cabbage with a cumin-based dressing. (The ample vegetable platter alone would be quite filling and can be had a la carte.) The dinner also includes the tempura package of vegetables in a heavy batter better saved for a fish fry.

We suggest spending a bit more money to indulge in one of the better fish dishes. Broiled cod and sole fillets are nicely done and generously served.

Keeping in mind that one comes here for the food and not for the ambience, try not to notice the dreary, unfinished storefront decor, more suited to an impoverished social service agency than to a restaurant. One hint: try to beat out your companion for a seat facing the window to Sixth Street; the rear view is pretty dismal.

No sugar or unnatural ingredients are used. Smoking is tolerated; bring your own wine if you wish. Credit cards or reservations? You must be kidding!

Open every day 4:30-11:30 P.M.

—Shelley Reback

NEW YORK CITY (MANHATTAN)

Madras Woodlands
310 E. 44th St.
212-986-0620

Even in a city noted for Indian restaurants, this attractive neighbor of the United Nations is a standout. The decor is warmly exotic (temple murals, hangings and sculpture, wall-to-wall red plush) without being intrusive; seating is comfortably uncrowded in the two rooms, and the service against a background of soft recorded music is efficient and friendly. But it is the food, deliciously different and remarkably reasonable, that stars.

Madras Woodlands is "pucca" vegetarian—meat, fish and even eggs are completely foreign to this kitchen, where the chefs prepare dishes from their native Madras, in southern India. The cuisine is largely based on cereals and legumes, prepared separately or ground together for breads, crepes and pancakes and combined with fresh vegetables and condiments for an incredible variety of soups, sauces, appetizers and curries.

While masalas (spice blends) are the key to all Indian cooking, seasonings in the south reflect the indigenous weather—hot, hotter, hottest. In fact, the British colonizers referred to the sambars and rasams (soups and sauces served with everything) as "pepper water." Most dishes here, however, are mild to medium, but manager Vijay Bhatia, noting an increasing trend toward fiery foods, encourages patrons to indicate their preferences.

The novitiate might try a Pu Pu Platter, which lives up to its Hawaiian name—a splendid sampling of filled crepes, patties, fritters, nuts and wafers with appropriate sauces and relishes. Add a salty lassi (frothy buttermilk drink), coffee or beer for a satisfying light lunch. Favorites are the complete luncheons and dinners served on the traditional thals (deep, round trays) containing small bowls of vegetable and grain combinations and sauces with a choice of breads, pickles and chutneys.

Unusual and interesting are the Medhu Vadai (deep-fried lentil donuts), the porridgelike Rava Iddly (steamed lentil patties), Uthappam (pancake with vegetable fillings), and the Uppumas (vegetables cooked with rice or wheat)—all served with rasams, sambars and chutneys. The house chutney is a fluffy coconut concoction, and it is placed on the table as soon as one sits down.

Special dinners include a glass of white wine, a selection of appetizers, curries, soups, salad and a choice of bread, dessert and beverage. The latter may be apple milk (a foamy blend), mango juice or Badham Kheer (almonds, rice and milk). Desserts include a variety of halvahs (puddinglike confections of cereal or vegetables with nuts and fruit), berfies (fudge-type sweetmeat), ice cream and fruit.

There's a full bar; wines are Italian imports. Smoking permitted. Minimum $5 on weekends. Major credit cards accepted.

Monday-Friday noon-2:30 P.M. and 5:30-10:30 P.M.; weekends 1-10:30 P.M.

– Vidya Chandra

NEW YORK CITY (MANHATTAN)

Pumpkin Eater
2452 Broadway
212-877-0132

Our correspondent cites Pumpkin Eater as an unusually good natural foods restaurant featuring vegetable, grain and fish dishes.

Smoking permitted. Bring your own beer and wine. No credit cards.

Open 11 A.M.-4 P.M. and 5-10:45 P.M. every day.

NEW YORK CITY (MANHATTAN)

Shalimar
39 E. 29th St.
212-889-1977

Although this attractive white-walled restaurant is not exclusively vegetarian, it has an extensive menu reflecting the diversity of Indian foods and of Indians themselves, most of whom are vegetarian. A forerunner of the explosion of Indian restaurants in New York, Shalimar opened in the 1960s in a neighborhood where Middle Eastern and Indian enterprises (spices, sweets, foods, utensils and textiles) comfortably coexist. Music (sitar, tabla) is live on weekends and on tapes during the week. The young staff is helpful and friendly.

The daily lunch special, served Monday-Friday noon-3 P.M., includes a choice of a vegetable and dahl (chickpeas, lentils or Indian legume) combination, a seasonal vegetable curry and a spicy fish dish (pomfret, if available), served with basmati (fragrant, long-grained) rice, fresh relish/chutney, and tea or coffee. The a la carte selections include a zingy Mattar Panir (fresh cheese and green peas) and an unusual Rajma-Urad (red and black beans blended in a light cream sauce).

But the big thing here is owner Vijay Bhatt's most recent innovation—daily regional specialties available at both lunch and dinner. Vegetarian days are Monday, Wednesday and Saturday; seafood on Tuesday, and fish on Friday. But chef Lucas Gomez really pulls out all the stops on Sunday with Gujarati (western India) Undihoo: a medley of six or seven vegetables steamed with lima beans and bananas and seasoned with small spicy balls of chickpea flour, fenugreek and cumin seeds. The result is a simply delicious combination of textures—silky smooth, crunchy crisp—and flavors—bitter, sweet and sour. Palate-boggling!

Choose from a variety of Indian breads and appetizers. Beverages include two lassi (yogurt) drinks, one salt and one sweet, and a masala (spiced) tea. Desserts: firni (custard flavored with rose water) and ras malai (cheese and milk confection) are for the sweet-toothed, but there is also a satisfying light carrot cake made in a Long Island kitchen and a rich mango ice cream churned up by a gentleman from New Jersey.

Smoking permitted. Complete bar, including Indian beer. Major credit cards accepted. A 15% service charge is added to the bill in lieu of tipping.

Open daily, noon to midnight.

—Vidya Chandra

NEW YORK CITY (MANHATTAN)

Souen
2444 Broadway
212-787-1110

Souen, a small macrobiotic restaurant on the Upper West Side, has its pleasant aspects; it's modestly priced, the help is friendly, the brick-walled room is cozy, and some of us feel quite at home among the over-the-hill counterculture types who eat there. With all that, one still expects good cooking, and Souen was ultimately disappointing.

The meals my dining partner and I had weren't the worst we'd ever eaten, but we agreed that they may have been the worst tempuras. The vegetables were soggy, the shrimp was limp and the batter was thick and sticky, all of which is what happens when the cooking oil isn't hot enough. The dipping sauce, a light brown liquid with a few scallion slices in it, was tasteless. I ordered a side dish of rice with sauce; the brown rice was fine, but the sauce looked like a glob of wallpaper paste and lacked flavor. My mu tea arrived warm, not hot. Desserts were offered – none of which sounded too interesting – but my friend and I had tasted enough by then to know we didn't want more.

It's possible we just ordered the wrong things. People around us were eating dinners that looked appetizing enough; then again, so did the tempuras. Souen has an excellent reputation, however, so we may have just hit it on a bad night.

Beer and wine served. No smoking. No credit cards.

Monday-Thursday noon-10 P.M.; Friday and Saturday until 11 P.M.; Sunday 4-10 P.M.

– Cheryl Morrison

NEW YORK CITY (MANHATTAN)

Spring Street Natural Restaurant & Bar
149 Spring St.
212-966-0290

Spring Street's well camouflaged; the front's an old-fashioned saloon, and the folk gathered around the bar don't look capable of distinguishing an alfalfa sprout from an avocado pit. Don't be discouraged. Past the bar is a large room, its walls sporting paintings befitting the artsy SoHo environs, its high ceilings displaying exposed pipes and fans straight out of a Sidney Greenstreet movie. The place has atmosphere.

It's also got great food. There's always a good selection of fish and seafood dishes plus one poultry entree for unreconstructed carnivores. Vegetarian dishes are abundant, with a basic selection of steamed and sauteed vegetables on the printed menu and specials chalked on the blackboard. On a recent visit, these included Eggplant Jarlsberg, Sauteed Okra Creole, String Beans in Garlic Sauce, Summer Squash Parmesan, and Cauliflower with Blue Cheese. There's always an eggless Tofu Souffle—spinach-mushroom one day, cauliflower-watercress another. A member of our party had the Super Salad, an enormous concoction that was well worth its price; it could easily have sated two people, with enough left over to keep a hutch of rabbits happy. We had Rice and Vegetables—sauteed vegetables, brown rice, beans, seaweed and sprouts—a generous platter of well prepared food. We shared an appetizer of baby eggplant sauteed and basted with ginger and tamari, and it was one of the highlights of the week for us.

Desserts include a fresh fruit salad, goat's milk and honey ice cream and a good variety of fruit pies. Some are made with sugar, some without; the staff knows which is which and is happy to tell you. Beverages include coffee, coffee-substitute, tea, cider and fruit juices, and there's that full bar in front with a good selection of wines.

Major credit cards accepted. Smoking permitted. Often crowded at peak hours.

Open 11:30 A.M.-1 A.M. every day. Limited menu before 4 P.M. and after 11:30.

—Lawrence Block

NEW YORK CITY (MANHATTAN)

The Ultimate Lotus
59 E. 56th St.
212-421-5580

At a glance, this Midtown establishment looks to be quite unremarkable, albeit comfortable, with its unobtrusive decor and white-clothed tables set well apart. In a city swarming with noteworthy Chinese restaurants, it is only the vegetarian menu that makes the Ultimate Lotus outstanding.

Most Chinese chefs offer a melange of sauteed vegetables, sauce them as often as not in chicken stock, and call the result Buddha's Delight. Other vegetable dishes like eggplant with hot garlic sauce generally contain meat. But there is a tradition of Chinese vegetarian cuisine, dating back to the emergence of the Buddhist and Taoist religions in the 12th century, and the chef here keeps that tradition alive.

A variety of vegetarian dishes, all well prepared, includes Szechuan Eggplant, Spicy Bean Curd, mixed vegetables either whole or julienne, and mushrooms with snow peas. Rather more remarkable are the specials here that mimic classic meat dishes while containing only vegetable ingredients. We're usually unimpressed by this sort of fakery—mock chopped liver at a dairy restaurant leaves us almost as cold as those slabs of texturized vegetable protein shaped like rashers of bacon and striped with red dye. But the fakery here really works. Our first course on a recent visit was the Vegetarian Duck, which looked and tasted uncannily like a piece of cold roast duck, skin and all. (If you don't have the right mind set for this sort of thing, you could wind up with an anxiety attack.) We were similarly impressed by Lotus Crisp and Steamed Bread, a chewy, tangy, meaty chunk of something-or-other served on a puff of steamed bread, garnished with scallions and topped with hoisin sauce. Sweet and Sour Mock Spareribs were a more recognizable fraud, but they did ape the flavor of the original dish to a surprising degree. Vegetarian Abalone and Mock Beef Stew are other entrees of this sort on the daily menu, and special banquets may be arranged featuring vegetarian essays of many of the classic dishes of China.

There's a full menu for carnivores, as well, and we've had good reports from meat-eating friends. While the place is no health food restaurant, there's a heightened nutritional consciousness; brown rice is available, and dishes may be ordered without salt or MSG.

Full bar service. Smoking permitted. Major credit cards accepted.

Open daily noon-10 P.M.

—Lawrence Block

NEW YORK CITY (MANHATTAN)

University Produce Restaurant
71 University Pl. at 11th St.
212-673-0634

The place certainly looks good. You enter a high-quality produce market on the ground floor, then descend a flight to the restaurant. There's an old tile floor, one brick wall with leaded glass windows and mellow pine wainscotting on the other walls. A little garden, artificially lit, thrives in the stairwell. It's a pleasant room, and the fruits and vegetables are, not surprisingly, as fresh as the daisies that bloom in the tabletop Perrier splits.

Eight salads are offered, at prices that struck us as fair enough, but the sandwiches are too high. We liked the Raw Veggie Salad, as well as the University Special Salad, a mix of oriental vegetables with ginger dressing. Sandwiches include lobster salad, shrimp salad and tuna salad. We had one called Cheese Geneve Elegante; it amounted to a pita bread pocket stuffed with melted Swiss and Muenster, with a side salad of sprouts, shredded carrots and lettuce. Very tasty, but about a buck too pricey. Omelets, soups and quiches are available.

Desserts are tempting, albeit sugared. On one visit we chose an apple crumb something-or-other. Another time we tried the Tropical Delight, a half-cantaloupe filled with grapes, raisins, walnuts and berries and topped with whipped cream. I don't know what was tropical about it; we were less than delighted.

Juices are freshly pressed, and the beverage list includes coffee, espresso and a variety of teas, herbal and otherwise. Bring your own wine and beer.

The menu advises that the principals "have long years of experience in the food business from Bio-Dynamic Farming in Europe to serving food on the tables of the most distinguished guests." Well, that's nice. Meanwhile, they run a nice restaurant. If they cut some of their prices by 30% or thereabouts, or if inflation catches up with their menu, they should do fine.

Smoking permitted. No credit cards.

Open seven days, 11:30 A.M.-10 P.M.

–Lawrence Block

NEW YORK CITY (MANHATTAN)

Vim & Vigor
157 W. 57th St.
212-247-8059

Across the street from Carnegie Hall, this original natural foods restaurant, established in 1945, appears to be little more than a lunch bar. The names on the menu are contrived to reflect the themes of music and dance suggested by the restaurant's venerable neighbor. Claiming a sincere desire to make your palate sing with pleasure and your body dance with good health, Vim & Vigor bills itself as a culinary Carnegie Hall, presenting the finest of the nutritious arts from the good old days of food, B.C. (before chemicals). The place is clean, efficiently run and busy.

If one can accept the cuteness of the menu, the fare fans a purist's enthusiasm. The food is well prepared and fresh. We tried the special of the day, chicken and soy casserole, which was quite tasty and very filling, and a bowl of fresh organic fruit that contained a wider than usual variety. The menu begins, *mais oui,* with Overtures (freshly squeezed "live" before your eyes) of vegetable and citrus juices and moves along to Preludes (the fruit juice quartet) of apple, papaya, strawberry-apple, or a house blend of unsweetened juices. A Soup Recital lists two, or three if gazpacho is in season.

The Sandwich Symphony, performed on 100% stone-ground whole wheat bread with a salad cup, offers six selections, including crunchy peanut butter with banana, honey and sesame seeds and tuna with a savory herb dressing served open-face and covered with mixed greens, cherry tomatoes and shredded cheddar cheese.

Rhapsodies in Green are the popular salads that include avocado and mushroom as well as soybeans and dill. For the less adventuresome, there are tuna salad, the Everything Salad (raw vegetables, cheeses, nuts and sprouts) and cottage cheese salad.

Hot Dish Masterworks include the daily specials, spinach quiche, Rice Provencal Serenade (organic brown rice steamed with a sauce of fresh mushrooms and tomatoes) and Vegeburgers with melted cheese or mushroom sauce, stuffed into a whole wheat pita and served with salad.

Shakes For The Dance of Health are the Fosse (strawberry yogurt with concentrated high-protein skimmed milk), the Baryshnikov (papaya juice, coconut, high-protein skimmed milk and yogurt) and the Joffrey (fresh fruit, high-protein skimmed milk and yogurt). The Nureyev is Vim & Vigor's super meal in a glass, containing Brewer's yeast, skimmed milk, ground sesame seeds, wheat germ, ground almonds, ginseng, molasses and honey.

For dessert, you may select the frozen yogurt sweetened with honey or one of the assortment of cakes, pies and other sweets offered daily. Beverages include milk, herb and regular teas, coffee, coffee-substitute and mineral water.

No smoking. No credit cards. Alcoholic beverages are not served, nor can wine and beer be brought in.

Monday-Friday 10 A.M.-8 P.M.; Saturday 10 A.M.-7:30 P.M.; Sunday 11 A.M.-7:30 P.M.

—*Nancy Chew*

NEW YORK CITY (MANHATTAN)

Whole Wheat 'n Wild Berrys
57 W. Tenth St.
212-677-3410

A few steps below street level, a dozen butcher block tables fill a cheery white-walled room, with additional seating in a back room behind the kitchen. Unless you're lucky enough to avoid peak hours, you may wish the place were larger. It does a turnaway business, which isn't bad for a restaurant that doesn't even know how to spell berries.

However you spell it, the food's first-rate. The Small Planet casserole of vegetables, rice, nuts and cheese is always available and always a good choice. Daily specials have included eggplant-walnut stew, manicotti and tofu-tahini casserole. There are always several fish dishes offered, and vegetable plates are available with or without rice, nuts, tofu, tahini and tomato sauce with cheese.

We're partial to the Everything Salad, a generous bowl of escarole, broccoli, sprouts, nuts and cheese. The tahini-based salad dressing is addictive; pour a little extra in the bowl and mop it up with the sourdough rye bread that comes with your meal.

Desserts are homemade and sugar-free, with Peanut Butter Ice Cream Pie and Double Carob Cake especially noteworthy. Beverages include coffee and coffee-substitute, along with a wide range of juices and teas, herbal and otherwise. Or bring your own wine.

Minimum $2 at lunch, $2.50 at dinner. No smoking. No credit cards.

Tuesday-Sunday 11:30 A.M.-4:30 P.M. and 5-10:45 P.M.; Monday dinner only.

—Lawrence Block

QUEENS

Quantum Leap
6564 Fresh Meadow La.
212-461-1307

Vegetarian cuisine is featured here with an emphasis on macrobiotic dishes. We have heard consistently good things about Quantum Leap. Desserts are sugar-free.

Bring your own alcohol. No credit cards. No smoking.

Tuesday-Thursday 5-9:45 P.M.; Friday and Saturday 5-10:45 P.M.; Sunday 4-9:45 P.M.

ROCHESTER

The Regular Restaurant
715 Monroe Ave.
716-271-1380

The macrobiotic influence is not hard to spot at this whole-food vegetarian restaurant. Oriental stir-fried vegetables are offered, along with dishes that employ such products as buckwheat noodles, ramen noodles, tofu and tempeh. Service is cafeteria style at lunch, with table service at dinner. No flesh foods are served, but there are egg dishes on the menu.

Nonsmoking section. No credit cards.

Tuesday-Saturday 11:30 A.M.-2:30 P.M.; Thursday-Saturday 5:30-9 P.M.; Sunday 4:30-8 P.M.

SEA CLIFF

Little Easter
64 Roslyn Ave.
516-676-9698

The regulars at Little Easter feel comfortable amid thrift-shop furniture, amateur paintings and small statuary. Desserts and beverages are listed on the blackboard next to the espresso machine. The old piano is ready for good, simple entertainment on a Saturday night, or there's Charlie Mingus or Richie Havens on the stereo.

The eclectic menu is not bashful about pairing Mexican and Japanese food, and it always works deliciously. Shiva's Dance, for example, is a tasty extravaganza on a huge platter: lightly breaded zucchini, broccoli and yams, slices of cucumber and tomatoes, cheese tortillas, curried rice, chutney, skewered and deep-fried vegetable and tofu cutlets, cheese and tomato lasagna, etc., etc.—all on escarole with a lovely aster in the middle. The price is steep, but we take home half for another meal in our own pie plate.

Our favorite here is the avocado sandwich—pita bulging with avocado, alfalfa sprouts, tomato, cheese and tahini dressing. Or order a fresh fruit creation, even if there's none on the menu. Salad and soup (the latter too thin) and warm, yeasty bread accompany main dishes, or they may be ordered separately. Remind the affable staff to stir the miso and vegetables in the pot before serving.

The staff will make spaghetti or a peanut butter sandwich for your children.

The bakers come and go here, so you take a chance on desserts. The superior ones use no sugar, but ask. When we last visited, a peach crisp was a little too sugary, but the chocolate cake was divine.

Beer and wine available. No smoking. No credit cards.

Monday-Thursday 6-10 P.M.; Friday and Saturday 6 P.M.-midnight; Sunday 5-10 P.M.

—Lillian Schiff

SYOSSET

Asparagii
Portobello Sq.
44 W. Jericho Turnpike
516-921-3838

On a rather hidden dead-end street, tucked among some tiny specialty shops, you'll find Asparagii, where you can treat yourself to delicious fresh food in light and airy surroundings. The bottom half of each wall is covered with knotty pine boards; the top half is painted white, which lends a feeling of spaciousness. The walls stretch toward a ceiling that's dotted with skylights. Vigorous hanging plants and potted trees provide pleasant greenery, while a wall of mirrors on one side makes the small restaurant seem much bigger than it actually is and creates more light.

Quiches are always good here. Every day brings a new special. A recent broccoli and tomato quiche was excellent—loaded with broccoli. Even the crust was delicious—very light and tender, not at all soggy. Quiche also can be purchased in combination with salad or soup. Other good choices are omelets (you can create your own with a wide variety of vegetables and cheese) and salads, which come with assorted greens, tomatoes, carrots, alfalfa sprouts, raisins and sunflower seeds. Dressings are outstanding; the dill dressing sampled recently was zesty and really added sparkle.

The delicious entrees come with salad and vegetable. They include chicken, fish and hamburger; all meat is raised organically.

Desserts are made with honey and are all quite good. Outstanding is the frozen yogurt, which you can adorn with a wide variety of fruit and/or nuts; the regular yogurt is delicious, too, and can be similarly adorned.

Herb teas, coffee, and delicious fruit sodas made with honey will satisfy the thirst admirably. Wine is offered, too.

Smoking "not encouraged," says the management. American Express and MasterCard accepted.

Monday-Thursday 11 A.M.-10 P.M.; Friday and Saturday until 1 A.M.; Sunday 4-10 P.M.

—Ann Jamieson

WATERTOWN

The Mouth Trap
141 Arsenal St.
315-782-6195

Off center of Public Square, a garden of greenery lines a narrow, brick-walled dining room filled with dark maple furniture. The crowd sometimes overflows into the counter space overlooking the kitchen. Wherever you sit, the aroma of fresh breads and soups is sure to stir up an appetite.

Stir-fried vegetables, served over brown rice and topped with nuts and seeds, is always an excellent choice. The entree changes daily; it might be quiche or an exceptional ratatouille. The Garden Salad, made of produce from nearby farms, makes for a complete meal, but the creamy rice pudding sweetened with honey is tempting even so.

A favorite breakfast is Almond Crunch, a granola-style cereal, or French toast, which is made with the Mouth Trap's own whole wheat bread with sesame seeds.

Beverages include Pero, fruit and vegetable juices, and a large selection of teas, and you can bring wine.

No smoking. Major credit cards accepted.

Monday-Saturday 7:30-10 A.M. and 11 A.M.-3 P.M.

—Jenise Williamson

WATKINS GLEN
Seneca Lodge
607-535-2014

At the tip of Seneca Lake, one of the beautiful Finger Lakes, just a mile from the Grand Prix race course, sits the rustic Seneca Lodge. The lodge is a cabin-colony resort reminiscent of the North Woods, with log construction, a huge stone fireplace in the dining hall and beamed ceilings. The Brubakers have owned Seneca Lodge since 1944, and they pay particular attention to the fare offered their guests. In years past they supervised the cattle herds on their farm to ensure that meat served in their restaurant could honestly be called organic. Their age makes it impossible to chase the cows around anymore, but it doesn't prevent them from raising and serving organic vegetables.

Although the dinner menu is dominated by meat and fish dishes such as Rainbow Trout Almondine and broiled scallops, a vegetarian entree called Our Famous Sunberger is a delight. All dinners include two vegetables and unlimited trips to the salad bar, which has been the mainstay of the restaurant's reputation for nearly four decades. The vegetables in the well-stocked bowls at the bar may be garnished with bran, kelp, sprouts and chickpeas. Breads and bran, banana or blueberry muffins are made at the lodge daily.

Breakfast of steel-cut oatmeal, juice, toast and beverage or whole wheat griddle cakes with pure New York maple syrup highlights the morning.

Coffee, wine and beer are available. Smoking permitted. MasterCard and Visa accepted.

Seneca Lodge opens April 1, the opening day of New York's trout season, and closes by Thanksgiving.

Breakfast is served 8-11 A.M.; lunch 11:30 A.M.-2 P.M.; dinner 6-9 P.M.

— Tom Terrizzi

WOODRIDGE

Vegetarian Hotel
P.O. Box 457
914-434-4455

For over 60 years, this Catskills resort has provided vegetarian meals and lodging in a refreshing rural setting. The clientele is overwhelmingly made up of elderly Jewish people, and the cuisine derives from traditional Jewish vegetarianism. Many of the dishes are the sort one finds at a dairy restaurant—vegetables trying to be something they are not, whether in the form of vegetarian chopped liver, vegetarian gefilte fish or a carrot roast we had which, which, while undoubtedly wholesome, was bland and uninteresting.

The usual complement of resort activities (swimming, dances, etc.) is offered, and frequent lectures by nutritional authorities are a feature. Meals are at pre-set times, and nonresidents may dine at the hotel for moderate fees. Accommodations are clean and comfortable. The Vegetarian Hotel won't be everybody's cup of Mock Chicken Soup—the pace suits the advanced age of the guests—but it's a classic and a Catskills institution. Write for a brochure if you're interested.

—Lawrence Block

North Carolina

CHAPEL HILL

Pyewacket Cafe
452 W. Franklin St.
919-929-0297

This restaurant, popular with University of North Carolina students, boasts homemade breads and soups along with hot entrees and an extensive sandwich selection. There are seven seafood entrees and 12 vegetarian dishes. Liquor is available, and there's an antique bar.

No credit cards.

Open Monday-Saturday 11:30 A.M.-midnight, and Sunday for brunch from 10:30 A.M.-3 P.M.

CHARLOTTE

People's Juice Bar
1618 Elizabeth Ave.
704-375-6953

The juice bar of the People's Natural Food Market, which is located in a remodeled old house near downtown Charlotte, does a brisk lunch business. You can stand at the counter or take your food out.

With the exception of a tuna salad, everything on the menu is vegetarian. I have yet to eat anything here which wasn't delicious, but one of my favorites is the avocado salad: pureed avocado over fresh vegetables, sprinkled with grated cheese and sunflower seeds and garnished with alfalfa sprouts. Sandwiches are available on whole wheat bread or (for a little extra money) pita, and there's a soup du jour to go with them.

Beverages include fruit and vegetable juices, smoothies and a number of more substantial drinks like the wicked pineapple-coconut shake. Herb teas are served, too.

No smoking. No alcohol. No credit cards.

Open 11 A.M.-5 P.M. Monday-Saturday.

—Jill Dubisch

CHARLOTTE

They Laughed at Edison
3200 Monroe Rd.
704-372-4312

Out of a formerly bland, uninspired pizza parlor, They Laughed at Edison has created a pleasant, cozy vegetarian restaurant with lots of wooden tables, green plants and cafeteria service. Lunch and dinner are served, and there are daily casserole specials in addition to salads, sandwiches and desserts.

Casseroles include carrot-mushroom loaf, broccoli, and Soy Gevalt—soybeans with black mushrooms, carrots and sour cream. These come with brown rice, a salad and a fresh whole wheat roll to make a filling meal. Rice with vegies sauteed in ginger and tamari sauce is a standard, and so is bean-of-the-day with rice. Salads include tabouli, fruit with or without yogurt, Tofunafish (tofu, black olives, onions and celery) and a sampler with guacamole or hommus, tabouli or sprout salad, a green salad and bread. Sandwiches include felafel, guacamole and cream cheese. The soups are homemade (and the mushroom I tasted was excellent).

Drinks include fruit and carrot juices, herb teas and coffee as well as some excellent imported beers and a prosaic selection of wines.

Desserts are sweetened with sugar or honey and labeled accordingly. The chocolate cheesecake (with sugar) is delicious and rich. The banana sour cream pie is also good, rich but with an unusual tart flavor.

Major credit cards accepted. Smoking area.

Hours: 11:30 A.M.-2 P.M. and 5:30-9:30 P.M. Tuesday-Saturday; 5:30-9:30 P.M. Sunday.

—Jill Dubisch

DURHAM

Somethyme
1104 Broad St.
919-286-1019

Somethyme is an institution in Durham. The first restaurant of its kind in the area, it's been in continuous, if not always profitable, operation for nearly a decade. Run by its employees, it's situated in an ordinary storefront, but it is a real gourmet establishment. Somethyme's reputation for subtle and exotic touches in food preparation causes long lines to form at the door.

Soups change daily (the split pea has a smidgen of curry), the vegetarian burritos are just hot enough, and the salad dressings are always made fresh, with many kinds of oils. The lemon-tamari house dressing is famous. At any time of day, a diner can choose among 12 kinds of omelets, several salads and sandwiches. Hot chili, from mixed beans combined with a spicy tomato sauce poured over brown rice with sour cream, is a real crowd pleaser. There's a delicious tabouli, too— puffed bulgur with herbs, lemon, olive and safflower oils, tossed with fresh vegetables.

Dinner entrees are less varied and more expensive. Heather Mountain, a baked potato topped with sauteed mushrooms and sour cream dressing, accompanied by tomato and avocado with blue cheese dressing, is favored by Duke University students, but it doesn't really challenge the cook. Plaki, however, is a great dish of fresh trout baked in a subtle sauce of lemon butter, sherry, tomatoes, onions and herbs, served with broccoli and rice. Somethyme offers at least two seafood selections a night.

Along with beer and wine, there are fruit drinks, "natural" sodas and coffees. Desserts are sweetened with sugar and honey.

Smoking is frowned on. No credit cards are accepted. Local musicians play on Friday and Saturday nights, passing a basket around for their pay. There's classical music on Sunday.

Lunch 11:30 A.M.-2:30 P.M. Tuesday-Saturday; dinner 5-9:30 P.M. seven days a week; Nighthyme (limited menu) 9:15-midnight Friday and Saturday; Sunday brunch, featuring Eggs Sardau (with spinach and hollandaise), from 11 A.M.-2 P.M.

—Sarah R. Shaber

RALEIGH

Irregardless Cafe
901 W. Morgan St.
919-833-9920

Near North Carolina State University, Irregardless Cafe is large, noisy, crowded and very busy. The long lines move quickly, though, and the food is worth the wait.

The cafe's enormous local popularity stems from the few concessions it has made to the nonvegetarian majority. It offers at least one poultry or seafood dish along with a vegetarian entree every day, serves mixed drinks as well as beer and wine, and caters shamelessly to the after-church crowd at its famous Sunday brunches. Everything, however, is prepared fresh from natural ingredients.

There is a set luncheon menu; the nightly specials are posted on a chalkboard. Each month, Irregardless distributes a guide to the nightly specials, and over any given month the specials are quite varied; in one week, the specials were Sweet and Sour Chicken, Spanakopita, Mediterranean Crepes, Viennese Spinach Roulade, Yaki-Meshi and Chicken Parmiagiana. Others have included Paella, Champagne Chicken, Calzone and Whole Wheat Pizza.

Brunch specials have included Fruit Waffle, Quiche Lorraine, Cape Charles Omelet (made with crabmeat) and Pancakes Oscar. The egg dishes come with tomato home fries and delicious homemade muffins. The brunch price includes orange juice and a bottomless cup of coffee.

Desserts and nonalcoholic drinks are unpredictable, but most are made from natural ingredients.

Smoking is frowned upon. No credit cards.

Lunch Monday-Saturday 11:30 A.M.-2 P.M.; dinner 5:30-9:30 P.M.; brunch Sunday 10:30 A.M.-2:30 P.M.

—Sarah R. Shaber

Ohio

AKRON

Gentle Lady
782 W. Market St.
216-374-5640

This once-vegetarian restaurant receives high marks for food, decor and service, but it now serves meat and doesn't tout itself as a natural foods eatery. There's plenty of meatless fare on the menu, however, because one of the owners is vegetarian.

Nonsmoking section. No credit cards. No alcohol.

Open Monday-Thursday 7 A.M.-10 P.M.; Friday until 11 P.M.; Saturday 9 A.M.-11 P.M.

CINCINNATI

Alpha
204 W. McMillan
513-381-6559

Alpha is sandwiched between the bar of the former arm-wrestling champ of Ohio, which features cheap beer on tap, and the back end of the Pickle Barrel Lounge on the south side of the University of Cincinnati campus. The restaurant compensates for its lack of atmosphere with a varied menu featuring five typed pages of vegetarian, breakfast, gourmet and fast food. Alpha tries to be all things to all people, and it sees itself as a five-star greasy spoon that sacrifices fancy decor for fine, inexpensive food. The orange vinyl chairs, speckled linoleum tables and simulated brick walls reinforce this reputation.

The popular vegetable special is a combination of steaming broccoli, cauliflower, corn, green peppers, carrots and mushrooms served over not-fully-cooked rice and covered with a somewhat bland, grainy cheddar cheese sauce. Other vegetarian offerings include the vegi-burger with cheese, 28 exotic omelets made with organic eggs, and the Epicurean Salad, which includes artichoke hearts, carrots, mushrooms and tomatoes. Ten varieties of fresh, steamed vegetables also are available.

Coffee, wine and imported beer are served. Smoking permitted. Credit cards accepted.

Wednesday-Monday 9 A.M.-11 P.M.

—*Lisa Spooner*

CINCINNATI

Lite Bite
Seventh and Race Sts.
513-369-6463

The Lite Bite is a triangular restaurant tucked away on the third floor of the downtown Shillitos department store. Glass walls and a couple of steps separate the restaurant from the store. Chrome trim and black-and-brown walls and floors give the Lite Bite a distinctively modern appearance. Bright pictures of fruits and vegetables decorate the walls. Two sides of the triangle are counters from which you can watch the speedy waitresses prepare your food. Giant stainless steel bowls of salad fixings face you as you eat.

We like the Light and Leafy—spinach, avocado, mushrooms and grapefruit sections with a sweet celery seed dressing. The soups—sometimes made with meat—are fresh daily. Our favorite dish is the pita (whole wheat, rye, sesame or white) stuffed with egg or tuna salad and served with a soup casserole. We also enjoy the refreshingly light high-protein shakes such as the Strawberry-Papaya Punch and the Pina-Papaya and the frozen yogurt shakes. Most of the desserts contain sugar, although a sugarless fruit cup and frozen yogurt are available.

Coffee. No alcohol. Smoking permitted. Shillitos's credit cards and Visa accepted.

Monday-Saturday 11 A.M.-4 P.M.; Saturday noon-5 P.M.

—*Lisa Spooner*

CINCINNATI

New World Food Shop
347 Ludlow
513-861-1101

On the northern edge of the University of Cincinnati campus, bordering the old and established neighborhood of Clifton, New World serves fresh, whole foods using no sugar, preservatives or artificial ingredients. It is a small, casual and friendly restaurant in the back of a health food store. The four rustic tables are separated from the kitchen by a counter from which the food is ordered.

Menu items vary weekly and are humorously highlighted on the cement walls. A sure bet is the tabouli, a generous portion of bulgur served over Bibb lettuce and topped with cherry tomatoes and carrot shavings—a meal in itself. Several other fresh garden salads are served with a choice of vinaigrette, creamy sesame, tofu or yogurt dressing. The avocado sandwich consists of avocado spread on whole wheat bread topped with melted white cheddar cheese, sprouts, lettuce and tomatoes. We also liked the Summer Noodles—watercress, mushrooms, cucumber and oriental vegetables in a chilled consomme. Desserts vary daily; they include rice pudding—a moist and cinnamony cakelike version—and honey cheesecake.

No coffee is served here, but there are herb teas and fruit drinks. No alcohol is served, but customers may bring their own. No smoking. No credit cards.

Monday-Friday 10 A.M.-8 P.M.; until 6 P.M. Saturday and until 5 P.M. Sunday.

—Lisa Spooner

CINCINNATI

Seventh House
915 Vine St.
513-421-9639

The Seventh House, hidden in the funk of downtown Cincinnati, serves vegetarian food prepared with no sugar or artificial preservatives. The floors are tile, the chairs are vinyl, and the burlap-covered walls are decorated with posters advertising Save the Seals, yoga and transcendental meditation along with announcements of menu additions.

The daily special and soup were especially good— cheesy potato soup, a delicious cheddar-potato combination garnished with chives, was served with steaming egg foo yung, which was covered with a thick soy sauce and served with brown rice. The whole wheat pita stuffed with hommus, sprouts, cabbage and onions was tasty but a tad dry. The Mexican Salad—lettuce, olives, green peppers, mushrooms, sprouts, sunflower seeds, hommus and guacamole—was somewhat more inspiring. The Top of the Wall cookies were small cement squares packed with almonds, raisins and oatmeal; perhaps at one time they were chewy.

No alcohol. Coffee served. Smoking permitted. No credit cards.
Monday-Friday 11 A.M.-3 P.M.

—Lisa Spooner

CINCINNATI

Spring Wheat
341 Convention Way
513-241-1600

Spring Wheat is directly off the skywalk—a network of second-story sidewalks overpassing the main streets of Cincinnati. The restaurant serves fast vegetarian lunches that would satisfy the most die-hard of meat eaters. Its dark paneled walls and tables, rust-orange rug, tapestries of wheat plants and hanging ferns create a warm and pleasant atmosphere.

A juice bar, which separates the restaurant from a health food store, serves 16-ounce blended juice drinks and ten varieties of high-protein shakes, which can be drunk in the restaurant or taken out to the skywalk benches. The most popular shake, the all-day energizer, is a delicious combination of papaya juice, protein powder, bananas and honey.

Several crisp, fresh salads brighten the counter. The fruit salads are a colorful combination of fruits in season. The food, served cafeteria style, is basic and healthful. We loved the chili with cheese, made with red kidney beans, green peppers and soy granules (which we swore were ground beef). Other favorites are the Pizza Bagel and the Melted Tuna Supreme (tuna on a whole wheat bun with tomatoes, sprouts and melted Swiss). The cookies, made with fructose, are rich and chewy, a must after lunch. Coffee is served.

No smoking. No alcohol. MasterCard and Visa accepted.

Open 11 A.M.-3 P.M. Monday-Saturday.

—Lisa Spooner

CLEVELAND
Genesis 1:29
12200 Euclid Ave.
216-421-9359

"And God said, 'Behold, I have given you every herb bearing seed, which is upon the face of all the earth, and every tree, in which is the fruit of a tree yielding seed; to you it shall be for meat.' " The verse tells the story at this cooperatively run vegetarian establishment. Meat and fish are not served, nor are coffee and alcohol available. On Fridays and Saturdays the place turns into a nonalcoholic night club after dinner, with only drinks served.

No smoking. No credit cards.

Open Monday, Tuesday and Thursday noon to 10 P.M.; Friday noon to 9 P.M.; weekends 2-10 P.M.

CLEVELAND
Govinda
15720 Euclid Ave.
216-566-8295

Remarkably inexpensive Indian food, with an all-you-can-eat policy that's a beacon for the gourmand. See our listing for Govinda in New York City for a lengthier report.

No credit cards.

Open 10:30 A.M.-5:15 P.M. Monday-Wednesday; until 8 P.M. Thursday-Saturday.

CLEVELAND HEIGHTS

Earth by April
2151 Lee Rd.
216-371-1438

The most popular natural foods restaurant in the Cleveland area, Earth by April has been widely praised for its gourmet cuisine, extensive salad bar, whole-earth decor and attentive service. Both seafood and vegetarian entrees are offered; among the latter, ratatouille and mushroom stroganoff are often mentioned with approval. Prices are high for a vegie restaurant, and reservations are advised.

Alcoholic beverages are served, and smoking is permitted. American Express, MasterCard, Diners Club, and Visa accepted.

Open Tuesday-Thursday 11:30 A.M.-3 P.M. and 5:30-10:30 P.M.; Friday and Saturday 11:30 A.M.-3 P.M. and 5:30-11:30 P.M.; Sunday 11 A.M.-3 P.M. and 5-9 P.M.

COLUMBUS

Seva Longevity Restaurant
2247 N. High St.
614-291-5591

Seva is a vegetarian establishment popular with Ohio State University students. We've heard good things about the vegetarian chili.

Beer and wine are served. American Express, MasterCard and Visa accepted.

Open 11 A.M.-11 P.M. every day.

YELLOW SPRINGS

Winds Cafe
230 Xenia Ave.
513-767-1144

In the back rooms of an old house on the village's main business street, the Winds is a pleasant surprise, with its low, wood-beamed ceilings, a fireplace, candles and fresh flowers on the oak tables, and paintings by local artists on the walls. While not specifically a vegetarian or natural foods restaurant, it always includes a vegetarian entree on its menu along with the chicken, red meat and seafood offerings and a good choice of omelets and salads.

Vegetarian entrees vary from week to week. Omelets are a real bargain, though the one we had was a bit underdone. The luncheon menu also offers hot sandwiches. Some appetizers and soups are vegetarian, too. The meatless Winds Chef Salad (lettuce, carrots, onion, celery, two cheeses, egg, avocado and sprouts) plus a basket of homemade whole wheat bread and hot herb tea makes a good, economical lunch.

Desserts and bread are homemade; some are sweetened with sugar, some with honey.

Service is sometimes slow, but late-night patrons don't care as they listen to live music on Friday and Saturday, with occasional performances by a string trio during dinner.

Alcohol and coffee are served. Smoking is permitted, but there is a nonsmoking section. MasterCard and Visa accepted.

Noon-3 P.M. and 6-10 P.M. Monday-Saturday. Cabaret 10 P.M.-1 A.M. Friday and Saturday.

—Lena Mae Gara

Oklahoma

STILLWATER

Garden of Eatin'
213 S. Knoblock
405-377-7199

The sheen of lacquered wood tables, spotlessly clean, brick walls and plants complete the decor of Garden of Eatin'. This tiny cafe, wedged into a row of small businesses just off the Oklahoma State University campus, has earned a reputation as one of the five best restaurants in town. The Garden offers a kaleidoscopic array of standards and daily specials on its three menus that keeps the crowds coming.

At breakfast, you may choose from omelets and other dishes made with locally produced fertilized eggs and served with toast and hashbrowns. Other options include cereal, with or without fresh fruit and yogurt, and French toast made of whole wheat, raisin or sweet bread and served with fresh fruit, butter and local honey.

The lunch menu of sandwiches is augmented by daily specials—our favorites—which are always delicious. Two of the best are the Potato Plate, a magnificent meal-in-a-skin that combines the baked potato with cottage cheese, sour cream, cheddar and paprika, and the chop suey, a tangy blend of brown rice, mushrooms and mandarin oranges, spiced with ginger.

A variety of breads and cream cheese is available at any time, and you can count on fresh ingredients in every dish. Coffee and a whole shelf of teas are available, and a honey-sweetened granola cookie, homemade cheesecake or a third dessert choice that changes completes a meal.

Smoking is permitted, but the owner hides the ashtrays. No alcohol. No credit cards. Minimum $1.35 at breakfast and lunch.

Monday-Saturday 9 A.M.-3 P.M.; Sunday 11 A.M.-3 P.M.

—Sharon Wright

TULSA

Middle Path Cafe
11th and Yale
918-936-7363

With a great deal of commitment, love and perseverance and some beautiful ideas, the owners of the Middle Path Cafe have shaped a worn building sagging with benign neglect into a comfortable, unpretentious restaurant. Hand-stitched patchwork quilts hang on the walls, and faced calico napkins are used on the varnished pine tables. Plants hang from natural rope macrame, as do basket-type light fixtures.

The Hot Toddy bread, dark and delicious, is baked in the cafe's own kitchen and sold through local health food stores. This bread is served as part of the regular menu, and croutons made from it add an extra touch to the vegetable soup and salad.

Not only do the cafe's operators bake their own bread and pastries (only natural sweeteners are used here), but the yogurt is cultured in their kitchen and the sprouts are cultivated by them as well.

These sprouts are included along with a delectable mixture of rice, olives, cheese, green pepper and squash as a stuffing for the vegetable crepes, which are topped with a sherry, sour cream and mushroom sauce, chopped fresh tomatoes, cashews and cheese. Entrees are served with soup and salad. Although no beef or pork is served, the menu includes broiled Danish cod and oriental chicken.

The entrees are available only after 5 P.M., but a variety of sandwiches is offered at all times. A tangy cream cheese and avocado and a very good chicken salad with black olives, cashews, celery and carrots are among them. Sandwiches are served on Hot Toddy bread and offered with a choice of soup or salad. The Munchie Platter, featuring black-eyed pea stew, vegetarian chili and a dish of yogurt topped with walnuts and almonds, also is part of the daily fare.

Certainly the carrot cake covered with a cream cheese and honey icing is a must.

Middle Path serves beer. The list of nonalcoholic beverages, along with teas and coffee, includes hot cider with free refills and an Orange Sunshine made with orange juice, lemon, honey and banana.

Smoking and nonsmoking sections. No credit cards.

Open 11:30 A.M.-9:30 P.M. Tuesday-Saturday.

—*Mary Ann West*

Oregon

COOS BAY

Hurry Back Sandwich Parlour
100 Commercial Ave.
503-267-3933

Walls of recycled gray wood, Spanish-tile table tops and burlap coffee sacks suspended from the rafters make the atmosphere of the Hurry Back Sandwich Parlour eclectic.

The menu offers an agreeable mix of salads, sandwiches, soups and sundaes, all prepared with fine ingredients and the kind of care that leads to delays in the service.

The soups vary from day to day. The chef favors dill in all of them. I have dined quite happily on the Soup Kitchen, a bowl of soup with warm bread, fresh fruit and sliced cheeses. The minestrone is an excellent blend of white beans and fresh vegetables in a tomato stock, topped with melted cheese.

A heady variety of cheese sandwiches is available, some served on a very good home-baked cheese-and-herb bread. There are two all-vegetable sandwiches on the menu, too. Meat sandwiches also are served, as is tuna salad with avocado and sprouts on an onion roll.

Desserts are limited to cheesecake sweetened with fructose, carrot cake and chocolate cheesecake. Two flavors of frozen yogurt usually are available in a cone or dish or in sundaes.

You can choose from a respectable selection of beers and wines. The house coffee is quite good, as are the espressos, and you can order an excellent cup of decaffeinated Colombian coffee.

Cash is the preferred tender at Hurry Back; personal checks are grudgingly accepted, but credit cards are out of the question. There's a nonsmoking section.

Monday-Thursday 11 A.M.-8 P.M., until 9 P.M. Friday and Saturday.

—Teri Albert

COOS BAY

Knight of Cups
1740 Ocean Blvd.
503-888-9531

A scant three miles from Highway 101 via Commercial Avenue and Ocean Boulevard, the Knight of Cups offers wholesome fare in a coffeehouse atmosphere. The single-room setting has an unusual array of tables and chairs, all of comfortably worn wood, and the effect of a genteel though slightly crowded parlor is heightened by the upright piano in one corner.

The blackboard menu varies, offering five to eight selections a day. I've enjoyed the rather hefty noodle kugel made with cheddar, Parmesan and cottage cheeses and topped with additional sour cream or cashews. A very generous bean burrito is served with sour cream atop a flour tortilla filled with cheddar, beans and an enchilada sauce that features red peppers in abundance.

Fish and meat dishes are available, as are a number of sandwiches—vegetarian on request. The seafood chowder is excellent, a creamy combination of fresh fish, shrimp and clams served with crackers. I recommend an accompaniment of the dark and hearty Russian rye bread.

The chocolate mousse pie is an airy confection of rich chocolate in a delicate graham cracker crust, topped with lots of fresh whipped cream. Other sweets frequently available are Boston cream pie and gingerbread served with whipped cream.

Coffees, espresso, hot chocolates, herb and black teas are available, as are fresh orange juice and "natural" sodas.

Entertainment is usually in evidence on the weekends, ranging from belly dancing troupes to balladeers. No alcohol. No credit cards. Nonsmoking section.

Open Monday-Saturday 11 A.M.-10 P.M.

—Teri Albert

COOS BAY

Stop 'N Eat, Inc.
Old City Hall
375 W. Central
503-267-5523

Fragrant East Indian cuisine is the surprise on the menu at this second-floor restaurant. The decor is mediocre at best, and fully half the fare is of the meat-and-potatoes variety, but the Indian selections are outstanding.

The vegetable curry is very good, its thick sauce supporting several vegetables. The curry dinner is served with plain boiled rice, one of two types of Indian bread (puri or parathas), either a simple tossed green salad or dahl (spicy lentil or split pea soup garnished with vegetables) and two of three chutneys: tomato, tamarind or mango. Beef, lamb and chicken curries also are available.

Not included with the curry dinners are the Indian appetizers. I recommend the vegetable samosas, crisp and spicy patties stuffed with potatoes and mixed vegetables. Additional Indian breads are offered as well—the paper-thin, crisply fried papadum and grilled parathas.

Portions at Stop 'N Eat are not large, and a very small quantity of chutney is expected to last one through an entire curry dinner.

Wine, beer and cocktails are served, and with some advance notice the cooks will prepare a fragrant spiced tea laced with hot milk, an ideal end to an Indian meal.

Credit cards accepted. Smoking permitted throughout the restaurant.

Tuesday-Saturday 5-11 P.M.

—Teri Albert

CORVALLIS

The Valley
136 S.W. Third St.
503-752-0933

In the downtown shopping area, almost hidden between larger businesses, the Valley restaurant is the favorite lunch (and breakfast and dinner) spot for food-particular people. Plants, antique accessories and brown cotton tablecloths make for a homey atmosphere.

All breads are made fresh daily, as are English muffins on Sunday mornings, with whole grains only and no sugar. Everything is made from the finest, freshest ingredients available; even the hamburgers are handmade when you order them, not frozen slabs of tasteless cardboard, and they're served on homemade buns with lettuce and tomato. The French fries are extra tasty, probably because they don't slice the potatoes for them until you order some.

Six vegetarian sandwiches are available, including the Veggie—avocado, cream cheese, alfalfa sprouts and tomato served on whole wheat bread. And there are eight meat sandwiches, in addition to four burgers.

The fish and chips is superior to anything we've eaten anywhere. And the Valley's got the best salad bar in town, with a wide selection of fresh vegetables, sprouts, homemade dressings and croutons. Soup lovers have a choice of three daily, and at least one of them will be vegetarian.

Dinners include a fish fry and steak; they come with soup and salad-bar privileges.

Desserts, made with sugar, include Olga's ice cream, a local brand made with fresh whole cream and fruits, no artificial flavorings or additives.

The Valley's own special coffee blend, ground by the staff, will please the most discriminating. Beer and wine are available. Smoking is permitted, but with the tall ceilings and fair ventilation it's not a problem for nonsmokers unless the restaurant is crowded. No credit cards. High chairs for little ones.

Monday 7 A.M.-5 P.M.; Tuesday-Friday 9 A.M.-9 P.M.; Saturday 8 A.M.-9 P.M.; Sunday 9 A.M.-2 P.M.

—Berniece L. Good

Pennsylvania

ALLENTOWN

Ann Ar Soup Bowl
913 Turner St.
215-821-0662

As the name implies, Ann Ar's specializes in hearty soups, complemented by wholesome salads and breads, but has expanded its menu to include some sandwiches and entrees.

The best bet here for lunch is still a bowl of the vegetarian vegetable soup, a tossed green salad with tahini dressing, a hot corn muffin and one of the delicious desserts such as the apricot mousse. It's a bargain, too.

Other good choices include the cream cheese and avocado sandwich with sprouts in whole wheat pita, and the Crab Mornay, with white sauce and cheese. There's one sandwich to be wary of: the oat bread of the Summertime Sandwich (cucumber, tomato, romaine and cottage cheese) tends to crumble, and you're left holding the cottage cheese.

The Soup Bowl's owner is Anna Rodale of Rodale Press, and many of the ingredients used at the restaurant are grown without chemicals at the firm's nearby experimental farm. No additives or preservatives are used in the cooking, and the fare is mostly vegetarian, although some sandwiches and some entrees include crab, turkey and ground beef.

The restaurant is in a two-story former carriage house, within easy walking distance of Allentown's main business and shopping areas, and the decor is warm and cheerful.

No alcohol. No credit cards. No smoking.

Tuesday-Saturday 11 A.M.-3 P.M. and 5-9 P.M.

—Linda Luther

BETHLEHEM

So Eat Already
22 W. Fourth St.
215-865-3440

There's so much to choose from here that deciding what to order is half the fun. The real pleasure, though, is in the tasting. The menu on the wall offers no less than 25 choices, all made with whole, natural ingredients. The atmosphere is informal—food is served deli style. A Rousseau-type mural takes up an entire wall and sets the natural tone for the restaurant. Lunchtime here can get pretty busy, but it's worth any wait.

So Eat Already excels in its always creative salads and sandwiches. One good choice is the Avocado Supreme, an open-face sandwich piled high with avocado slices, zucchini, cucumbers, tomatoes, mushrooms, green peppers and sprouts, topped with melted cheese. The thick slice of rye bread at the base is covered with tahini.

Another good bet is the gazpacho, a tangy, peppery blend of fresh vegetables, or an omelet. For those with more traditional tastes, the restaurant offers sandwiches made with preservative-free meat. Daily specials are offered, too.

Almost all the baking, from whole grain breads to pies, is done on the premises.

No alcohol is served, "but you can bring your own wine, and we'll gladly join anyone in a glass," says the manager. No smoking. No credit cards.

Monday-Saturday 9 A.M.-9 P.M.

—Linda Luther

EASTON

Nature's Way
145 Northampton St.
215-253-0940

Simple and good vegetarian sandwiches and fresh juices are the primary fare at the juice and snack bar in this natural foods store. Eating here is informal; there are seats for four at the counter, and the menu is on the blackboard.

A good bet is the Syrian sandwich, whole wheat pita bread stuffed with hommus and sprouts. Other tasty creations include the vegie sandwich, tofu salad sandwich and pita pizza. Most sandwiches are reasonably priced.

To quench your thirst, try the fresh carrot juice or any of the other vegetable juices such as beet or celery, or herb teas. No coffee is available here, but Nature's Way does offer a coffee-substitute.

By far the best dessert is the tofu pie, a creamy delight on a whole wheat crust, especially good when topped with apricots. It's so delicious you have to keep reminding yourself it's a really healthful dessert.

No credit cards. No smoking. No alcohol.

Open 11 A.M.-2 P.M. every day officially, but the owners try to accommodate snack-bar customers during all hours the store is open.

—Linda Luther

EMMAUS

Food Naturally
301 Main St.
215-967-3600

Food Naturally offers quick, wholesome food at a reasonable cost—salads and snacks as well as quiches, sandwiches and hot entrees like vegetarian chili and vegetable tempura. Originally a snack bar in a health food store, Food Naturally moved up the street in 1981 to become a sit-down restaurant that can accommodate 31. The service is extremely friendly.

The specialty here is the Healthwich, a delicious combination of lettuce, shredded carrots, cheese, tomatoes, cucumbers and sprouts stuffed into whole wheat pita bread and topped with either oil and vinegar or herb mayonnaise. Other sandwiches include tofu salad, tuna salad, and tahini and honey. In the hot-food category, the outstanding dish is homemade quiche, a creamy pie in whole wheat crust that outdoes many at fancier establishments.

The snack bar offers an array of fruit juices and a soup of the day.

No smoking. No credit cards. No alcohol.

Open Monday-Saturday 11 A.M.-7:30 P.M., but closed from 2-4:30 P.M. Saturday.

—Linda Luther

NARBERTH

Over the Rainbow
856 Montgomery Ave.
215-664-8589

What's over the rainbow? If not a pot of gold, at least a taste of heaven, right on Philadelphia's Main Line. The atmosphere is one of simple elegance with the exclusivity necessitated by a seating capacity of 40.

Tastebuds awaken to the light and refreshing gazpacho and remain ecstatically alert throughout the meal. The blackboard menu, which changes daily, features chilled and hot soups, king-size salads, inspired chicken dishes, inventive vegetarian cuisine, quiches, and gourmet burgers made from organically raised Australian cattle. The chickens are bred sans hormones, too, and the vegetables are organic whenever possible. No artificial anything is allowed.

Showcased in glass bowls, the colorful salads taste as good as they look. The distinctive Rainbow, Spinach, Tropical, Nicoise and Pizza salads would satisfy the average dinner appetite.

A generous house salad, topped with tofu herbal, Parmesan vinaigrette or tomato dressing, accompanies the entrees. The Fate, a chickpea, green pea, yogurt, green pepper and mushroom casserole, is divinely accented, and the shrimp, tomato and cheese pie in whole wheat crust is a meal for the gods.

Equally high quality prevails in the dessert menu, which includes carob brownies and other moist and flavorful pastries. A cup of turbinado sugar adorns the cloth-covered tables, but fructose is used in the cooking.

Coffee is available, and so are herbal teas, Pero, goat's milk and other healthy beverages. You can bring wine. No smoking. No credit cards.

Open for lunch Monday-Saturday, dinner (until about 9 P.M.) Tuesday through Saturday.

—Steven Hochman

NEWFOUNDLAND
White Cloud
Route 447
717-676-3162

Quartered in a converted house, this country inn serves only "good food that is good for you," says its managers. Meals using whole grains, fresh fruit and vegetables from their organic garden are prepared without preservatives or additives. Guests wait to be served in a dining room overlooking the neatly manicured lawn, with classical music playing softly in the background. The owner, George Wilkinson, circulates among the guests, stopping to inquire where they're from and to chat amiably for a few minutes.

There's a self-service salad table from which tomatoes, cucumbers, alfalfa sprouts, green peppers and a yogurt-mayonnaise dressing can be added to a basic tossed salad. Most entrees are sauteed or steamed vegetables with brown rice. More exotic ones are the Cheesebake (cottage cheese, cheddar and spinach), Cheese-nut Balls in Mexican Sauce, "Veal" Parmesan (melted cheese over breaded tofu in tomato sauce) and my favorite, Baked Nut Loaf with Mushroom Sauce. Two choices of soup are offered. A side order of a home-grown vegetable is included with the dinner, as are whole grain and banana breads.

Three juices, eight herb teas, milk, coffee (served with a frown), coffee-substitute and blender drinks are available. Desserts range from a large scoop of Haagen-Dazs ice cream to carob-peanut pudding, fruit crunch and carrot cake (with or without a sugar icing). The carrot cake was exceptionally moist and tasty—not overly carroty.

Absolutely no smoking. Meat, fish and alcohol are not served, but guests may bring their own wine. the only sugar used is in the icing. Reservations preferred.

In summer, meals are served seven days a week: breakfast 8-10:30 A.M., lunch noon-2:30 P.M. and dinner 6-8:30 P.M.; lunch and dinner are served continuously from noon-8:30 P.M. Sunday. Winter hours vary, so call ahead.

—*Susan Hamburger*

PITTSBURGH

Cornucopia
328 Atwood St.
412-682-7953

Lasagna with green noodles is a specialty at this all-vegetarian restaurant. A grilled broccoli sandwich is also popular. The ice cream is homemade.

No smoking. No credit cards.

Tuesday-Sunday 10:30 A.M.-10 P.M.

QUAKERTOWN

Nonesuch
Clymer Rd.
215-536-8005

Wholesome lunches are the goal at the snack bar of the Nonesuch natural foods store, which is on a long, winding country road but isn't difficult to find.

Sandwiches, salads and soups are the primary fare, and customers can either sit at the counter (which seats five) or at two small tables. Waits can be long.

Specials are offered each day, and the snack bar excels in its tofu dishes. A good bet is the tofu chapati, a combination of herbed tofu and shredded carrots wrapped in a paper-thin, tasty chapati. Another is the tofu taco with a slice of quiche, at times available on a bargain-priced "super special." Still another goody is tofu-stuffed mushroom caps. An array of fresh fruit juices and healthful milk shakes is available. The carrot juice, made to order, seems a bit overpriced. Natural ice cream is the main dessert offering.

No smoking. No credit cards. No alcohol.

Monday-Friday 10 A.M.-3 P.M., until 5 P.M. Saturday.

—Linda Luther

Rhode Island

NEWPORT

Paradise Juices
381 Thames St.
401-846-5763

Newport's only fruit and vegetable juice bar is just a short walk from the main tourist area and offers a welcome rest from the hectic confusion so common to the town in the summertime. Hand-painted Pennsylvania Dutch motifs decorate the front door and invite the visitor inside where tropical drinks and vegetable sandwiches are prepared. There are two serving rooms and a counter for carry-out orders. The front room is bright and cheerful with plenty of windows, plants and a couple of tables. The back room has been decorated with lingering in mind. Daily newspapers and current magazines on the large oak tables encourage a guest to stay just a bit longer. The sign above the door reads, "There are no strangers in Paradise," and owners Anne Yale and Pat Allen-Bartlett are always on hand to greet guests with warmth and friendliness.

The menu is changed daily to take advantage of seasonal specials, but regular drinks include the Rosanna Banana-Dana, a blend of pineapple, coconut and bananas, and the Aquidneck Sunrise, orange and grapefruit juices. One sandwich favorite is avocado with sprouts and a dressing of yogurt and dill or curry, and another is melted cheese on whole wheat Syrian bread.

Snacks are available, too—banana chips, for example, or papaya strips. There's coffee and a wide selection of herb teas, and in the fall and winter an aromatic pot of mulled cider is offered, along with homemade gingerbread.

Honey is used for sweetening, and the cheese in the

sandwiches is rennetless, relying on vegetable oil instead of the animal fat found in most cheeses.

Smoking permitted in the back room, away from food preparation. No credit cards. No alcohol.

Open daily 10 A.M.-10 P.M. in summer, but hours vary a little in winter, so check.

–Edna Owens

NEWPORT
Yesterday's
28 Washington Sq.
401-847-0116

A turn-of-the-century saloon, Yesterday's specializes in old-fashioned quality and a friendly atmosphere. The abundance of plants, mirrors and stained glass all gives one the feeling of stepping back in time when entering the front door.

Yesterday's brings quality food to everyone, meat eater and vegetarian alike. The food contains no preservatives and is never purchased frozen or canned. Each meal is prepared to order; only the soup is made ahead of time. The grapefruit juice is freshly squeezed each morning, and it alone is worth the trip. Other specialties are a savory onion soup, a delectable salad dressing made with herbs and honey, and apple strudel.

The menu features eight salads, and the Euell Gibbons Salad is a meal in itself. Each day the board has at least one vegetarian meal. In the evening, vegetarian meals are always available from the menu or on special request. The breads are Syrian, French, dark or light rye, onion roll or bulkie roll.

Service is fast and efficient as well as friendly. Biggie Korn, owner of Yesterday's, feels that listening to his customers is the only way to present them with what they want, so a lot of the items on the menu have been added because of customer suggestions, including the Mexican selections.

Smoking permitted. Coffee and herb teas available. No credit cards. There's jazz on Wednesday and Sunday, and occasional entertainment at other times.

Open daily 11 A.M.-11 P.M.; Friday and Saturday 11 P.M.-2 A.M. for entertainment only.

–Edna Owens

PROVIDENCE

Amaras
231 Wickendon St.
401-621-8919

Our correspondent has high praise for the cooking at this well-appointed restaurant, with special praise for a pie of carrots, parsnips, cream cheese and mushrooms. Among the sandwiches is a TLT: tofu, lettuce and tomato.

South Carolina

CHARLESTON

Sprouts & Krauts Food Emporium
Marion Square Mall
803-722-6726

Sprouts & Krauts calls itself "the great restaurant alternative" and lives up to its claim. It's near the center of historic downtown Charleston in a mini-mall fashioned from an old department store building. The atmosphere is light and friendly—a fun place with cafeteria service. The bilevel dining area is filled with green plants (for sale) and sunshine from numerous skylights.

Imagination is a main ingredient here. The vegetable soup is light and clear with crisp vegetables, in contrast to the heavy gumbos served all over town. The South-of-the-Border sandwich, pita bread filled with refried beans, onion, green pepper and Swiss cheese and topped with sour cream, is worth getting used to. My teenage son raves about the chicken lasagna: "Not only is it really good, but they give you lots of it." The bratwurst with German potato salad is also excellent.

Soups, coffee and iced tea are made with distilled water. Try a choconana shake of yogurt, carob powder and bananas, a meal in itself. Most desserts are made with natural sweeteners. The giant chocolate- or carob-chip cookies are perfect for a midafternoon snack.

Domestic and imported beers are available, as well as "natural" soft drinks, and there's a limited wine selection.

Nonsmoking section. American Express, MasterCard and Visa.

Monday-Saturday 11:30 A.M.-9 P.M.; Sunday 11:30 A.M.-3 P.M.

—C. Mitchell Carnell, Jr.

Tennessee

MEMPHIS
The Good Life
3125 Poplar Ave.
901-327-9755

If you are looking for a quick lunch and some good food, this is your best bet. It is ideally located in the center of Memphis. You can eat at the stand-up snack bar, carry out your order or just shop in the store, which owner and operator Helen Hellsman says is certified organic.

Prices are reasonable. The snack bar features all kinds of salads and a special Good Life Vegetable Loaf. No meat is available; tuna is the only fish offered. Desserts are not sweetened with sugar. A tasty blend takes the place of coffee here. You could bring your own wine if you wanted, but most people don't. Smoking is not permitted. MasterCard and Visa are accepted.

The snack bar is open 11 A.M.-2:30 P.M. Monday-Friday.

—Ann Hughes Sayle

MEMPHIS
Norris Health Foods
4624 Poplar Ave.
901-683-3984

Norris Health Foods has a store section and a snack bar. The atmosphere is pleasant, not fancy. This establishment does a bustling business, so you know the fare is good. You can eat at the snack bar or carry out your meal. All sorts of natural foods are served, mainly in sandwiches. There is no static menu; the daily specials are written on the blackboard each morning.

Norris's uses Worthington's meat substitutes; no meat or fish is served. Coffee-substitute replaces the real thing. There's no alcohol served, and customers usually don't bring their own. Desserts are sweetened with honey and fructose.

No smoking. MasterCard and Visa accepted.

Open 9 A.M.-4:30 P.M. weekdays; 9 A.M.-4 P.M. Saturday.

—Ann Hughes Sayle

MEMPHIS

Whole Foods of Germantown
1779 Kirby Pkwy.
901-755-3700

In the beautiful and booming section known as Germantown, you'll find Memphis's only true restaurant of the vegetarian/natural foods persuasion, and it's one of the best restaurants in the city of any type. It will charm you from the minute you walk through the door. Fresh flowers and warm colors make the French provincial atmosphere really welcoming. Whole foods is certainly a fun and attractive place for a sit-down meal. People are friendly here, we've noticed, and eager to be of help.

The cooking is every bit as first-rate as you might expect from such a clean, cheery place. A bulletin board shows the hot entree of the day. You can choose from the menu, too: it lists a wide variety of sandwiches and salads. Hearty Boy is a delightful sandwich with everything from mushrooms to avocado on it. Candlelight dinners are planned for Thursdays. Customers may bring their own wine. No meat or fish (except tuna) is served.

No smoking. MasterCard and Visa accepted.

Open 10 A.M.-7:30 P.M. Monday-Saturday; noon-6 P.M. Sunday.

—Ann Hughes Sayle

NASHVILLE

Good Life Health Foods
213 Fifth Ave. North
615-254-3777

In historic downtown Nashville, country music capital of the world, you will find an excellent lunch spot called Good Life

Health Foods. We think they should change the name to Great Life, because the food is so good. The owners have worked hard to restore the old building that houses their restaurant; the atmosphere is relaxing and pleasant. Natural unfinished wooden planks form the walls, and a veritable jungle of plants creates an outdoorsy feeling.

There's a different specialty each day. Hot sandwiches, salads and vegetarian casseroles delight the palate. Most popular is steamed vegetables with rice. No meat is served; tuna is the only fish available. Desserts are honey-sweetened and excellent. Doesn't fruit-filled crumb cake sound appealing?

You can bring your own wine to enhance the meal or just enjoy the wide variety of nonalcoholic beverages served—coffee and fruit and vegetable juices included. Don't worry about smokers spoiling your meal, either; smoking isn't allowed.

MasterCard accepted.

Open 11 A.M.-2:30 P.M. Monday-Friday.

—Ann Hughes Sayle

NASHVILLE
The Grateful Breadbox
121 N. 21st St.
615-327-1105

Here's the heart of health food in Nashville. This sandwich shop and bakery is a neighbor of the Vanderbilt University campus. Owner Salem Forsythe chose a location small enough to keep overhead down and take-out business up. No more than 25 customers can crowd around the few tables and the counter inside, where the decor is the ever-popular pine slab and plants. Weather permitting, another 20 can enjoy the outdoor dining.

The bakery supplies breads and natural pastries to more than a dozen area wholesalers, and complimentary trays of baked goods with butter are always available in the restaurant to promote the genuinely kind atmosphere of the place.

For breakfast, there is whole wheat or honey Danish to go with fresh-ground Mocha Java or French roast coffee, or you can order several varieties of toast, homemade yogurt or granola with milk.

Sandwiches and salads offer a complete run of the garden accompanied by Swiss, cheddar and cream cheeses from natural dairy processes. A tofu spread is made with olives, sweet peppers, celery, garlic, onions, tomatoes and sprouts. Carrot and orange juices are processed in the restaurant.

Last visit, free hard cider was offered to anyone interested. No alcohol is sold, but Tennessee's BYOB law allows consumption. Black bean was the soup of the day, and the usual vintage soft rock was providing nice sounds.

No credit cards. No smoking inside. Distilled water is offered gratis. A small, health-oriented lending library is located by the cash register and the public-notice wall.

Open 7 A.M.-7 P.M. Monday-Saturday.

–Bill Conrad

NASHVILLE

Laughing Man
1927 Broadway
615-327-1388

A block east of Vanderbilt University is a most logical location for Nashville's best-known health food restaurant, which offers a pleasant retreat from the blue-plate specials that predominate on this city's restaurant scene.

The decor is decidedly natural in the old, high-ceilinged commercial building. New slab pine covers the walls. Plants crowd the windows on both ends of the room and hang from a suspended lattice overhead. Macrame wall hangings, assorted old prints and resin-coated tables complete the set.

The owners maintain a policy of no meat, no fish, no sugar and no smoking. You can purchase a cup of coffee, and you can bring your own spirits, but the Laughing Man doesn't sell any alcohol.

At lunchtime, avocado, cheese, tomato, sprouts and sauteed mushrooms are featured ingredients of sandwiches. For fans of soy in disguise, there's a soyburger. Pita bread is available for a little extra money.

What separates Laughing Man from the sandwich-and-soft-drink category, however, is its cooked offerings. Reliable staples include beans as well as vegetables with rice, but you can venture into Indian curry, crepes du jour and even a Mexican-natural approach to tostada with guacamole and chips or burritos.

MasterCard and Visa accepted.

Open 7 A.M.-9 P.M. Monday-Saturday; Sunday 11 A.M.-3 P.M.

—*Bill Conrad*

NASHVILLE

Lifeline
4910B Charlotte Ave.
615-373-1847

This one's not on the main drag of Music City, U.S.A., but the food is good and you'll be glad you came. In a laid-back atmosphere, 20 people can enjoy food that's as good as if it were cooked with loving care at home. You serve yourself from a cafeteria-style counter, so save your tips. The regular customers who know about this place may beat you to it if you don't allow a safe margin of time before meals.

Be sure to try the meatless chili or spaghetti. For dieters and salad specialists, there are fruit salads as well as regular salads. The oat burger promises an unusual and zesty taste for those adventurous enough to try it. There are many other sandwiches on the menu, all vegetarian.

Lifeline serves no meat, no fish, no coffee and no alcohol, and it's not the sort of place where people usually bring their own wine. Desserts are sweetened with honey, and your bill is sweetened by the reasonable prices.

Smoking permitted. MasterCard accepted.

Open 11 A.M.-5 P.M. Sunday through Friday.

—*Ann Hughes Sayle*

Texas

AUSTIN

Garden Cafe
413 W. 23rd St.
512-472-2668

The plain wood exterior is papered with handbills. The interior is festooned with hanging baskets and potted plants. Large windows add to the garden atmosphere. The wait for a table is patiently endured by the regulars during the crowded noon hour; evenings are less crowded.

In a retail area adjacent to the University of Texas, the cafe caters to a mixture of students, store clerks, shoppers and the university staff. The average customer is young and casually dressed. A scattering of university administrators and suburban shoppers raises the average age as well as the standard of attire and attests to the quality of the food.

For a light lunch, the fruit salad with yogurt is consistently good. The Mountains are slices of whole wheat bread piled high with lettuce, sprouts, and your selection of vegetable, avocado or mushroom, topped with grated cheese and broiled. For dinner, try the popular tempuras; the vegetable and mushroom are excellent, and the shrimp is okay, but I've never found the fish acceptable.

No smoking. No credit cards. No coffee or alcohol, and—with a few exceptions—no sugar.

Monday-Saturday 11 A.M.-9:30 P.M.

—C. *Wesley Allen*

AUSTIN

Good Food Store Cafe
2720 Hancock Dr.
512-453-8783

This cafe is a snack bar in the corner of a natural food grocery. Any time during the day you will find several of the 14 seats occupied by shoppers and others who come in just for a snack. Its reputation as a good snack bar is substantiated by experience, but lunch crowds can bog down the casual service.

The low-priced natural and organic fare includes sandwiches (try the avocado), tacos, salads and chalupas (recommended, but variable). The smoothies, made from fruit in season, are outstanding.

No meat, fish, sugar, coffee or alcohol. Smoking permitted. MasterCard and Visa accepted.

Monday-Saturday 11 A.M.-6:30 P.M. (after 6, drinks only).

— C. *Wesley Allen*

AUSTIN

Health Kitchen
403 W. Sixth St.
512-478-3022

A superb luncheon salad bar! Serve yourself, and agonize over the choices: crisp lettuce, tender spinach and alfalfa sprouts in large bowls surrounded by carrots, onions, celery, three other kinds of sprouts and an array of other vegetables. Walk in, make your salad, choose your drink and enjoy your meal.

Near downtown, the Health Kitchen is crowded with office workers and shoppers at lunch hour. The decor is plain and simple. The chairs are of varying lineage. A sit-down bar extends along one wall, health food posters decorate another. A large front window and hanging baskets provide a proper environment for your meal.

The salad bar is only available from 11 A.M.-2 P.M. At other hours there is a good vegetarian and natural foods menu: order and pick up your food at a counter in the rear. Soup is popular; the mushroom is not creamed, and the fresh mushroom flavor can be appreciated. Chalupas, fresh-squeezed juices, sandwiches (the ones in the refrigerator are second-best) and quiche provide fare for a steady stream of customers during the day.

Follow the advice on a poster and the example of others, and clear your own dishes to the cart. You declare what you ate and pay at the register as you leave. The result: good food at reasonable prices.

No smoking. No meat, sugar, alcohol or coffee. MasterCard and Visa accepted.

Monday-Friday 9 A.M.-5:30 P.M., Saturday until 5.

—C. *Wesley Allen*

AUSTIN

Juice Factory
4501 Guadalupe
512-454-8349

This restaurant serves a clientele that ranges from beards to bald heads, with the average well on the younger side. Their mutual interest is sufficient servings of flavorful vegetarian meals at very reasonable prices. The dinners are a delight for the epicure of vegetarian and natural foods.

Each day of the week there is a different selection of six international meals, all well prepared and well seasoned. The servings are ample. The repertoire includes: Mid-Eastern Casserole, eggplant parmesan, Vegifu Pie and spinach cream pie. The herb-seasoned Russian Peasant Pie (whole wheat crust, potato, carrot, onion and cabbage) is excellent. The vegetables in the Chinese dinner are cooked until barely tender and served on excellent brown rice.

Besides the dinners, there are sandwiches, salads, chalupas, tacos, soup and chips. For an enjoyable sandwich, try the Squirrel's Treat (organic peanut butter with honey and banana) or a vegetable submarine.

The peppermint tea is good, but the smoothies rate below average; fresh-squeezed orange and carrot juices are available.

Desserts, sweetened only with honey, include ice cream, cake and pie.

No smoking. No alcohol, meat, fish, eggs or sugar. No credit cards.

Open 10 A.M.-9 P.M. every day.

—C. *Wesley Allen*

AUSTIN

Saferway Cafe
801 Rio Grande
512-474-9398

The second floor of an old mansion surrounded by large trees is a pleasant setting for this strictly vegetarian natural foods restaurant. Inside, a mixed assemblage of chairs and tables is usually more than half occupied for the evening meal. A special dinner each day is described on a chalkboard at the head of the stairs.

The dinner is an international meal; each day of the week the recipe is from a different country. One excellent dinner was artichoke noodles and mushrooms served with stuffed cabbage on sprouts, accompanied by Jewish egg bread. The delicate seasoning attests to the care of the staff.

The organic salad bar is popular and available any time. A fruit salad, soup of the day, and a wide range of sandwiches deserve consideration. Tea is available hot or cold, a special flavor for each day. Smoothies, juices, shakes and spring water are available, too. Pass up the nonalcoholic wine.

The service is casual, and the attire is informal; jeans, cut-offs, sandals, T-shirts and occasional swim suits are standard in warm weather.

The definition of vegetarian here excludes meats, fish, coffee and sugar. No smoking or credit cards.

Open every day 11 A.M.-9 P.M., dinner beginning at 6 and Sunday brunch until 2:30 P.M.

—C. *Wesley Allen*

HOUSTON

Gallery Inn
9336 Westview
713-932-7503

Looking for candlelight atmosphere? Try an evening at the Gallery Inn. The manager calls his place a "healthy" foods restaurant and promises to prepare any food to your specifications, including weighing portions and cooking with low sodium. The high prices reflect the upper-middle-class neighborhood of Northwest Houston. Diners are surrounded by American Indian art, and the menu carries out this theme.

Try the salad called Alabama-Coushatta (Sam Houston joined this local tribe); you get a large plate of fresh spinach, mushrooms, hard-boiled egg, tomatoes and onion with a side bowl of house dressing. If you prefer to toss your own, the salad bar has an attractive selection.

Soups vary, and sandwiches come with names like the Native (avocado under melted cheese) and the Gringo (chicken, tuna or egg salad). All are garnished with fruit in season and served on whole wheat bread. Sandwiches are served all day, but dinner hour begins at 6. The menu includes seafood and meat dishes, too.

Coffee, tea, juice, soft drinks, smoothies and milk are available, and there's full bar service. There is packaged sugar or artificial sweetener on your table; some cooking is done with honey, some with sugar. The carrot cake has chunks of dates and nuts and a cream cheese icing. Bread and desserts are baked next door at Ye Seekers Horizon Health Food Store (owned by the same organization that owns the restaurant but operated separately), some of them from flour ground on the premises (but some contain refined white flour, so watch out).

Nonsmoking section. Major credit cards accepted.

Monday-Thursday 11 A.M.-8:45 P.M.; Friday and Saturday until 9:45 P.M.

—Mary D. Wade

HOUSTON
Hatters
Cowperwood Regency Building
6001 Savoy Dr., Suite 103
713-789-9232

Hatters, on the first floor of a new executive office building in Southwest Houston, takes a natural approach to fast foods. Aimed at the office worker, this small, bright shop is a deliberate attempt to provide an alternative to the hamburger stand.

The menu, with an Alice in Wonderland theme, features sandwiches on brown bread, served in paper boats with cherry tomatoes, carrot sticks and curly lettuce. The Mad Hatter (avocado and cheese), the Teapot (chunky tuna salad and cheese), and the Dormouse (egg salad, cheese and sunflower seeds) all bristle with alfalfa sprouts unless you request otherwise. A peanut butter sandwich with raisins, bananas, nuts and honey also is available. All sandwiches are available in half-sizes, with slightly-more-than-half prices.

The usual vegetable salad (White Rabbit) and fruit salad (Queen of Hearts) as well as the Cheshire Chef (including ham and turkey) are served with Italian or house dressing.

Hatters provides ashtrays on all ten tables. Beer, wine and coffee are served. No credit cards.

Hours: strictly for the coffee break and lunch crowd; Monday-Friday 7:30 A.M.-3:30 P.M.

—Mary D. Wade

HOUSTON
Health Seekers
2946 S. Shepherd
713-526-9268

Looking reminiscent of the Walgreen's it once was, this restaurant/ food store operates in an older commercial area. A half-dozen counter stools remain in place at the former soda fountain. Eight booths and numerous tables bring seating to 125.

The menus list the usual avocado and egg salads as well as chicken and tuna. Many of the salads are available as cold sandwiches or as hot, open-face sandwiches served on Texas-size whole wheat bread slices. There is a vegetarian chili, and the Health Burger is ground round steak on a seven-grain bun. Daily soup or casserole specials are posted on the blackboard. No garnishes are served with the dishes.

Smoothies come in at least seven fruit flavors, and the apple-banana is exceptional. Baked goods are served, too; some are made with sugar, some with honey. Coffee and teas are served; no alcohol.

Smoking permitted. MasterCard and Visa accepted.

Monday-Saturday 11:30 A.M.-8 P.M.; Sunday until 5.

—Mary D. Wade

HOUSTON

Hobbit Hole
1715 S. Shepherd
713-528-3418
and
10001 Westheimer
713-783-9170

Although the interior of the near-downtown restaurant on South Shepherd is intended to create a Tolkien world, diners in humid Houston may prefer the garden out back, where large fans keep the wind chimes singing.

Servings are generous, with small sizes available. Avocados are featured, beginning with a Bilbo Baggins sandwich (guacamole, tomatoes and safflower mayonnaise). Far Downs (egg salad, tomato and sunflower seeds) can include a layer of guacamole for a little extra money. All sandwiches are served on Hobbit Hole's own fresh-baked whole wheat bread.

Quiche, cheese tacos and fish are served, but no meat. Vegetable salads are all good, but the yogurt-honey dressing makes Frodo's Fruit Salad something special. Desserts are yogurt-based, or there's ice cream. No sugar is used anywhere, only honey.

Beverages include fresh fruit juices, but the house specialty is smoothies—blends of fresh fruit, honey and ice. Beer, wine, liquor, herb tea and milk are available.

Major credit cards accepted. Smoking permitted in the garden only at South Shepherd, but frowned on at Westheimer.

Monday-Thursday 11 A.M.-10:30 P.M.; Friday and Saturday until 11 P.M.; Sunday 3-8:30 P.M. at the South Shepherd restaurant and noon-8 P.M. at the Westheimer location.

—Mary D. Wade

HOUSTON

Pineapple Tree
6108 Westheimer
713-977-7938

Located on one of the city's major thoroughfares, next to a shopping center, Pineapple Tree seats 40 in a cheerful room and offers much more than strictly vegetarian fare.

The house specialty is spinach lasagna made from five kinds of cheese, spinach noodles and pounds of steamed spinach under a thick tomato sauce filled with mushrooms and herbs. Other vegetable casseroles include quiches, either mushroom or zucchini. Tabouli, a Lebanese salad of bulgur, chopped parsley, cucumbers and tomatoes topped with a dressing of safflower oil, tamari, lemon juice and garlic, comes in small and large sizes. There are tuna and chicken salad sandwiches as well as poached trout.

Desserts include the usual yogurt sundaes and pastries; some of the pastries contain sugar, but an effort is made to warn the patrons about them. Good herb tea is available, but no coffee. No alcohol is served, and bringing your own is discouraged.

No smoking. MasterCard and Visa accepted.

Monday-Saturday 11 A.M.-10:30 P.M.; Sunday 12:30-9 P.M.

—Mary D. Wade

Utah

SALT LAKE CITY

Khyber Kitchen
870 S. 900 East
801-531-7826

The Khyber Kitchen, says a flier, "is very much like a small restaurant on a side alley in Beirut, Damascus, Istanbul, Tehran, Kabul or Peshawar. The atmosphere, music and everything take you right to some far-off corner of the Middle East, and the taste-tingling food remains in your memory long after you have eaten."

While that last claim strikes us as open to interpretation, the offerings are inviting. Six full dinners are available, representing cuisines of Afghanistan, Persia and India-Pakistan, as well as Arabian, Arabo-Turkish and Indo-Afghan styles.

No alcohol or drugs allowed on the premises. No smoking. No credit cards.

Noon-2 and 5-8 P.M. daily.

—Lawrence Block

SALT LAKE CITY

Susan's Cafe
154 E. 200 South
801-364-4096

This small restaurant offers vegetarian natural and organic foods, and many of the recipes were developed by the owner. Omelets and selected meats are served, and other dishes are simple but tasty combinations of whole grains, vegetables and legumes. No sugar or white flour is ever used, and no drugs or alcohol are allowed on the premises. Coffee and tea are available.

Small smoking section. No credit cards.

Monday-Friday 11 A.M.-7 P.M.; Saturday 11-5 P.M. Closed Sunday.

—Lawrence Block

Vermont

BRATTLEBORO
Common Ground
25 Eliot St.
802-257-0855

This spacious, homey restaurant, founded in the late 1960s and still run by a collective, is a southern Vermont countercultural institution and a must-visit for health-conscious New England vacationers. Indoors are large old oaken tables where customers can eat family style with strangers if they wish. There are small tables, too, indoors as well as on the second-floor terrace.

Common Ground is mostly vegetarian, but its menu includes fish and chicken. A broiled haddock dish was lightly cooked and flaky, although the smell of the fish suggested that it was not as fresh as it might have been. A skewer of vegetables was broiled lightly, too, so that the tomato wedges, broccoli, carrots, onions and mushroom caps on it were still crisp. The salad bar is so-so.

At night there's often guitar-playing by locals. Nonsmoking section. No credit cards. Beer and wine are served, as are coffee and herbal and black teas.

Monday-Saturday 11:30 A.M.-4 P.M.; Wednesday-Sunday 5:30-9 P.M.; Sunday brunch 10:30 A.M.-1:30 P.M.

—*Cheryl Morrison*

BURLINGTON
Fresh Ground Coffee House
175 Church St.
802-864-9663

If you want to eat inexpensively, this is where to go. This Vermont-style cafeteria—pine floors, barn-siding walls, taped classical-jazz-folk music, poster prints and plants—offers a variety of vegetarian foods that will be as kind to your pocketbook as you want them to be.

One low-priced meal is the Beggar's Banquet—a bowl of homemade soup, a slice of whole wheat bread, a red-ripe apple, a slice of cheddar and tea or coffee. If you want to go whole hog, there's vegetarian lasagna at the other end of the scale, still reasonably priced. In between there is a hot, open-face hommus topped with tomato, cheese and sprouts, and there are vegetable platters.

Beverages include beer and wine, hot and cold cider, coffee-substitute, cappuccino (mine was more like cafe au lait) and mineral water. Beware of the desserts if you don't want to get clogged with refined white sugar.

On Friday and Saturday nights, there's live entertainment from 9 to 1.

Nonsmoking section. No credit cards.

Monday-Thursday 11:30 A.M.-9 P.M.; Friday and Saturday until 4 A.M.; Sunday 10 A.M.-2 P.M.

—Linda Santucci

MONTPELIER
Gitano Jazz Cafe
24 Elm St. (Jailhouse Common)
802-229-4468

"We run the gamut food- and price-wise," says owner Carlos Montoya Jr. Vegetable, fish and meat dishes coexist at Gitano, a 19th-century jailhouse restored in a simple, modern style. The most fanciful object, and the focus of the decor, is the hand-painted pressed tin ceiling that towers nearly three stories from ground level.

At a Sunday brunch, the Ensalada de Chiapas, best described as a banana guacamole served on head lettuce, was good and interesting but not as soul-satisfying as the toasted homemade cornbread. The Spanakopita was chock full of spinach, and the tomato bisque was deliciously chunky (although mislabeled). Other items at brunch included German Apple Pancakes, honey-almond granola and Eggs Benedict.

In keeping with the cafe mode, light fare such as fruit and cheese, hommus salad, pates and sandwiches are always available. Dinner entrees, like fillet of sole served with a wine-and-cheese sauce, stir-fried vegetables with hommus and rice, and Chicken Vermouth, are inexpensively priced.

Some desserts are made with honey, molasses or maple syrup, but the day I was there all the desserts were sugar-based, and the cheesecake always is. Soups are mostly vegetable-based. Homemade breads are often wheat, oatmeal and rye, and white flour is nearly always mixed with whole grain flours. Herb teas, hot and cold cider, mineral water and full bar service are available.

Every weeknight is special: Monday is movie night, Tuesday features all the spaghetti you can eat, Mexican specialties preside on Wednesdays, Thursday is crepe night, and on Fridays there are free steamers from 4-6 P.M.

Smoking permitted. MasterCard and Visa accepted.

Monday-Saturday 11:30 A.M.-2:30 P.M. and 5:30-9:30 P.M.; Sunday 10:30 A.M.-2:30 P.M.

—Linda Santucci

MONTPELIER

Horn of the Moon Cafe
8 Langdon St.
802-223-2895

Just off Main Street on a former commerce lane that's fast becoming a row of artisans' shops is the Horn of the Moon. Its community involvement is apparent from the bulletin boards and the work of local artists on the walls.

Breakfast is the main event here, and dedication to vegetarianism is evident in the menu. Vermont maple syrup heads the list of natural sweeteners, of course.

Breakfast features sauteed tofu, mushrooms and onions with tahini, a mushroom monterey omelet and a different special every morning.

There are dozens of choices for lunch, all delectably natural and drawing heavily on local products. The Vermont Special is a delicious homemade soup that contains local produce; it's served with cider, a mini-loaf of whole wheat bread, locally made cheddar cheese, butter and sprouts. Most of the lunch menu is available for dinner, as are a variety of quiches and the ever-present specials. Wednesday is Mexican night. No meat or fish is served. There's Haagen-Dazs ice cream for dessert.

No smoking, credit cards or alcohol, but you can bring your own wine or beer. Brown sugar sits on the table in bowls, but honey and maple syrup are the only sweeteners used in the cooking.

Monday and Tuesday 7 A.M.-3 P.M.; Wednesday-Saturday until 8:30 P.M.; Sunday 9 A.M.-1 P.M.

—Barb Mraz

RUTLAND

The Emperor of Ice Cream
40 Center St.
Rutland Beach
802-775-2022

The Emperor of Ice Cream lists its address as Rutland Beach, even though it's three hours from seagulls or salt air. Owners Chinsley and Turiansky feel that if you sell ice cream, your place should be on the shore. Alas, theirs is nestled in the Green Mountains, but it's much more than an ice cream parlor, offering a wide selection of vegetarian, natural and Chinese dishes. Some meat is served but there's no fish.

Unfortunately the waitresses must scurry to a second-floor kitchen, but it doesn't disturb the patrons lounging comfortably in leather chairs.

Of the sandwiches, my favorite is avocado, cheese, sprouts, tomato, mushrooms and lemon-tahini dressing served on whole wheat pita or a choice of bagel (such as herb or onion). The combination of the creamy lemon-tahini and the crunchy sprouts is excellent. A chef's salad, without meat, is offered plain or in pita bread. The Emperor's homemade dressings include oil-and-vinegar and herb mayonnaise as well as tahini.

Among the desserts, there is a big emphasis on fresh fruits

and yogurt. Honey and carob ice cream are available, but they pale in comparison to other choices. Although the sundaes are expensive, they are worth the splurge; Haagen-Dazs or Louis Sherry ice cream is topped with toffee bars, walnuts, fresh whipped cream, and sauces, liquors or fruits.

Wine and a full bar are available, and there's a great selection of international coffees and teas. Smoking permitted. No credit cards.

Monday-Saturday 7 A.M.-10:30 P.M.

—Sandra Stillman Gartner

SPRINGFIELD

Penelope's
30 Main St. (on the square)
802-885-9186

It looks like it should be a health food restaurant—knotty pine, plants, stained glass, brick—and, as Penelope's employees say, it's the closest thing to it in the area. What it is, though, is a half-breed. (That's the way of Vermont; with a sparse population, one must appeal to a wide market.) Lunch is inexpensive here; dinner is moderate.

Using organically grown produce whenever they can, the cooks include vegetarian selections on every menu. At dinner, there are fresh seafood entrees. Yogurt and fresh fruit, cheese boards, a vegetarian sandwich, omelets, a vegetable casserole (broccoli au gratin the day I was there) and salads are standard lunch fare. On my tossed salad with an abundance of fresh vegetables, the honey-lime dressing was especially good. They even leave the peel on the potatoes in the potato salad. A variety of burgers and sandwiches is available, too.

Soups are mostly meat-based, although there's a vegetarian soup a couple of times a week. Desserts would be considered generally unwholesome by nutrition-conscious diners—they contain white sugar (though honey's used, too). But Penelope's is famous for its pies, like pecan and sour cream-raisin.

The wine list is more than adequate. Beer and liquor are served, too, as are herbal teas.

Smoking permitted. MasterCard and Visa accepted.

Monday-Thursday 11:30 A.M.-9 P.M.; Friday and Saturday until 10 (upstairs). Downstairs open Sundays 4-11 P.M.

—Linda Santucci

STOCKBRIDGE

Annabelle's Restaurant and Tavern
Route 100 at Route 107
802-746-8911

Actually this is a culinary oasis that shelters patrons from the exigencies of mountain wilderness, because not for many miles can one find the quality of food, ambience and entertainment that this place provides. You can dine in the glass-walled splendor of a greenhouse or by the fireside in the old farmhouse. The restaurant is a subsidiary of a luxury-home builder, and its atmosphere is a skillful marriage of old woods and new glass.

The cuisine likewise reflects this eclectic meld. Though tending to be continental and French in orientation, with a constantly changing menu Annabelle's is able to satisfy the varied palates of generations of locals, newcomers and visitors.

Fish and meat comprise the majority of the entrees on their mostly nouvelle cuisine menu, but Annabelle's always has at least one vegetarian listing, and if the kitchen is not too busy the chef will cook according to your preference. In the summer months, most of the vegetables are organically grown, and organically raised venison and native wild rabbit can sometimes be obtained. The soups include some with vegetable or fish bases as well as those with meat and poultry stocks.

Brown rice is served occasionally, and many of the home-baked breads contain half whole wheat flour. Some desserts are made with honey, some with sugar.

Nonalcoholic drink concoctions (some made with Haagen-Dazs honey ice cream), herb teas and a large selection of domestic and imported wines and beers are available.

Major credit cards accepted. Smoking permitted.

Open every day from 11:30 A.M. through dinner.

—Linda Santucci

STOWE

Stowe Away
Mountain Rd. (Route 108)
802-253-8972

Walking into this 1950s ski lodge, one would never suspect its down-home country restaurant of frijoles and salsa or chalupes and chimichangas. But once you get a whiff of warming enchiladas, you know this isn't ordinary American nourishment; for the Southwest, perhaps it would be, but in New England a chimichanga is rare.

The Stowe Away serves mainly Mexican vegetarian meals. Chef Michael Henzel, son of hosts John and Leah Henzel, cultivates his own organic vegetables in season. One red meat item (Chile Verde) is served, and there are chicken dishes and usually a few fresh fish entrees during the summer.

I had the vegetable-based Swiss chard soup, which was delightfully light for a cream soup. Though slightly overbaked, the tostada and cheese enchiladas (both made with corn tortillas) were the best of the combination plates.

Breads are whole grain. Honey or maple syrup is used for sweetening, as in the cheesecake and delicious homemade honey ice cream. Sopaipillas—deep-fried dough squares—are made with whole wheat flour and honey; ditto for the apple pie. Herb teas and Perrier are sold along with coffee, beers, wines and liquors.

Carte Blanche, MasterCard and Visa accepted. Smoking permitted.

Breakfast (non-Mexican but just as wholesome) and dinner are served daily during the on season, mid-December to April. In the summer, the Stowe Away is closed on Tuesdays and the hours vary, so call ahead. Lunch is never served.

—Linda Santucci

STRAFFORD
The Stone Soup
802-765-4301

Stone Soup isn't a vegetarian restaurant, but a gourmet chef who relies heavily on whole foods makes the vegetarian selections outstanding—expensive, but worth it.

At its postcard setting on the green of a typical New England village, Stone Soup features soft recorded classical music and antique lighting. Would you believe an overhead bulb softened with an authentic well-starched antique petticoat? And the food is served on dishes made by local potters.

A meal might include cold strawberry soup or hot cream of celery with cashews, a dish of hors d'oeuvres, warm zucchini bread (which I enjoyed) and a visit to the salad bar. Desserts are made with a minimum of refined sugar, with honey or with Vermont maple syrup.

I had an international specialty—Eggplant Champignon, stuffed with a delicate blend of mushrooms and herbed bread crumbs and served with spiced rice and blanched vegetables.

Beer and wine served. Major credit cards accepted.

Wednesday-Sunday, 6-11 P.M., but dinners aren't served after 9.

—Barb Mraz

WESTON
Cobble Hill Farm
802-824-5427

A 300-acre family farm where meals are served to the public and paying guests are accepted for stays of a weekend or longer. The owners describe themselves as offering "meatless cuisine including quiche, crepes, soups, sandwiches, salads, fruit pies and home-baked bread. We can adjust our cuisine for those with special dietary needs."

Virginia

FALLS CHURCH
Mother Nature's Store
5167 Leesburg Pike
703-998-5100

See listing for McLean location.

McLEAN
Mother Nature's Store
1429 Center St.
703-893-1322

The atmosphere of this combination health food store/cafeteria is down home: everyone on a first-name basis, homemade wooden tables, laid-back music from a local radio station.

It takes some time to wade through the menu displayed above the counter. In spite of some cutesy titles, the sandwiches are worth waiting in line for. Favorites include the Golden Meadow (open-face avocado, mushrooms, sprouts and tomato under melted Muenster), Peanut Butter Delight (a scrumptious blend of their own peanut butter, cream cheese and honey, sprinkled with nuts and raisins, cinnamon and unsweetened coconut, topped with banana slices) and Mother Nature's Special (avocado, mushrooms, cucumbers, sprouts, tomato, sour cream and sesame seeds), all served on seven-grain bread. Ham, turkey and tuna are offered for nonvegetarian tastes.

The next dilemma is deciding what to wash the sandwich down with. You can choose from a dazzling array of fruit juices such as apple-banana, apple-boysenberry and papaya-honey, or exotic combinations such as high-pro shakes, banana smoothies or ZAPs (bananas, strawberries and orange juice). For the less adventurous there are iced tea, coffee and a coffee-substitute.

You can also enjoy homemade soup or inspiring salads. There's carrot cake or apple cobbler for dessert.

No smoking. No alcohol. MasterCard and Visa accepted; $10 minimum.

Monday-Saturday 9 A.M.-6 P.M.; Sunday 11 A.M.-4 P.M.

—Candice F. Ransom

NORFOLK

Potpourri
749 W. Princess Anne Rd.
804-627-4293

At Potpourri when your waitress asks how everything is, she really wants to know. The staff here is young, cheerful and concerned, a combination resulting in excellent service. Two carpeted platforms turn a large room into several cozier areas and the tiled floor, old-style ceiling fan and photography displays complete the hospitable scene.

Vegetarian specials are offered daily and run the gamut from avocado to zucchini dishes. A typical day might offer a guacamole salad plate or vegetarian shepherd's pie. The Enchilada Potpourri is a menu staple but varies in its filling, so ask before ordering. Those filled with beans were deliciously spicy and attractively offered with cauliflower and fruit garnishes. Included in the price is the soup of the day (a rather unsuccessful gazpacho when we visited).

Also offered daily are a vegetarian quiche and a fish special as well as a meat dish. There are the usual selections of salads. The zesty buttermilk dressing is a better bet than the house dressing. Also on the menu is a variety of sandwiches made on your choice of bread, pita, whole wheat, rye, Kaiser roll or English muffin.

Desserts, some of which contain sugar, include Haagen-Dazs ice cream, cheesecake and strudel (made with honey) in addition to one or two made daily at Potpourri. The homemade pie of peaches and strawberries and the carrot cake (made with honey) were excellent. Coffee, tea, soft drinks, fresh lemonade and juices are available, as well as yogurt shakes and 34 kinds of imported beer. An extensive list of wines and champagnes is also available.

On Sunday, Potpourri is a popular place to brunch. The variety is enough to make a choice quite difficult. There are seven types of crepes before you even get to the ones with fruit or preserves. A spinach and feta cheese omelet was delicious, but passing up one of cauliflower and almonds or cheese blintzes or French toast wasn't easy.

Smoking permitted. American Express, MasterCard and Visa accepted.

Hours: 11:30 A.M.-midnight Monday-Thursday; to 1 A.M. Friday and Saturday; Sunday 10:30 A.M.-11 P.M.

—*Anne Wickstrom*

RICHMOND

Grace Place
826 W. Grace St.
804-353-3680

Sitting under a canopy of trees at the Grace Place, it's hard to believe that you're in the heart of Richmond's Fan district and just a block away from its hub of activity, Virginia Commonwealth University. The friendly, relaxed staff, fresh flowers or plants on each table and a guitarist playing softly add to the feeling of peacefulness you'll have while eating on the patio behind the building. Inside, check out the natural food shop on the first floor before going upstairs to the restaurant, with its warm oak tables and many plants.

The large menu includes soup du jour, which might be a tasty gazpacho summer soup or mushroom winter soup, as well as a selection of seven salads with a house dressing based on pureed vegetables. The Shepherd's Dinner—soup, bread and cheese, fresh fruit or green salad and nuts—is a bargain.

There are daily specials as well as regular entrees that include vegetarian chili, served with bread and salad, and Avocado Rescue: fried rice and sauteed vegetables topped with a legume pate and an avocado broiled au gratin, served with soup and salad. A la carte selections include fried rice, sauteed vegetables, beans du jour and a quarter of a quiche.

Desserts, like the bread, are made on the premises and do not contain sugar. The carrot cake was unusually light, and the cheesecake was delicious. Also available are carob brownies, and sundaes and ice cream sodas made with natural ingredients.

In addition to the fruit juices, teas, decaffeinated and gourmet coffees and natural fruit sodas, wine and an unusual choice of beers are offered. The wine and natural soda coolers are not as successful as their catchy names.

The menu warns that naturally prepared foods take a little extra time, so the Grace Place is not for those in a hurry. The lunch menu includes some sandwiches, and at tea a pared-down menu is available.

No credit cards. Smoking discouraged. Entertainment nightly and for Saturday lunch.

Open 11:30 A.M.-3 P.M. for lunch, 3-5 P.M. for tea, 5:30-9 P.M. for dinner in the winter and until 10 P.M. in summer.

—Anne Wickstrom

VIRGINIA BEACH

The Bosom of Abraham
2107 Atlantic Ave.
804-428-8118

In the heart of Virginia Beach's resort strip, among the motels, pancake houses and souvenir shops, sits the Bosom of Abraham, a Middle Eastern restaurant where you'd least expect to find one. Although the entrees all include meat, fish or poultry, there is plenty on the rest of the menu to delight a vegetarian. It's the perfect place for a group that includes both meat-and-potatoes eaters and vegetarians.

As you enter the Bosom, there's a living-room-style waiting area that you'll appreciate during the busy tourist season. Brass and copper utensils on rough-hewn paneling and cleverly painted greenery add visual interest to the dining area. Our waitress not only was friendly and helpful, but she refilled our basket of pita bread without being asked.

Start with a raw vegetable tray with its tangy dip or hommus, served with pita bread. You also could pick the stuffed grape leaves, soup of the day, or either of two seafood cocktails.

One salad choice is tabouli: parsley, onions and tomatoes mixed with crushed wheat, lemon and oil. A good bet is the felafel, a tasty, filling vegetarian burger served on pita bread. There is a daily fish special, and broiled Cornish hen is a menu staple.

For dessert there is Haagen-Dazs ice cream or baklava as well as a carrot cake made with honey. The Bosom of Abraham has full bar service, freshly squeezed juices, coffee and an assortment of herbal teas. Turkish coffee is available, too.

Smoking permitted. American Express, MasterCard and Visa accepted; $5 minimum on charges.

Summer hours: 11:30 A.M.-2 A.M. daily. Winter hours: 11 A.M.-3 P.M. Wednesday-Friday; 5 P.M.-midnight Wednesday-Sunday, but winter hours may vary, so call ahead.

—Anne Wickstrom

Washington

ELLENSBURG

Valley Cafe
105 W. Third St.
509-925-3050

Driving through central or eastern Washington, one is best advised to pack a lunch unless one is traveling via I-90. In that case, the Valley Cafe can offer a reprieve from the diet restrictions imposed by the average North American restaurant.

Formerly known as Outrageous Taco (the sign is still there), the Valley Cafe offers relaxed vegetarian dining in a funky style. Local artists circulate shows monthly on the spacious walls, and live music can be heard Friday and Saturday nights. Roomy wooden booths and a Depression-era counter provide adequate seating.

Some meat is offered in the various combinations of Mexican food, in whole wheat pizza and in sandwiches on French or homemade whole wheat bread. The bread is baked by the workers daily; the management here is a collective called the Rainbow Farm.

All the food is made up to your specifications. Homemade soup changes daily, but it's guaranteed to have a vegetable base. Both regular and rennetless cheese are available; sugar and honey are used here, and the pastries are made with whole wheat and white flour.

Good offerings are the Courageous Burrito or Quesadillas (which offers a choice of any three of six vegie toppings), both complete meals in themselves. So are the enchiladas. Prices are fair for the bountiful portions. Skip the guacamole and chips; the chips are baked dry and the guacamole is bland.

Other hot entrees here are the steamed vegies and the delicious house specialty, the Garbanzo Burger, which is served with mushroom gravy, salad and bread.

For breakfast there are omelets, hashbrowns, French toast and Huevos Rancheros—a Mexican omelet served on a tortilla.

Wine and beer are available, and a juice bar offers fresh carrot juice and smoothies. No credit cards. Smoking permitted.

Monday-Thursday 7:30 A.M.-9 P.M.; Friday and Saturday 7:30 A.M.-10:30 P.M.

—*Anthony Greene*

ISSAQUAH

Barn Swallow
Gilman Village Mall
206-392-6069

If you find yourself famished and are at a point ten miles east of Seattle on I-90, relief is near. Take Exit 17, proceed into Issaquah to the Gilman Village Mall, and find your way to the Feed Store there. Inside is the Barn Swallow, serving lunches Monday through Saturday, 10 A.M.-4 P.M.

Good salads and sandwiches are the fare. A vegetarian soup of the day is offered, too: borscht on Monday, broccoli with zucchini on Wednesday, corn chowder on Friday and vegetable in between. The avocado and cream cheese sandwich is a worthy purchase, and the large luncheon salad is a better than average bowl of greens.

Fresh-ground coffee, herb teas and a variety of juices provide additional sustenance. Domestic or imported beer also is available. A specialty here is the frozen natural yogurt, untainted by sugar, preservatives or other chemicals.

No smoking. No credit cards.

—*Anthony Greene*

SEATTLE

Cafe Loc
407 Broad St.
206-682-7663

The Buddha on the counter gazes benignly at the customers. Your hostess, Minh Chanh Huynh (pronounced Min Chen Win) greets you warmly as you enter this clean, cheerful cafe across from Seattle Center, home of the Space Needle.

This small, intimate restaurant is a must for vegetarians. The Vietnamese vegetarian cuisine here is unsurpassed by any other oriental food in Seattle. All dishes here are prepared fresh and with exacting skill. Food is prepared to your specifications, but note that chicken stock is used in the soups unless you specify otherwise.

Call ahead at least half an hour and Huynh will prepare her very special vegetarian egg roll dish for you—rice paper wrappers filled with vegetables and tofu, wok-fried to a golden brown. Place portions of the freshly grated carrots, bean sprouts, chopped cucumber and mint sprigs on a broad lettuce leaf, add an egg roll, roll the leaf tightly and dip it into the delicious sauce that's provided. A gourmet delight!

Other specialties include cashews and vegetables, broccoli tofu, vegetable soup, sweet-and-sour tofu with vegetables and curried tofu or vegetables, hot as you like. Seafood is available, too.

Sweets include fried bananas, lychee nuts and a delightful and unusual Mexican soda, made from soursop fruit, called Guanabana. Freshly made pure soybean milk is available year-round. Delicious iced coffee is served in summer, the hot version all year.

For special occasions, a unique seven-course vegetarian dinner is available for parties of eight or more. Reservations for this must be made 24 hours ahead.

Smoking permitted, but outdoor dining provides escape in the summer. No credit cards.

Monday-Saturday 11 A.M.-3 P.M. and 5-8 P.M.

—*Anthony Greene*

SEATTLE

Cheri's Cafe
112 Broadway East
Capitol Hill
206-324-8027

Inside the Broadway Arcade mini-mall, modern fast-food service decor with a touch of high-tech flair adorns Cheri's Cafe. Cheri's is a favorite with Capitol Hill shoppers and business people and caters to both ends of the protein spectrum.

The cafe is basically self-service; check the blackboard near the door for the daily special. Prices are modest. A different vegetarian casserole each day nearly makes up for the lack of atmosphere. If you like it hot and fresh, come early for lunch; batches of the daily are made up ahead and kept in a warming oven all day. Some regular patrons here insist the flavors are better when mingled at the end of the day; each to his own.

Soups are made with or without meat bases, depending on the cook's preference, so inquire before ordering. Entrees include vegetable quiche, ratatouille, and probably best of all, spanakopita, a Greek dish made with feta cheese and phyllo dough and served with tzatziki, a cold yogurt and cucumber soup. Portions are fair but not bountiful, and fresh greens are average. The sandwich selection contains only two meatless entries, a cream cheese with avocado and an Egg Supreme.

There's sugar in some desserts, honey in most. Bottled carbonated fruit juices are available, as well as tea and coffee. No alcohol.

No credit cards. Smoking permitted.

Open 9:30 A.M.-8 P.M. Monday-Friday; 11:30 A.M.-6 P.M. Saturday.

—Anthony Greene

SEATTLE
Golden Temple
3505 N.E. 45th St. (east of the Univ. of Wash.)
206-523-2321

Inside the conventional American business edifice found at this address, an exotic enterprise conducts a thriving service. Rebirthing, meditation, Eastern philosophy and other esoteric topics are discussed among the patrons while the placid, turbaned workers bustle about the tables taking orders and serving food. The serene air is enhanced by tasteful color schemes and jazz or Indian music low in the background.

Only dinner is available, though it comes in a wide variety. If possible, it would be wise to fast a day ahead in order to savor the simple flavors of the heavy breads and entrees. The specialty of the Temple is Adi Shakti Enchiladas, which comes with a salad and a side of refried beans. Another touted dish is Bhajan's Banquet, a mildly curried vegetable dish mixed with mung beans and rice. Daily specials are offered.

Cheese is rennetless, and the Mexican-style beans are lardless. No sugar is used; honey sweetens the desserts, including the widely distributed Golden Temple honey ice cream available here in sundaes.

Since the restaurant is a spiritual training ground, meals are prepared by members of the Guru Ram Das Ashram Family. The food here tends toward the simple results of beginning vegetarian cooking.

No liquor. No smoking. No credit cards.

Open Tuesday-Saturday 4:30-9:30 P.M.

—Anthony Greene

SEATTLE
Sunlight Cafe
1029 N.E. 65th St.
206-522-9060

Adhering to a philosophy of providing wholesome vegetarian food at reasonable prices, the Sunlight Cafe has become one of

Seattle's ports in the storm of inflation. The clientele is young and hip; many customers are borderline vegetarians attracted by the varied cuisine, congenial workers and comfortable atmosphere. Short waits may be in store during lunch and dinner hours, but service is efficient.

Daily specials are listed on the blackboard. For lunch or dinner, try the new house specialty, the Ceresburger—a mixture of soybeans, bulgur, millet and vegetables, which comes with a cheese topping and a salad. It is delicious, as is the Garbanzoburger alternate. Other sandwich fare: egg salad, creamy cheese, peanut butter and melted cheese, all on bread baked here daily.

Dinner includes several choices—sauteed vegetables (served on brown rice, prepared to your taste), a different casserole each day, a tempting lasagna thick with cheese and the economical Combination Special (check it out with the waiter). Each entree comes with soup and salad.

There's a full range of teas and fruit juices. Fruit smoothies are popular here, as is the Lassai, a blend of buttermilk, yogurt and honey with or without banana. The coffee is good, and the price includes a refill.

Real buttermilk goes well with the breakfasts, served on Sunday only. Pure Vermont maple syrup is served on the waffles, French toast and hotcakes. For something different, try the Sunlight Scramble, a tasty blend of properly sauteed vegetables and tofu served with hashbrowns and an English muffin.

For dessert, there's fruit! The Sunlight Fruit Salad is refreshing and pleasing, covered with a delicious honey-almond dressing. No sugar is used here.

No credit cards. No liquor. No smoking.

Lunch Monday-Friday 11:30 A.M.-2:30 P.M.; dinner 5-9 P.M. Monday-Thursday and Saturday, Friday until 10; breakfast Sunday 10 A.M.-2 P.M.

—*Anthony Greene*

SEATTLE

Vitium Capitale
Corner Market Building, Suite 32
Pike Place Market
206-624-5290

Crepes? When in the mood for continental cuisine, try this unpretentious establishment in the Pike Place Market. The completely meatless menu offered here ranges from a simple butter crepe to the elegant and exotic curried broccoli crepe, served with banana, walnuts and yogurt. Beverages are a specialty here and include many variations on cappuccino and espresso as well as fresh carrot and orange juices.

The restaurant is situated on the second floor of the Corner Market Building, and the carnival atmosphere of the market is left behind as soothing strains of modern jazz or classical music sweeten the air.

Breakfast and lunch are served daily, but a unique vegetarian dining experience is offered on Thursday, Friday and Saturday nights, when a five-course gourmet dinner is prepared for intimate dining. Reservations for these dinners must be made 48 hours ahead. You may order from a selection or defer to the chef. A different entree is offered each night. No meat is served; fish by request. The meal includes a nonalcoholic aperitif such as fruit nectar, salad, soup, entree with a side vegetable, bread, dessert (no sugar is used here; the Fruit Flambe is excellent) and beverage. Examples of entrees include mushroom cutlets, Creole gumbo, eggplant parmesan and Szechuan vegetables.

No credit cards. Smoking allowed; no restrictions. No alcohol is sold; use discretion if you bring your own.

Hours: Sunday-Wednesday 9:30 A.M.-8 or 9 P.M. (depending on the crowd); Thursday-Saturday 9 A.M.-4:30 P.M. and 7-9:30 P.M. by reservation only.

—Anthony Greene

SPOKANE

Dan's Select Food and Eating Establishment
W. 621 Mallon
509-327-8058

Dan's is a delightful fuel stop for sightseers or shoppers in the historic Flour Mill on the banks of the Spokane River. It's nestled in the lower level across from a pottery shop, and one can see the intimate dining area and take a good look at what is going on in the kitchen upon approaching. The atmosphere is open and friendly, and the fare is salads, soups and sandwiches.

Not to be missed is the specialty, Bowla Tostada, which features a generous serving of Dan's secret-recipe beans topped with green peppers, onions, tomatoes, sprouts, black olives, mushrooms, avocado and a yummy Mexican sauce plus sour cream. The sandwiches showcase mozzarella, cheddar or Swiss cheese with lots of crisp vegetables and toppings on whole wheat bread or rolls. The hot sandwiches are a meal in themselves, especially the Cheese Bubbly, with two kinds of cheese and tomatoes, and the Italian Sub, filled with cheese, olives, onions and everything else.

Top off the meal with some peanut butter cookies (containing no sugar, like all the desserts here) and coffee, herb tea, fruit juice or cider. They'll have to roll you out the door!

No meat or fish is served at Dan's. No smoking. No alcohol. No credit cards.

Hours: 10 A.M.-5 P.M. except Friday, when Dan's is open until 9 P.M., and Sunday, when it's closed. Longer hours holidays and summer.

–Linda L. Higbee

Wisconsin

MADISON
Country Life Restaurant
2465 Perry St.
608-257-3286

Country Life is a fully vegetarian restaurant emphasizing whole grains, natural foods, and organic vegetables insofar as possible.

No smoking. No credit cards.

Sunday-Thursday 11:30 A.M.-2 P.M. and 4:30-7:30 P.M.

MILWAUKEE
Abu's Jerusalem of-the-Gold
1978 N. Farwell
414-277-0485

We walk through the doorway and survey the place. Greasy spoon. Seating for 24. Five customers, two men behind the counter. We choose a table by the grape drink and lemonade dispensers. We stare at the menu above the stoves. "Abu's Healthful and Natural Foods," it reads. Suddenly we hear, "Hey! Hey! What do you want? Do you know what you want?" And so we meet Abu.

If you aren't ready for lots of spice, you aren't ready for Abu's cooking. Abu, an Arab, offers Middle Eastern food exclusively, right down to the Turkish coffee. He serves at least 13 meatless dishes, as well as some with meat. Our favorites are the meatless kibbes (Abu spells them "kubby" and replaces lamb with peppers), felafel and eggplant-and-spinach pies, made with a slightly sweet dough. The tabouli salad—a mixture of bulgur, parsley, mint, tomatoes and spices—is fresh and good. Abu claims to use vegetables from his own garden. Unfortunately for his tahini and baba ghanoush, Abu serves microwaved frozen pita.

Avoid the desserts, unless you're utterly devoted to honey. They're apt to contain refined sugar, too.

Abu has no feeling for what much of America has come to think of as atmosphere. At his little place Middle Eastern song blares from one speaker. Two pictures of Jerusalem, a piece of embroidery and yellowed newspaper reviews hang on the wall. Service, too, is minimal. But where else can you sit talking and eating good food, virtually undisturbed for two hours, while Abu, his friends and customers shout, scold and laugh around you? Abu is his own atmosphere.

No credit cards. No alcohol is served, but you may bring your own wine. Smoking permitted.

Open 10 A.M.-10 P.M. daily.

—*Katherine Kaehler*

MILWAUKEE

Downtown Tea House & Natural Foods
412 E. Wisconsin Ave.
414-277-9599 (Carry-out: 277-9505)

The Downtown Tea House is probably the most authentic natural foods restaurant in the area. Formica butcher-block tables and bentwood caned chairs under hanging plants create a clean, light atmosphere. The staff adds informality, but the Tea House lacks the traditional Milwaukee *gemutlichkeit*.

The vegetarian entrees are all good. My favorite is the cheese and vegie sandwich, a fastidious layering of tomato, lettuce, shredded carrots, mayonnaise, raw milk cheddar and alfalfa sprouts on two slices of seven-grain bread (one of the nicest breads I've tasted). Another good choice is the hot spinach tartlet, a firm spinach and mushroom souffle topped with melted Swiss cheese, garnished with a hot pepper and served with "natural" potato chips. Meat, fish and fowl are on the menu, too.

Desserts are made with honey, and special nutritional beverages and a full line of herb teas are available. And on a cold Milwaukee day, nothing tastes as good as a mug of hot, spicy, natural cider.

No alcohol. No smoking. Major credit cards accepted.
Monday-Friday 11 A.M.-5 P.M.; Saturday until 4.

—Katherine Kaehler

MILWAUKEE

Eggcetera
424 E. Wisconsin Ave.
414-273-8222

Eggcetera is off the lobby of the grand Pfister Hotel, and its specialty is the omelet. The menu lists 32 variations on that theme, and 12 are meatless.

Among the omelets, my favorite is the Ruby—a marvelous surprise of cranberries and almonds—but I have enjoyed every meal I've eaten at Eggcetera. The Naturelle (eggs and butter), the Provencale (tomato, onion, parsley and garlic) and the Romanoff (with marinated strawberries) all are prepared and served with the distinctive Pfister touch. The omelets are garnished with fruit and accompanied by crusty Italian bread.

Not in an omelet mood? Try the salad buffet or the Crepe de la Florentine, deliciously seasoned not-quite-creamed spinach rolled in a crepe and covered with a sharp cheddar sauce.

The atmosphere at Eggcetera is composed and relaxing. The large terraced rooms are covered in red, the waiters wear tuxedos, and a pianist plays softly in the background. A perfect spot for brunch or a business luncheon.

Good, strong coffee is offered. Alcohol is served, but it's expensive. Nonsmokers' seating available. Reservations recommended, especially for large parties.

Major credit cards accepted.

Monday-Friday 11:30 A.M.-2 P.M.; Sunday 10 A.M.-3 P.M.

—Katherine Kaehler

MILWAUKEE

Fire-light Inn
3510 N. Oakland Ave.
414-961-0699

Behind the Fire-light Inn's university-neighborhood-joint exterior lurks a gourmet experience for the vegetarian as well as the carnivore.

Begin by sampling a few wines at the wine bar, free of charge. For an appetizer, I recommend the spicy guacamole and home-made chips. Settle into the warmth of the burnt orange and brown interior, where the thickly cushioned booths, hanging plants and shuttered windows encourage a pleasant, comfortable meal.

The star of the vegetarian entrees is the Cashew Calava. A blend of cashews and mild cheddar sauce over tender avocado chunks and brown rice, this unusual dish literally melts in your mouth. Another delicious choice is the Italian combination plate—a pairing of eggplant parmesan and manicotti accompanied by thick slices of bread and a mound of alfalfa sprouts. The fresh ricotta cheese lifts this dish out of the ordinary. If you like Mexican food, and I mean real Mexican food, try the Mexican combination plate of bean tostada, enchilada and burrito.

Also on the menu are six vegetarian salad entrees, two tofu entrees, quiche and nut loaf (with outstanding mushroom gravy). All are served with salad or soup. The hot dishes arrive much too hot to eat—a real difference once you're aware of what you've been missing.

Desserts are another adventure. Try the carrot cake, gingerbreadlike, full of raisins and nuts, and topped with cream cheese icing. Or the creamy cheesecake. Both come with a big dollop of unsweetened whipped cream. If you can still move, the Fire-light showcases a variety of hot drinks, ice cream drinks and fancy coffees. The cooks avoid refined sugar and flour.

The wine list is rare for a restaurant of this type, especially in the Midwest. MasterCard and Visa accepted. Smoking permitted.

Open Monday-Thursday 11 A.M.-10 P.M.; Friday and Saturday 11 A.M.-11 P.M.; Sunday 4-10 P.M.

—Katherine Kaehler

Canada

Nova Scotia

HALIFAX

Sanford's Second Storey
1823 Hollis St.
902-423-4560

The rich aroma of fish and vegetable chowder leads us up the stairs to Sanford's Second Storey in Halifax's Historic Properties. The setting is a soothing blend of chocolate and cream colors with rows of potted ivy framing the windows and softly whirring ceiling fans that take you back to Casablanca.

The menu—the same for lunch and dinner—features hearty soups and salads, all with a whole wheat roll from Sanford's own bakery. The Waldorf Salad blends apples, celery, nuts and raisins in a honey-yogurt sauce. In the sandwich department, Nature's Reuben—sauerkraut, tomatoes and cheese broiled on rye—is another tasty choice. The specialty is Sanford's Quiche, a lightly seasoned vegetable, egg and cheese pie with a generous helping of salad. The Chef's Wok is sometimes disappointingly limp and cool, but the meatless lasagna is a reliable favorite. Appetizers, crepes and omelets round out the menu.

There are four honey-sweetened desserts; the giant serving of hot blueberry cake is heartily recommended. Drinks include juices, cider, coffee, regular and herb tea, spring water, wine and beer.

Smoking permitted. Major credit cards accepted on bills over $5.

Monday-Friday 11 A.M.-10 P.M.; Saturday noon-10 P.M.

—*Sheila Simpson*

Ontario

KINGSTON
Scarecrow Natural Foods Restaurant and Coffee House
169A Princess St.
613-548-7338

At the well-established Scarecrow, the atmosphere is back-to-the-land casual. The walls are covered in weathered barn board and hung with quilts. The furniture is natural wood; each table has its own small potted plant. Located above a store on Kingston's main street, the place is always crowded at noon.

Scarecrow offers a full menu: omelets, pancakes, open-face sandwiches, quiche, casserole entrees and a large variety of beverages and desserts. Everything is fresh, whole grain, and unadulterated. Portions are huge. All the food is delicious. Though somewhat out of the mainstream of North American diets, none of the food here is difficult even for conservative eaters to accept; the most different thing is probably curry. They go easy on the soybeans and heavy on the cheese and sprouts.

Full liquor license. Smoking and nonsmoking sections. Entertainment by jazz and folk musicians until 1 A.M. Thursday-Saturday. MasterCard and Visa accepted.

Monday-Wednesday 11 A.M.-8 P.M.; Thursday-Sunday 11 A.M.-1 A.M.

—Tricia Van Luven

KINGSTON
Sunflower Natural Food Restaurant
2-20 Montreal St.
613-542-4566

The menu at Sunflower, which is just a block off the main street, is not as extensive as Scarecrow's, but it offers salads, open-face sandwiches, homemade soups, desserts and main-dish casseroles that change every week.

The furniture consists of refinished old dining room tables, split in half, and pressback chairs. The wainscotted walls are papered with cream-colored burlap and hung with tastefully framed graphics. The mood is quiet here, with no canned music.

Although the food lacks variety and is perhaps a little heavy in the soybean department, it is fresh, well prepared and delicious. Portions are large.

The seating capacity is smaller than at Scarecrow, but one never encounters the crowds, perhaps because of the strict no-smoking policy. Beer and wine are available with meals. MasterCard and Visa are accepted.

Monday-Thursday 9 A.M.-8 P.M.; Friday and Saturday until 9 P.M.

—Tricia Van Luven

TORONTO

Annapurna Vegetarian Restaurant
138 Pears Ave.
416-923-6343

Despite its somewhat unpromising location in a basement behind a highrise, Annapurna is a cheerful little place. Several portraits of spiritual leader Sri Chinmoy beaming from the white stuccoed walls are the only sign that it is run by a religious group. And unless you insist on eating Japanese style at a low table (great for kids), you'll never have to wait, a boon considering Toronto's burgeoning population of restaurant-goers.

Wholesome, tasty food is served here at bargain prices. The daily special, which recently included minestrone, spinach quiche with vegetable rice and mixed salad, is always a good choice. But the kitchen really shines in its small but delicious selection of South Indian dishes. Try the Masala Dosai, a crepe filled with spiced potato and served with homemade coconut chutney, or the spinach curry, mild or hot as you request, with warm, fresh puri or chapati to mop it up.

All desserts are homemade. Ask the staff which ones are

sugar-free. Especially recommended are the cheesecake with ricotta whip, the carob cake and the wonderful Indian sweets. My favorite is berfi, a gorgeous fudgelike concoction of milk powder, butter and sugar. Beverages include juices, coffee-substitute and a variety of teas—if you can resist the mango milk or a glass of rose-scented lassi.

No alcohol. No smoking. No credit cards.

Monday-Saturday noon-9 P.M.

—*Alyse Frampton*

TORONTO

Cow Cafe
406 Dupont St.
416-961-8341

The decor of this small, unpretentious converted storefront is limited to a nice collection of theater posters and some bright checked tablecloths. With only five tables in front and limited family-style seating in the rear, peak hours can be crowded. Service is uneven.

Soups are usually excellent, spinach bisque being a particular favorite. Salads also are good; a recent assortment included mixed greens, bulgur, coleslaw, Waldorf and marinated zucchini and mushroom. The seasoning of the guacamole and hommus plates veers from inspirational to weird. Of the hot entrees sampled, a buttery, flaky cabbage strudel was marvelous, but lasagna was disappointingly bland and overpriced.

Many people come here just for the beverages and desserts. In fact, a separate menu is needed for the 24 kinds of tea, herbal and otherwise, various coffees, juices, mineral waters and fruit frappes. Chances are that some of the splendid desserts are sugar-free; unfortunately, chocolate-brandy mousse and the sinfully rich sour cream-Brazil nut torte are not among them.

No credit cards. No smoking. No alcohol.

Tuesday-Saturday noon-2:30 P.M. and 6-10 P.M.; Sunday 6-10 P.M.

—*Alyse Frampton*

TORONTO
Govinda's Natural Foods Buffet
1280 Bay St.
416-923-8858

Peach-robed Hare Krishna disciples operate this pleasant, airy cafeteria amid the chic boutiques and discotheques of Yorkville. Although you can pick up a copy of "Back to Godhead" along with your meal, service is friendly and nonevangelical. And even at peak hours, the place is never crowded.

A small assortment of fresh, well-seasoned Indian vegetarian dishes are prepared strictly from whole foods. Practically the entire menu can be sampled in the Govinda Special, which includes soup (bean or vegetable) or mixed salad, two curried vegetables and rice, a piping hot, buttery chapati, beverage and dessert. Less ravenous diners may order most of these items separately at modest prices. The chapati sandwich, bursting with vegetables and homemade mayonnaise, makes a fine, light lunch. Rather greasy pakoras or vegetable fritters and samosa with chutney also are available.

For dessert there are creamy carob ice cream and several intriguing Indian sweets that seem to have withstood adaptation to sugar-free cooking. Try laddu, a rich candy made from chick-pea flour, butter and honey. Beverages include herb teas, cider, orange juice and yogurt shakes.

No smoking. No credit cards. No alcohol.
Monday-Saturday noon-8 P.M.

—*Alyse Frampton*

TORONTO
The Parrot
325 Queen St. West
416-366-4147

Only early birds beat the line in front of this popular place, and service can be maddeningly slow, but it's worth the wait. Original art hangs on the exposed brick walls, the tablecloths are fresh, and a slice of fluted lemon floats in each glass pitcher of table water.

The same attention to detail and a genuine interest in good cooking show in a menu that changes often, drawing on an imaginative and expanding repertoire of dishes from international vegetarian cuisine. One lunchtime yielded a delicate cream of pumpkin soup, lovingly garnished with sour cream and flecks of fresh dill, and a robust Greek salad studded with chunks of feta cheese and oil-cured olives. Dinner might be Bagna Cauda (a platter of vegetables with a little tub of warm garlic-butter sauce) and aromatic Linguine al Pesto or stuffed eggplant with pilaf. Fish dishes are sometimes offered, and there is an excellent Sunday brunch with the best Eggs Hollandaise in town.

Lovely fresh fruit tarts crowned with a puff of whipped cream are a specialty, but sugar-free desserts such as a fruit with yogurt or natural ice cream are always available. Teas, coffees and juices are served, and there is an interesting, reasonably priced wine list.

Smoking section. Visa accepted.

Tuesday-Saturday noon-2:30 P.M. and 6-10 P.M.;
Sunday noon-2:30 P.M.

—Alyse Frampton

TORONTO
Spice of Life
830 Yonge St.
416-961-5207

The decor at Spice of Life seems to be an attempt at Scandinavian simplicity; despite hanging plants and the exposed brick wall, the place is cavernous and a little cold. But the ample seating ensures that you'll rarely have to wait, and the service is satisfactory.

A few meat dishes appear on a menu that otherwise offers vegetarian fare prepared from whole foods. Good lunch specials, which include dessert and beverage, are Soup and a Bun, Garden Salad or the Mexican Specialty. Purists may argue, but to my mind the restaurant is worth a visit primarily for its Mexican offerings— generous portions of burritos with cheese, tacos with refried beans, enchiladas with cheese, all served with homemade chili sauce. Other good dinners are Today's Vegetable Dish and various omelets.

Desserts are homemade and sugar-free. Try the apple crisp or the carrot cake or a warm, buttery banana muffin. Fruit and yogurt smoothies, cider, and special teas are available in addition to regular tea and coffee.

No credit cards. No smoking. No alcohol.

Monday-Saturday 11:30 A.M.-11 P.M.

—*Alyse Frampton*

TORONTO

United Bakers Dairy Restaurant
338 Spadina Ave.
416-362-1298

United Bakers has been serving business people from Toronto's garment district for more than 60 years, and if you arrive when they do, between 11:30 A.M. and 2 P.M., you might have to squeeze in at the long arborite counter. That's okay; at least there the motherly waitress can bend over you and you won't have to shout your order.

Don't be waylaid by the fresh and plentiful salmon and sardine salads, the vegetables or fruit with sour cream or the other simple standbys of kosher dairy cooking. Have instead the Vegetarian Chopped Liver, a flavorful, coarse-textured pate made from soybeans and vegetables, or the tart and refreshing spinach borscht. Follow it with one of the wonderful dishes on which the restaurant rests its reputation: golden blintzes with sour cream or applesauce, noodles swimming in cottage cheese and butter, crispy latkes. Pickled pike and gefilte fish, served sweet or peppered, shouldn't be missed, either, unless your regimen doesn't include fish.

Some of these dishes and all of the desserts are made with refined sugar and flour. Desserts are uninspiring, with honey cake and apple cake the best of the lot. Beverages run to coffee, tea, juice and soft drinks.

Smoking permitted. No credit cards. No alcohol.

Monday-Thursday 6 A.M.-7:30 P.M.; Friday until 7 P.M.

—*Alyse Frampton*

WINDSOR

Himalaya Dining Room
841 Ouellette Ave.
519-258-2804

To step into this converted Victorian house on a busy main street is to enter another land as well as another era. The architecture has been altered to simulate an East Indian temple. The air is heavy with the sweet smell of spices. This tiny family-operated restaurant features East Indian and French cuisine. Chef Oza, who was born in Jaipur, India, believes the proper combination of foods is essential for good health.

Meat and fish dishes are included in the menu along with vegetarian entrees such as Palak Paneer (spinach and cheese) or Vegetable Korma Curry. Try an interesting vegetable side order like Dal Sambhar (curried lentils). Oza will plan your entire menu if you ask.

The chef admits that some of his many sweets are made with sugar, but others are made with honey and, for the purist, there are mango slices or papaya cubes. Teas and coffees are offered, and there's a full bar.

Smoking permitted. Diners Club and MasterCard accepted.

Open 5-11 P.M. daily.

—*Ruth Ryan Langan*

Quebec

MONTREAL

Le Commensal
2115 St. Denis St.
514-845-2627

A converted storefront operated on a shoestring budget, Le Commensal nevertheless manages to offer a good range of vegetarian food at reasonable prices. It is a small restaurant, tastefully decorated with homey furnishings. The food is served cafeteria style by two friendly and warm people.

The daily soup, served with bread, is usually a good bet, especially if you are partial to hearty varieties such as lentil or split pea. For the main course, customers have a choice of about ten dishes. Chickpeas with cumin, lentil stew, noodles with tomatoes and cucumber salad are typical offerings. Most of the dishes available, though simple, are well prepared and tasty, and portions are generous.

To drink, there is spring water or juice. No alcohol is served, but customers may bring wine. Cereal drink, coffees and an assortment of herbal teas also are available.

Desserts are plain but good. You may choose from among rice pudding, stewed prunes, baked apples and similar dishes. Honey is the only sweetener used.

Smoking allowed. No credit cards.

Open for lunch and dinner every day except Sunday.

—Harriet Schleifer

MONTREAL

Madhu Bhanda
5922 Sherbrook St. West
514-861-9035
and
1175 Crescent St.
514-861-8131

Madhu Bhanda is the most successful vegetarian restaurant in Montreal, with locations in the west end of the city and in the downtown area. While the west end Madhu Bhanda is a simple and pleasant snack bar, with a counter and booths, the downtown restaurant is attractively furnished with small tables, plants and pictures on the walls. At both, the staffs are exceptionally friendly and cheerful, and the owner is often found working in the kitchen.

Food at both locations is the same, but the downtown branch offers two choices of soup and casserole for the daily special, which is consistently delicious and filling and offers much variety. Soups are generally hearty—lentil and Mexicana Vegetable are two of the most popular. The casseroles are rice- or noodle-based, with assorted vegetables and sauces. Other excellent meals are the felafel and hommus plates and sandwiches and the lentil burgers; there is a selection of sandwiches and omelets. All bread here is whole wheat.

Beverages include natural apple, carrot and orange juices and protein shakes. Alcohol is not served, but customers may bring in wine. Coffee, coffee-substitute and herb teas are served.

For dessert, there is a selection of cakes and squares, made with honey, as well as apple crisp and ice cream. The carrot cake and apple crisp are especially good.

Smoking is discouraged at the West End location, and half the downtown restaurant is reserved for nonsmokers. No credit cards.

The West End Madhu Bhanda is open for lunch and dinner every day, but the downtown location is closed weekends.

—*Harriet Schleifer*

MONTREAL

Le Vent d'Est
964 Rachel St. East
514-524-2100

Le Vent d'Est is the only Montreal restaurant serving vegetarian food that can be described as elegant. Varnished pine furniture, hanging plants and candlelight combine to create a subdued and lovely atmosphere. The staff is courteous and professional, and all dishes are prepared and served with an eye to their appearance.

Salads are excellent and beautifully creative. Any of the several varieties offered—hommus, watercress or seaweed, to name a few—would make a fine light meal. Tempuras are a specialty of the house, and it is easy to tell why. Both fish and vegetable tempuras are offered, and all are a delight to the palate. Heavier dishes include an excellent tofu platter and Japanese noodles with vegetables or shrimp. The whole wheat rolls served with every meal are baked on the premises.

A wide choice of wines is offered at reasonably low prices. Several combination juices also are served; the strawberry-apple is perhaps the best of these. Numerous coffees and herb teas are available, too.

Desserts also are made on the premises. The chocolate cake with strawberry sauce is heavenly, but you won't be disappointed if you select one of the pies or pastries. All desserts are sweetened with honey or maple syrup.

Smoking permitted throughout, but most of the clients refrain. No credit cards.

Tuesday-Saturday 11:30 A.M.-2 P.M. and 5-10:30 P.M.; open for breakfast on Sunday.

—Harriet Schleifer

Your Favorite Places

If in your travels you come across some good restaurants that aren't listed in this book, you can use these pages to make notes on them for future trips. If you'd like to write up a review for us to include in future editions of this book, please look over the section on "How To Become A Reviewer" in the Introduction, for suggestions on what kind of information to gather and how to write it up.

Your Favorites

Your Favorites

Your Favorites

Your Favorites

Your Favorites